The New South
Carolina Cookbook

The New South Carolina Cookbook

Collected and Edited by the
South Carolina Family
and Community Leaders

University of South Carolina Press
Columbia, South Carolina

© 1997 University of South Carolina

Published in Columbia, South Carolina, by the
University of South Carolina Press

Manufactured in the United States of America

01 00 99 98 97 5 4 3 2 1

Library of Congress Cataloging-in-Publication Data

The new South Carolina cookbook / collected and edited by the South
    Carolina Family and Community Leaders.
        p.   cm.
    Includes index.
    ISBN 1–57003–112–6
    1. Cookery, American—Southern style.   2. Cookery—South Carolina.
I. South Carolina Family and Community Leaders.
TX715.2.S68N48 1997
641.5—dc20
                                                                    96–9972

CONTENTS

PREFACE

The South Carolina Cookbook was originally published in 1953 by the South Carolina Council of Farm Women and has since been revised and/or reprinted eight times. The name of the organization has changed since then to South Carolina Home Demonstration Council, South Carolina Extension Homemakers Council, South Carolina Association for Family and Community Education, and, now, to South Carolina Family and Community Leaders (FCL).

The purpose in preparing the original cookbook was not only to present many of the recipes used in the state, but also to provide the principles of cooking which preserve food value and quality of foods. Recipes were contributed by members of the organization and other interested parties throughout the state.

Changes in nutritional guidelines over the years led the South Carolina Family and Community Leaders in 1990 to determine that a new South Carolina cookbook should be published. Over 500 recipes were contributed by members of the organization. These were sent out to other FCL members and tested for accuracy and taste. The recipes were also analyzed by nutritionists for nutritional content before inclusion in the new cookbook. Some traditional recipes from the old cookbook were included which may not reflect today's

nutritional standards, but the nutritional analyses will allow users to determine if these meet their personal dietary standards. The end result is a new cookbook with new recipes making up an estimated 50–60% of the book while the remainder are repeats of traditional recipes from the original book.

Southern recipes, although extremely tasty, are not generally known for their healthful benefits according to today's dietary standards. The recipes in this book are included as submitted by the individual contributors and may or may not reflect today's standards. In addition, changes and substitutions in recipes may change the resultant quality of the product (taste, texture, etc.). This, then, becomes a matter of experimentation for the preparer to determine if the resultant product has the quality and taste to fit his/her needs.

A special chapter called "Altering Recipes" is included in this cookbook showing how to change recipes and make substitutions that will make the products more healthful. It is devoted almost exclusively to showing ways to reduce fat, calories, cholesterol, and sodium in the diet by making changes and substitutions in recipes. The information in this section is taken from North Central Regional Extension Publication 473, *Altering Recipes*, written by Patricia Redlinger, Iowa State University extension food science specialist, and Diane Nelson, Iowa State University extension communication specialist. The complete publication is available from Extension Distribution, ISU, Ames, IA for $1.

Three groups of special recipes have been marked specifically throughout this cookbook as follows:

+ Recipes which may be useful for "Cooking for a Crowd"
√ Recipes called "Palmetto Favorites," which are traditional favorites in South Carolina
★ Recipes "Lower in Fat"

Because of preparation method or choice in ingredients, some recipes have been marked for consideration when selecting foods lower in fat. This does not mean that recipes without the check are unhealthy. Most any food can be part of a healthy diet when eaten in smaller serving sizes and less frequently. Use the tips on altering recipes to make any recipe more healthful. Remember, the key to a healthy diet is balance, variety, and moderation.

An "Information" section is also included which provides information on weights, measures, substitutions, food values, the Food Pyramid, meal planning, and table setting and service. The user of this cookbook will find it a source for frequent reference. It is hoped that this combination of the past and present awill make this cookbook a very usable and valued book for years to come.

Clyde T. Mounter, Ed.D., C.H.E.
SCFCL State Advisor
Clemson University

ACKNOWLEDGMENTS

Appreciation is expressed to the members of the South Carolina Family and Community Leaders for furnishing ideas and recipes and to their cookbook committee composed of Mrs. Betty Baker, Chair; Mrs. Bee Cochran; Mrs. Bobbie Earle; Mrs. Mary Nell Fairey; and Mrs. Betty McGregor. Additional thanks go to Dr. Tom Mounter, State Advisor; Dr. Mildred Cody, Georgia State College; Dr. Rose Davis and Mrs. Libby Hoyle, food and nutrition specialists; and other members of the Clemson University Cooperative Extension Service staff for their help in planning and editing the material. A special thanks goes to Ms. Judi Mounter for the many hours spent entering information into the computer and proofing the final copy.

Agencies providing educational material used in the cookbook were as follows: Clemson University Cooperative Extension Service, Winthrop University Dacus Library Archives, United States Department of Agriculture, the National Home Economics Association, and Iowa State University Extension Service.

The South Carolina Family and Community Leaders has no reason to doubt that recipe ingredients, instructions, and directions will work successfully. Sample recipes were tested and evaluated by FCL members. These recipes are family favorites, and many have been handed down through generations. The recipes are a composite of South Carolina from the Blue Ridge Mountains to the Atlantic Ocean.

Nutritional analyses are provided for the recipes since many people are concerned about calories, fiber, fat, cholesterol, and sodium intake in their diets. The figures listed are the best estimates based on the capabilities of the program used. Nutrient contents may vary due to differences in preparation and selection of ingredients. Keep in mind that recipe substitutions such as the use of low-fat dairy products can make a dish more healthful.

INTRODUCTION

The people of South Carolina possess a rich heritage in recipes that were handed down by their ancestors from England, Scotland, Ireland, France, and Germany. In addition, typically Southern recipes have been developed to use products produced in the state, such as cornmeal, grits, sweet potatoes, turnip greens, collards, peaches, melons, fresh-water fish, and seafoods. These recipes have helped to make South Carolina well known for its excellent cookery.

The South Carolina Cookbook was first published in 1953 by the South Carolina Extension Homemakers Council. Since that time, it has been revised and reprinted eight times. The royalties from the sale of this book have been used to establish scholarships at Winthrop College, South Carolina State University, and Clemson University.

In recent years developments in the field of nutrition regarding the effects of fats, cholesterol, and salt in the diet have become an increasing concern. Many of the recipes in the original cookbook contain high quantities of these ingredients, making them at-risk foods by today's dietary standards. With this in mind, the South Carolina Family and Community Leaders decided it was time to print an entirely new cookbook with most recipes reflecting today's dietary recommendations while maintaining the taste and quality of traditional Southern cookery. Some traditional recipes are included which may not reflect these standards, but each recipe has a nutritional analysis that will permit users to determine if it meets their personal dietary guidelines.

Several hundred members of the South Carolina Family and Community Leaders contributed their favorite recipes to compose the greater part of the cookbook, while the remainder have come from interested persons throughout the state. Thus, a variety of recipes are offered to the experienced and the amateur cooks who wish to improve their culinary arts and add variety to their meals. The user of this cookbook will find it a source for frequent reference.

The South Carolina Family and Community Leaders hope that you will make daily use of the cookbook in preparing wholesome, nutritious meals for your family. Brides found that a copy of the original cookbook was a welcome wedding gift. It is hoped that *The New South Carolina Cookbook* will be just as popular.

Clyde T. Mounter, Ed.D., C.H.E.
SCFCL Advisor
Clemson University

SOUTH CAROLINA FAMILY
AND COMMUNITY LEADERS HISTORY

ORGANIZATION

The South Carolina Family and Community Leaders (FCL) was organized at Winthrop College in June 1921. It is composed of FCL Clubs throughout the state. These clubs are organized into county councils.

The purpose of the state association is to develop, strengthen, and correlate the work of the county associations in the state and their efforts to assist people in promoting all interests pertaining to the higher standards of living in homes and communities. The state association represents the common interests of the county associations in planning cooperative educational work and advising with Extension representatives in determining statewide policies.

Programs are developed to help people keep abreast of state and national affairs. The work of the council is reviewed and an educational program of work adopted for each year.

The county organizations of Family and Community Leaders, composed of members in FCL Clubs, have as their objectives to raise the standard of home and community life; to develop leadership and initiative among people in the promotion of those movements which are for the upbuilding of community life; to bring together members of FCL Clubs in the county for those ends; and to act as aids to extend the work of the Extension Home Economists.

Family and Community Leaders Clubs are organized by Extension Home Economists in natural communities and hold meetings in homes, schools, churches, club rooms, and community rooms. Officers are elected and chairs are appointed to help develop yearly educational programs of work.

HISTORY

In the early 1900s an interest developed in improving agriculture and rural life. The United States Department of Agriculture, in cooperation with state governments and farm organizations, developed programs to accomplish this aim. They recognized that they must reach the youth and homemakers with educational programs if home and family living were to improve. Home economics research was being conducted on some land-grant college campuses. It was felt that the findings of this research could be applied to rural life through an educational program for homemakers.

In South Carolina, O. B. Martin, Superintendent of Education, developed a keen interest in these opportunities for youth and, with the help of Seaman Knapp, who provided the leadership for the early Extension concept, provided opportunities for teachers to participate in training for youth clubs such as corn clubs and tomato clubs. Marie Cromer, a teacher in Aiken County, led the way for girls' clubs in South Carolina in 1916. Another teacher, Dora Dee Walker, also became interested in girls' clubs and then extended it to women's clubs. These two women were employed by Winthrop College to conduct an Extension program for women and girls.

In 1914 the Smith-Lever Act was passed by Congress providing for an educational program in agriculture and home economics, and related areas, in all states. Because the plan provided for cooperation of federal, state, and county governments, the program offered by each land-grant college became known as the Cooperative Extension Service. Additional home economists were employed to lead the home economics program for women and youth. The first official home demonstration club in South Carolina was organized in Sumter County in 1916. Other clubs were rapidly organized throughout the state.

The first two County Councils of Farm Women, composed of members of the home demonstration clubs, were organized in Calhoun and Abbeville Counties in 1919. The South Carolina Council of Farm Women was organized at Winthrop in June 1921. Subsequently, the name was changed to South Carolina Home Demonstration Council in 1957, and to South Carolina Extension Homemakers Council in 1966. In 1967 the Palmetto Home Demonstration Council officially joined the South Carolina Extension Homemakers Council. The present name, South Carolina Family and Community Leaders, was adopted in 1995.

The original plan for the homemakers

clubs was for a project leader in each club to receive specific training from the Extension home economist and teach the lesson in the monthly club meeting. In this way individuals were sharing their knowledge, making it possible for the County Extension home economists to serve large numbers of people.

The clubs proved to be an effective method for reaching large numbers of homemakers with home economics information. The clubs were also the core of group action for community improvement, and the county council became a leader in countywide improvements. In South Carolina the FCL groups have achieved outstanding accomplishments. The projects include compulsory education; a public health unit in every county; beautification of homes and highways; establishment of public libraries in every county with bookmobile service; the enrichment of cornmeal and grits; establishment of county farm markets; rights of women to serve on juries; highway safety, especially defensive driving courses; integration; citizenship caravan for public policy; aid to the Peace Corps; and many other progressive projects throughout the years.

The clubs' and councils' education committees indicated a broad interest in local, national, and international concerns, some of which extend beyond the Extension program emphasis—citizenship, cultural arts, family life, health, international relations, public relations, safety, and leadership.

The club and council system is recognized as one of the most effective informal adult educational systems in the world. No other such system of adapting current research findings for application and wide diffusion is known. Leaders throughout the county, state, and national levels have emerged from the Family and Community Leaders organizations.

The South Carolina Family and Community Leaders (SCFCL) is affiliated with the Country Women's Council of USA (CWC), the Associated Country Women of the World (ACWW), and the Master Farm Homemakers Guild (MFHG). Members of the SCFCL who have served as national or regional officers are: Mrs. W. T. Humphries, NEHC Southern Regional Director; Mrs. Crosby Newton, NEHC Southern Regional Director; Mrs. C. D. Sowell, NEHC Legislative Chair; Mrs. F. N. Culler, NEHC Citizenship Chair; Mrs. W. E. Cochran, CWC Secretary; and Mrs. Henry Buff, NEHC Director—Southern Region, MFHG President, ACWW Area President, and CWC Chair.

Throughout its existence, the organization has been assisted by the Clemson University Cooperative Extension Service, and much has been accomplished under the state leadership of Miss Edith P. Savely, Miss Christine S. Gee, Miss Lonnie I. Landrum, Miss Harriet Layton, Mrs. Marion B. Paul, Miss Juanita Neely, Miss Jane G. Ketchen, Mrs. Sara A. Waymer, Mrs. Sallie P. Musser, Dr. Ruby Craven, Dr. Virginia Greene, Dr. Myrle Swicegood, Dr. Sara A. Bagby, and

the present state adviser, Dr. Clyde T. Mounter.

In seventy-five years of existence, the organization has had twenty-three presidents as follows:

Mrs. Bradley Morrah*	Mrs. W. E. Cochran
Mrs. L. C. Chappell*	Mrs. J. A. Seaber Sr.*
Mrs. E. W. McElmurray*	Mrs. Joe R. Johnson
Mrs. J. Whitman Smith*	Mrs. Ralph Gates
Mrs. J. L. Williams*	Mrs. Herman Haynie
Mrs. Landrum Sellers*	Mrs. Dayton Swintz
Mrs. C. D. Sowell*	Mrs. Henry Buff
Mrs. O. J. Smyrl*	Mrs. Joe Ridley
Mrs. Gordon Blackwell	Mrs. Skippy Rizer
Mrs. M. H. Lineberger*	Mrs. Bobbie Earle
Mrs. Irvin Hawthorne	Mrs. Mary Nell Fairey
Mrs. F. N. Culler	
* Deceased	

Based on materials compiled and written by Mrs. Bee Cochran, State FCL Historian.

The New South
Carolina Cookbook

INFORMATION

MEAL PLANNING

Meal planning is essential for Americans if they wish to enjoy better health and reduce the chances of getting certain diseases. The Food Guide Pyramid was developed by the United States Department of Agriculture (USDA) after research on what Americans eat, what nutrients are in these foods, and how to make the best food choices.

The Pyramid will help you choose what and how much to eat from each food group in order to get the nutrients you need and not too many calories, or too much fat, saturated fat, cholesterol, sugar, sodium, or alcohol.

Products are now being required to provide new food labels with nutritional information. The labels will serve as a guide in helping you select products for a healthy diet. (See sample label on p. 4.)

The Pyramid focuses on fat because most Americans' diets are too high in fat. Following the Pyramid will help you keep your intake of total fat and saturated fat low. A diet low in fat will reduce your chances of getting certain diseases and help you maintain a healthy weight. You will also learn how to control the sugars and salt in your diet, and make lower sugar and salt choices.

DIETARY GUIDELINES

Eat a variety of foods to get the energy, protein, vitamins, minerals, and fiber you need for good health.

Maintain healthy weight to reduce your chances of having high blood pressure, heart disease, stroke, certain cancers, and the most common kind of diabetes.

Choose a diet low in fat, saturated fat, and cholesterol to reduce your risk of heart attack and certain types of cancer. Because fat contains over twice the calories of an equal amount of carbohydrates or protein, a diet low in fat can help you maintain a healthy weight. (See Food Guide Pyramid, p. 5.)

Choose a diet with plenty of vegetables, fruits, and grain products which provide needed vitamins, minerals, fiber, and complex carbohydrates and can help you lower your intake of fat.

Use sugars only in moderation. A diet with lots of sugars has too many calories and too few nutrients for most people and can contribute to tooth decay.

Use salt and sodium only in moderation to help reduce your risk of high blood pressure.

If you drink alcoholic beverages, do so in moderation. Alcoholic beverages supply calories but little or no nutrients. Drinking alcohol is also the cause of many health problems and accidents and can lead to addiction.

SERVING SIZE

The number of servings you need from each food group depends upon the number of calories you need, which, in turn, is dependent on your age, sex, size, and how active you are.

3

Consistent serving sizes in both household and metric measures. →

Nutrition Facts

Serving Size 1 cup (228g)
Servings Per Container 2

Amount Per Serving

Calories 260 Calories from Fat 120

	% Daily Value*
Total Fat 13g	**20**%
Saturated Fat 5g	**25**%
Cholesterol 30mg	**10**%
Sodium 660mg	**28**%
Total Carbohydrate 31g	**10**%
Dietary Fiber 0g	**0**%
Sugars 5g	
Protein 5g	

Vitamin A 4%	•	Vitamin C 2%
Calcium 15%	•	Iron 4%

* Percent Daily Values are based on a 2,000 calorie diet. Your daily values may be higher or lower depending on your calorie needs:

		Calories:	2,000	2,500
Total Fat	Less than		65g	80g
Sat Fat	Less than		20g	25g
Cholesterol	Less than		300mg	300mg
Sodium	Less than		2,400mg	2,400mg
Total Carbohydrate			300g	375g
Dietary Fiber			25g	30g

Calories per gram:
Fat 9 • Carbohydrate 4 • Protein 4

Nutrients required on nutrition panel are those most important → to the health of consumers.

Percent of daily value indicates how a food ← fits into the overall daily diet.

Reference values can be adjusted, depending on a ← person's calorie needs.
(Adapted from the *FDA Consumer*)

Conversion guide provides caloric value of the energy-producing nutrients. →

Food Guide Pyramid
A Guide to Daily Food Choices

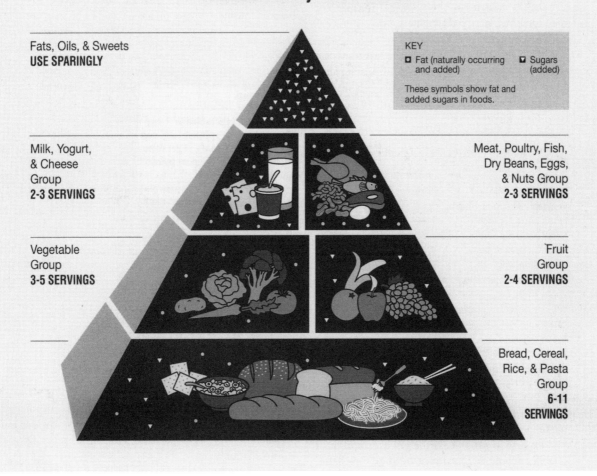

Fats, Oils, & Sweets
USE SPARINGLY

KEY
☐ Fat (naturally occurring and added)
☑ Sugars (added)

These symbols show fat and added sugars in foods.

Milk, Yogurt, & Cheese Group
2-3 SERVINGS

Meat, Poultry, Fish, Dry Beans, Eggs, & Nuts Group
2-3 SERVINGS

Vegetable Group
3-5 SERVINGS

Fruit Group
2-4 SERVINGS

Bread, Cereal, Rice, & Pasta Group
6-11 SERVINGS

1,600 calories is the average amount for many sedentary women and some older adults.

2,200 calories is the average amount for most children, teenage girls, active women, and sedentary men. Pregnant and breast-feeding women may require more.

2,800 calories is the average amount for teenage boys, many active men, and some very active women.

It is hard to determine the amount for children. However, preschool children need food from each of the five groups. It is important that they have the equivalent of two cups of milk a day.

Servings Per Calorie Level

	1,600	2,200	2,800
Bread Group Servings	6	9	11
Vegetable Group Servings	3	4	5
Fruit Group Servings	2	3	4
Milk Group Servings	2–3*	2–3*	2–3*
Meat Group (ounces)	5	6	7
Total Fat (grams)	53	73	93
Total Added Sugars (tsp.)	6	12	18

*Women who are pregnant or breast-feeding, teenagers, and young adults to age 24 need 3 servings.

The amount of food that counts as a serving is listed on the following pages. If you eat a larger portion, count it as more than one serving. For example, a dinner portion of spaghetti would count as two or three servings of pasta.

Be sure to eat at least the lowest number of servings from the five major food groups listed below. You need them for the vitamins, minerals, carbohydrates, and protein they provide. Just try to pick the lowest fat choices from the food groups. No specific serving size is given for the fats, oils, and sweets group because the message is **USE SPARINGLY**.

Milk, Yogurt, and Cheese

½ cup of milk
yogurt
1½ ounces of natural cheese
2 ounces of process cheese

Meat, Poultry, Fish, Dry Beans, Eggs, and Nuts

2–3 ounces of cooked lean meat, poultry, or fish
½ cup of cooked dry beans, 1 egg, or 2 tablespoons of peanut butter count as 1 ounce of lean meat

Vegetable

1 cup raw leafy vegetables
½ cup of other vegetables, cooked or chopped raw
¾ cup of vegetable juice

Fruit

1 medium apple, banana, or orange
½ cup of chopped, cooked, or canned fruit
¾ cup of fruit juice

Bread, Cereal, Rice, and Pasta

1 slice of bread
1 ounce of ready-to-eat cereal
½ cup cooked cereal, rice, or pasta

THE FOOD GROUPS

Breads, Cereals, Rice, and Pasta

These are the foods that provide complex carbohydrates (starches) which are an important source of energy, especially in low-fat diets. They also provide vitamins, minerals, and fiber.

Starchy foods are not fattening. It is what you add to these foods or cook with them that adds most of the calories—for example: margarine or butter on bread, cream or cheese sauces on pasta, and the sugar and fat used with the flour in making cookies.

To get the fiber you need, choose several servings a day of foods made from whole grains, such as whole-wheat bread and whole-grain cereals.

Choose most often foods that are made with little fat or sugars. These include bread, English muffins, rice, and pasta.

Baked goods made from flour, such as cakes, cookies, croissants, and pastries, count as part of this food group, but they are high in fat and sugars.

Go easy on the fat and sugars you add as spreads, seasonings, or toppings.

When preparing pasta, stuffing, and sauce from packaged mixes, use only half the butter or margarine suggested; if milk or cream is called for, use low-fat milk.

Vegetables

Vegetables provide vitamins, such as vitamins A and C and folate, and minerals, such as iron and magnesium. They are naturally low in fat and also provide fiber.

Different types of vegetables provide different nutrients. For variety, eat: dark-green leafy vegetables (spinach, romaine lettuce, broccoli); deep-yellow vegetables (carrots, sweet potatoes); starch vegetables (potatoes, corn, peas); legumes (navy, pinto, and kidney beans, chickpeas); other vegetables (lettuce, tomatoes, onions, green beans).

Include dark-green leafy vegetables and legumes several times a week—they are especially good sources of vitamins and minerals. Legumes also provide protein and can be used in place of meat.

Go easy on the fat you add to vegetables at the table or during cooking. Added spreads or toppings, such as butter, mayonnaise, and salad dressing, count as fat.

Use low-fat salad dressing.

Fruits

Fruits and fruit juices provide important amounts of vitamins A and C and potassium. They are low in fat and sodium.

Choose fresh fruits, fruit juices, and frozen, canned, or dried fruit. Pass up fruit canned or frozen in heavy syrups and sweetened fruit juices unless you have calories to spare.

Eat whole fruits often—they are higher in fiber than fruit juices.

Have citrus fruits, melons, and berries regularly. They are rich in vitamin C.

Count only 100 percent fruit juice as fruit. Punches, ades, and most fruit "drinks" contain only a little juice and lots of added sugars. Grape and orange sodas do not count as fruit juice.

Meat, Poultry, Fish, Beans, Eggs, and Nuts

Meat, poultry and fish supply protein, B vitamins, iron, and zinc. The other foods in this group—dry beans, eggs, and nuts—are similar to meats in providing protein and most vitamins and minerals.

Choose lean meat, poultry without skin, fish, and dry beans and peas often. They are the choices lowest in fat. Some lean choices from beef are roasts/steaks: round, loin, sirloin, chuck arm. Pork choices are roasts/chops: tenderloin, center loin, ham. Veal choices include all cuts with the exception of ground. Choices from lamb are roasts/chops: leg, loin, fore shanks. Good choices of chicken and turkey would be light and dark meat without the skin. Fish and shellfish are low in fat; those marinated or canned in oil are higher.

Prepare meats in low-fat ways. Trim away all the fat you can see. Broil, roast, or boil these foods instead of frying them.

Go easy on egg yolks; they are high in cholesterol. Use only one yolk per person in egg dishes. Make larger portions by adding extra egg whites.

Nuts and seeds are high in fat, so eat them in moderation.

Milk Products

Milk products provide protein, vitamins, and minerals. Milk, yogurt, and cheese are the best sources of calcium.

Choose skim milk and nonfat yogurt often. They are lowest in fat.

1½ to 2 ounces of cheese and 8 ounces of yogurt count as a serving from this group because they supply the same amount of calcium as 1 cup of milk.

Cottage cheese is lower in calcium than most cheeses. One cup of cottage cheese counts as only one half-serving of milk.

Go easy on high-fat cheese and ice cream. They can add a lot of fat (especially saturated fat) to your diet.

Choose "part skim" or low-fat cheeses when available and lower-fat milk desserts like ice milk or frozen yogurt.

Fats and Added Sugar

Fat and added sugars are concentrated in foods from the Pyramid tip—fats, oils, and sweets. These foods supply calories but little or no vitamins and minerals. By using these foods sparingly, you can have a diet that supplies needed vitamins and minerals without excess calories.

Some fat or sugar symbols are shown in the food groups. That is to remind you that some food choices in these food groups can also be high in fat or added sugars. When choosing foods for a healthful diet, consider the fat and added sugars in your choices from the food groups, as well as the fats, oils, and sweets from the Pyramid tip.

In general, foods that come from animals (milk and meat groups) are naturally higher in fat than foods that come from plants. But there are many low-fat dairy and lean meat choices available, and these foods can be prepared in ways that lower fat.

Fruits, vegetables, and grain products are naturally low in fat. But many popular items are prepared with fat, like french-fried potatoes or croissants, making them higher fat choices.

The amount of fat you can have depends on your calorie needs. The Dietary Guidelines recommend that Americans limit fat in their diets to 30 percent of calories. This amounts to 53 grams of fat in a 1,600-calorie diet, 73 grams of fat in a 2,200-calorie diet, and 93 grams of fat in a 2,800-calorie diet.

You will get up to half this fat even if you pick the lowest fat choices from each food group and add no fat to your foods in preparation or at the table.

You decide how to use the additional fat in your daily diet. You may want to have foods from the five major food groups that are higher in fat—such as whole milk instead of skim milk. Or you may want to use it in cooking or at the table in the form of spreads, dressings, or toppings.

If you want to be sure you have a low-fat diet, you can count the grams of fat in your day's food choices using the Pyramid Food Choices Chart and compare them to the number of grams of fat suggested for your calorie level.

You do not need to count fat grams every day, but doing a fat checkup once in a while will help keep you on the right track. If you find you are eating too much fat, choose lower-fat foods more often.

Eating too much saturated fat raises blood cholesterol levels in many people, increasing their risk for heart disease. The Dietary Guidelines recommend limiting saturated fat to less than 10 percent of calories, or about one-third of total fat intake.

All fats in foods are mixtures of three types of fatty acids—saturated, monounsaturated, and polyunsaturated.

Saturated fats are found in largest amounts in fats from meat and dairy products and in some vegetable fats such as coconut, palm, and palm kernel oils.

Monounsaturated fats are found mainly in olive, peanut, and canola oils.

Polyunsaturated fats are found mainly in safflower, sunflower, corn, soybean, and cottonseed oils, and some fish.

To avoid too much saturated fat, follow the Food Guide Pyramid, keeping your total fat within recommended levels. Choose fat from a variety of food sources, but mostly from those foods that are higher in polyunsaturated or monounsaturated fat.

Cholesterol

Cholesterol and fat are not the same thing. Cholesterol is a fatlike substance present in all animal foods—meat, poultry, fish, milk and milk products, and egg yolks. Both the lean and fat of meat and the meat and skin of poultry contain cholesterol. In milk products cholesterol is mostly in the fat, so lower-fat products contain less cholesterol. Egg yolks and organ meats, like liver, are high in cholesterol. Plant foods do not contain cholesterol.

Dietary cholesterol, as well as saturated fat, raises blood cholesterol levels in many people, increasing their risk for heart disease. Some health authorities recommend that dietary cholesterol be limited to an average of 300 mg or less per day. To keep dietary cholesterol to this level, follow the Food Guide Pyramid, keeping your total fat to the amount that is right for you. It is not necessary to eliminate all foods that are high in cholesterol. You can have three to four egg yolks a week, counting those used as ingredients in custards and baked products. Use lower-fat dairy products often and occasionally include dry beans and peas in place of meat.

Sugars

Choosing a diet low in fat is a concern for everyone; choosing one low in sugars is also important for people who have low calorie needs. Sugars include white sugar, brown sugar, raw sugar, corn syrup, honey, and molasses. These supply calories and little else nutritionally.

To avoid getting too many calories from sugars, try to limit your added sugars to 6 teaspoons a day if you eat about 1,600 calories, 12 teaspoons at 2,200 calories, or 18 teaspoons at 2,800 calories. These amounts are intended to be averages over time. The patterns are illustrations of healthful proportions in the diet, not rigid prescriptions.

Added sugars are in foods like candy and soft drinks, as well as jams, jellies, and sugars you add at the table. Some added sugars are also in foods from the food groups, such as fruit canned in heavy syrup and chocolate milk.

Salt and Sodium

You do not necessarily have to give up eating salt, but most people eat more than they need. Some health authorities say that sodium intake should not be more than 3,000 milligrams (mg) a day; some say not more than

2,400 mg. Much of the sodium in people's diets comes from salt they add while cooking and at the table. One teaspoon of salt provides about 2,000 mg of sodium.

Go easy on salt and foods that are high in sodium, including cured meats, luncheon meats, and many cheeses, most canned soups and vegetables, and soy sauce. Look for lower-salt and no-salt-added versions of these products at your supermarket. Information on food labels can help you make food choices to keep sodium moderate.

MEASURES, WEIGHTS, AND SUBSTITUTES

Measures

4 ounces	¼ pound
16 ounces	1 pound
3 teaspoons	1 tablespoon
4 tablespoons	¼ cup
5⅓ tablespoons	⅓ cup
8 tablespoons	½ cup
16 tablespoons	1 cup
2 tablespoons (liquid)	1 ounce
1 cup	8 fluid ounces
2 cups	1 pint (16 fluid ounces)
4 cups	1 quart
4 quarts	1 gallon
dash	less than ⅛ teaspoon

All measurements for recipes in this book are level. You will be more successful in your cooking if you learn always to measure ingredients accurately.

FLOUR—Flour should always be sifted before measuring. Place dry measuring cup on flat surface. Sift flour lightly into cup to prevent packing. Fill cup to overflowing and level off with spatula.

SUGAR—Sift sugar before measuring if it contains lumps. Use same procedure as for flour.

BROWN SUGAR—Pack firmly into measuring cup and level off with knife or spatula.

BUTTER/SHORTENING—If you do not have ¼-, ½-, and ⅓-cup-size measuring cups, you may quickly measure those amounts of butter/shortening in a cup measure by partly filling cup with water. For example, if you want ⅓ cup shortening, fill cup with water to ⅔ cup mark. Then add shortening until water level reaches 1 cup mark.

LIQUIDS—Liquids are measured in standard measuring cup with an extended lip to prevent spilling. Place measure on level surface. Read with eye on level with markings on measure.

BAKING POWDER, SALT, SPICES—Use standard measuring spoons. Heap ingredients in spoon. Level off with spatula.

Canned Food Sizes

8 ounces	1 cup
Picnic (10½–12 ounces)	1¼ cups
Vacuum (12 ounces)	1½ cups
No. 300 (14–16 ounces)	1¾ cups
No. 303 (16–17 ounces)	2 cups
No. 2 (20 ounces)	2½ cups
No. 2½ (27–29 ounces)	3½ cups
No. 3 cylinder (46 ounces)	5¾ cups
No. 10 (6½ pounds)	12 cups

Comparative Weights and Measures

Food	Measure	Weight
Apples	3 cups sliced	1 pound
Bananas	2 cups sliced or 1½ cups mashed medium	1 pound
Bread	1 cup soft crumbs	1½ slices
	½ cup dried crumbs	2 slices
Butter	2 cups	1 pound
	½ cup	¼ pound or 1 stick
Cabbage	5 cups shredded	1 pound head
Carrots	3 cups shredded	1 pound
Cheese (American or Cheddar)	4 cups	1 pound
Chocolate morsels	1 cup	6 ounces
Cocoa	1 cup	¼ pound
Coconut (flaked or shredded)	5 cups	1 pound
Coffee	40 cups perked	1 pound
Crackers (graham)	1 cup fine crumbs	14 squares

Food	Measure	Weight
Crackers (saltine)	1 cup finely crushed	28 crackers
Crackers (vanilla wafers)	1 cup finely crushed	22 wafers
Cream (whipping)	2 cups whipped	1 cup (½ pint)
Eggs	1 cup	5 large eggs
Eggs (whites)	1 cup	8 eggs
Eggs (yolks)	1 cup	12 eggs
Flour (all-purpose)	4 cups	1 pound
Flour (cake)	4½ cups	1 pound
Green pepper	1 cup diced	1 large
Lemon	3 tablespoons juice	1 medium
Lemon (grated rind)	2 teaspoons	1 medium
Lettuce	6¼ cups torn	1 pound head
Macaroni	2¼ cups cooked	4 ounces (1 cup)
Marshmallows	1 cup	11 large
Nuts (peanuts)	2¼ cups nutmeats	1 pound
Nuts (pecans)	2 cups nutmeats	1 pound
Onion	½ cup chopped	1 medium
Orange (juice)	⅓ cup	1 medium
Orange (grated rind)	2 tablespoons	1 medium
Peaches	2 cups sliced	4 medium
Pears	2 cups sliced	4 medium
Potatoes (white)	2 cups cubed/1¾ cups mashed	3 medium
Raisins (seedless)	3 cups	1 pound
Rice (long-grain)	3 cups cooked	1 cup
Spaghetti	5 cups cooked	8 ounces
Strawberries	4 cups sliced	1 quart
Sugar (brown)	2½ cups firmly packed	1 pound
Sugar (granulated)	2 cups	1 pound
Sugar (powdered)	3½ cups unsifted	1 pound

Equivalent Substitutions

1 cup self-rising flour	1 cup all-purpose flour plus 1 teaspoon baking powder and ½ teaspoon salt
1 cup cake flour	1 cup sifted all-purpose flour minus 2 tablespoons

1 cup all-purpose flour	1 cup cake flour plus 2 tablespoons
2 tablespoons flour	1 tablespoon cornstarch
1 teaspoon baking powder	¼ teaspoon soda and ½ teaspoon cream of tartar
1 egg	2 egg yolks (in custard)
1 egg	2 egg yolks plus 1 tablespoon water (cookies)
1 cup sour milk or buttermilk	1 tablespoon vinegar or lemon juice plus fresh milk to equal 1 cup
1 cup commercial sour cream	1 tablespoon lemon juice plus evaporated milk to equal 1 cup or 3 tablespoons butter plus ⅞ cup sour milk
1 cup honey	1¼ cups sugar plus ¼ cup liquid
1 (1-ounce) square unsweetened	3 tablespoons cocoa plus 1 tablespoon butter or margarine
1 clove fresh garlic	1 teaspoon garlic salt or ⅛ teaspoon garlic powder
1 fresh onion	1 tablespoon instant minced onion
1 tablespoon fresh herbs	1 teaspoon dried herbs or ¼ teaspoon powdered herbs
¼ cup chopped fresh parsley	1 tablespoon dehydrated parsley
1 teaspoon dry mustard	1 tablespoon prepared mustard

DEFINITIONS

BAKE—To cook by dry heat; usually done in an oven. When applied to meats, it is called ROASTING.

BARBECUE—To roast an animal slowly on a gridiron, or over coals in a specially prepared trench. The animal may be left whole or cut in pieces. While cooking, it is basted with a highly seasoned sauce.

BASTE—To moisten meat or other food while cooking to add flavor and to prevent drying of the surface. The liquid is usually melted fat, meat drippings, water, or water and fat.

BEAT—To make a mixture smooth or to introduce air by using a brisk, regular motion that lifts the mixture over and over.

BLANCH (precook)—To pretreat in boiling water or steam. Used to inactivate enzymes and shrink food for canning, freezing, and drying.

BLEND—To mix thoroughly two or more ingredients.

BOIL—To cook in water or a liquid in which bubbles rise continually and break on the surface. The boiling temperature at sea level is 212°F.

BRAISE—To brown meat or vegetables in a small amount of shortening, then to cook slowly in a covered utensil in a small amount of liquid.

BREAD—To coat with bread crumbs alone, or to coat with bread crumbs, then with slightly beaten egg or milk, and again with crumbs.

BROIL—To cook by direct heat. Grill.

CANDY—(1) When applied to fruit, fruit peel, or ginger, to cook in a heavy syrup until plump and transparent, then drain and dry. Product is also known as crystallized fruit, fruit peel, or ginger. (2) When applied to sweet potatoes and carrots, the term means to cook in sugar or syrup.

CARAMELIZE—To heat sugar or foods containing sugar until a brown color and characteristic flavor develop.

CHOP—To cut into pieces with a sharp tool.

CREAM—To work one or more foods until soft and creamy, using the hands or a spoon or other implement. Applied to shortening and sugar in place of BLEND.

CUT—(1) To divide food materials with a knife or scissors. (2) To incorporate shortening into dry ingredients with the least amount of blending.

DICE—To cut into cubes.

DREDGE—To sprinkle or coat with flour or other fine substance.

FOLD—To combine by using two motions, cutting vertically through the mixture and turning over and over by sliding the implement across the bottom of the mixing bowl with each turn.

FRICASSEE—To cook by braising; usually applied to fowl, rabbit, or veal cut into pieces.

FRY—To cook in shortening; applied especially (1) to cooking in a small amount of shortening; also called sauté or pan-fry and (2) to cooking in deep fat, also called deep-fat frying.

GLACÉ—To coat with a thin sugar syrup cooked to the crack stage. When used for pies and certain types of bread, the mixture may contain thickening but is not cooked to such a concentrated form, or it may be uncooked.

GRILL—See BROIL.

GRIND—To reduce to particles by cutting, crushing, or grinding.

KNEAD—To manipulate with a pressing motion accomplished by folding and stretching.

MARINATE—To treat with a marinade (an oil-acid mixture which is usually a kind of salad dressing). Used to tenderize and add flavor.

MELT—To liquefy by heat.

MINCE—To cut or chop into very small pieces.

MIX—To combine ingredients in any way that effects a distribution.

PAN-BROIL—To cook uncovered on a hot surface, usually a frying pan. The fat is poured off as it accumulates.

PAN-FRY—To cook in a small amount of shortening. See FRY.

PARBOIL—To boil until partially cooked. The cooking is usually completed by another method.

PARCH—To brown by means of dry heat.

PARE—To cut off the outside covering. To peel.

PASTEURIZE—To treat liquids such as milk and fruit juices with heat from 140 to 180°F.

PEEL—To strip off the outside covering.

POACH—To cook in a hot liquid, using precautions to retain shape. The temperature used varies with the food.

RENDER—To free fat from connective tissue by means of heat.

ROAST—To bake; applied to certain foods, such as meats. See BAKE.

SAUTÉ—To brown or cook quickly in a small amount of shortening with frequent turning. See FRY.

SCALD—(1) To heat a liquid to just below the boiling point. (2) To dip poultry in moderately hot, not boiling, water to loosen feathers before picking.

SCALLOP—To bake food, usually cut in pieces, with a sauce or other liquid. The top is commonly covered with crumbs. The food and sauce may be mixed together or arranged in alternate layers in the baking dish, with or without crumbs.

SEAR—To brown the surface of meat by a short application of intense heat; used to develop flavor and improve appearance, although shrinkage is increased.

SIMMER—To cook in a liquid at a temperature of about 185°F. Bubbles form slowly and break below the surface.

STEAM—To cook in steam with or without pressure. The steam may be applied directly to the food, as in a steamer or pressure cooker.

STEEP—To allow a substance to stand in liquid below the boiling point for the purpose of extracting flavor, color, or other qualities.

STEW—To simmer or boil in a small quantity of liquid. When applied to meat, simmering temperature is used.

STIR—To mix food materials with a circular motion for the purpose of blending or securing a uniform consistency.

TOAST—To brown by means of direct heat.

WHIP—To beat rapidly to produce expansion, due to incorporation of air. Applied to cream, eggs, and gelatin dishes.

TEMPERATURE AND TIME TABLES

Deep-Fat Frying

Use a deep kettle half-filled with fat or oil. Heat and test. The temperature is important because the fat must be hot enough to form a coating on the food instantly but not too hot, for this will cook the outside before the inside is done. (See deep-fat frying temperatures below.) Fry a small amount of food at a time and, when golden brown, drain on paper towels. Test fat from time to time during the frying process.

Clarifying Fat. Cool fat after using and clarify by cooking in it a few slices of potato. Heat slowly; cook potatoes until slightly brown. Remove potatoes, strain, and cool. Fats may thus be used a number of times.

To Egg and Crumb. Dry bread, roll into crumbs, sift, and season. Beat eggs until yolks and whites are mixed. Add 1 tablespoonful of milk or water to each egg. Roll food in crumbs, dip into egg, drain, and roll in crumbs again. Put aside until ready to fry.

Type of product	Temperature of fat degrees F.	Approx. time required to brown a 1-inch cube of bread in hot fat *seconds*
Doughnuts	350–375	60
Fritters		
Oysters, scallops, soft-shell crabs		
Fish		
Croquettes	375–385	40
Egg plant		
Onions		
Cauliflower		
French-fried potatoes	385–395	20

Oven Temperatures

Term	Temperature (degrees F.)
Very slow	250–300
Slow	325
Moderate	350–375
Moderately hot	400
Hot	425–450
Very hot	475–500

Roasting

Kind of roast	Oven temperature	Internal temperature	Approximate min. per pound
Beef ribs (Standing)	300°F		
Rare		145°F	18–20
Medium		160°F	22–25
Well-done		170°F	27–30
Beef ribs (Rolled)	300°F	Add 10 min. per pound to above	
Pork (Fresh)	350°F		
Loin, 3–4 pounds		185°F	35
Shoulder		185°F	30–35
Ham		185°F	30–35
Butt		185°F	50–55
Pork (Cured)	300°F		
Ham, 10–12 pounds		170°F	25
Half ham		170°F	30
Large ham		170°F	20
Tender ham		150°F	15–20
Lamb	300°F	180°F	30–35
Veal	300°F	170°F	25–30

Broiling

Ham (cured) ½-inch thick	20 minutes	Steak 1-inch thick (medium done)	8–10 minutes
Ham (cured) 1-inch thick	30 minutes	Steak 1-inch thick (well done)	12–15 minutes
Lamb chops ¾-inch thick	10–15 minutes	Steak 2-inches thick	35–40 minutes
Lamb chops 1½ to 2-inches thick	25–30 minutes	Veal chops, breaded or floured	40–45 minutes
Pork chops, single	20 minutes		

Sugar Temperature Test

Temperature	Test	Cold water test	Use
230–234°F	Thread	Syrup dropped from spoon spins 2-inch thread	Syrup
234–240°F	Soft ball	Syrup can be shaped into a ball but flattens when removed from water	Fudge, fondant
244–248°F	Firm ball	Syrup can be shaped into a firm ball which does not flatten when removed from water	Caramels
250–266°F	Hard ball	Syrup forms hard ball, although it is pliable	Divinity, popcorn balls
270–290°F	Soft crack	Syrup separates into threads that are not brittle	Taffies
300–310°F	Hard crack	Syrup separates into hard, brittle threads	Brittle
330°F			Caramelize

EVERYDAY HERB GUIDE

BASIL—Member of mint family with leaves 1½ inches long, has mild aromatic odor, warm, sweet flavor with slight licorice taste. Tastes good with tomatoes, peas, squash, lamb, fish, eggs, tossed salad, cheese, duck, and potatoes. Available whole and ground.

BAY LEAF—Green, aromatic leaf of laurel tree, has pungent flavor. Tastes good with vegetable and fish soups, tomato sauces and juice, poached fish, and meat stews. Available as whole leaf.

CHERVIL—Member of parsley family with feathery leaves, has mild, delicate flavor. Tastes good with egg and cheese dishes, chicken, peas, spinach, green salads, and cream soups. Available whole and ground.

DILL—Fruit of parsley family, has aromatic odor with delicate caraway flavor. Tastes good with fish dishes, cream and cottage cheese, potatoes, fish and vegetable salads, pickles, and tomatoes.

FENNEL—Dried fruit of herb in parsley family, consists of tiny yellowish-brown seeds with licorice flavor. Tastes good with soups, fish dishes, sauces, sweet pickles, bread, and rolls. Available whole and ground.

MARJORAM—Member of mint family with aromatic odor. Tastes good with fish chowders, vegetable soups, eggs, cheese dishes, stews, roast chicken, beef, lamb, pork, and stuffings. Available whole and ground.

MINT—Dried leaf of peppermint or spearmint plant, with strong, sweet odor and tangy, cool taste. Tastes good with jellies, fruit juices, candies, frosting, cakes, pies, lamb, ice cream, potatoes, peas, and chocolate desserts. Available whole (dried), flakes and as fresh sprigs.

OREGANO—Member of mint family, light green in color, with strong, aromatic odor and pleasantly bitter taste. Tastes good with tomato sauces, pork and veal dishes, pizza, vegetable and fish salads, and chili. Available whole and ground.

PARSLEY—Tiny green leaf growing in clusters on low plant, mild, slightly tangy flavor. Tastes good with meat, vegetables, soups, eggs, and cheese. Available whole, ground, and as flakes.

ROSEMARY—Leaf of evergreen shrub, with appearance of curved pine needle, has aromatic odor with slightly piney taste. Tastes good with poultry stuffing, veal and lamb roasts, potatoes, cauliflower, fish, and duck. Available whole and ground.

SAGE—Shrub of mint family, with pleasant aromatic odor and warm, slightly bitter taste. Tastes good with stuffings, pork roasts, sausages, poultry, and hamburgers. Available as leaf, rubbed, and powdered.

SAVORY—Member of mint family, has aromatic odor, pungent flavor. Tastes good with eggs, meat, salads, chicken, soups, and stuffings. Available whole and ground.

TARRAGON—Leaf and flower-top of plant, has pungent flavor resembling licorice. Tastes good with fish sauces, egg and cheese dishes, green salads, pickles, vinegar, chicken, tomatoes, and sauces for meats and vegetables. Available whole and ground.

THYME—Member of mint family, with short brown leaves, has warm, aromatic odor, pungent flavor. Tastes good with soups, clam chowders, stuffings, beef, lamb, veal, pork, oysters, eggs, cheese, bean and vegetable soups, fish. Available whole and powdered.

TABLE SETTINGS

Principles of Table Service

Good Balance—Table utensils and decorations should be arranged in an orderly manner, equally spaced, and not crowded. Silverware, napkins, china, and glassware should form lengthwise and crosswise lines on the table.

Harmony and Color—The table coverings, napkins, decorations, dinnerware, glassware, and food should be chosen with their colors in mind to make sure that they look good together.

Suitability—Select things for the table which are suitable to each other, or the occasion, and to the menu.

Distinction—The table can be covered with charm and simplicity by using imagination, originality, and a few inexpensive accessories. Every time the table is set, a picture is created.

Setting the Table

A well-set table adds much to the enjoyment of a meal. Clean linens, china, silver, glassware, and attractive flower arrangements can do much toward putting a person in the right mood to enjoy a meal.

The way in which a table is to be set depends upon the food to be served. Some rules that apply at all times are:

1. Allow 20 to 24 inches for each person or "cover." The space taken up by the glass, silver, linen, and china for each person is called the cover.
2. The plate is placed in the center of the cover 1 inch from the edge of the table.
3. Silver is placed on the table in the order in which it is to be used from the outside in toward the plate. All silver is placed 1 inch from the edge of the table. Butter spreaders, if used, should be placed on the bread and butter plate.
4. Place the knife at the right of the plate with cutting edge toward the plate. The spoon is placed at the right of the knife with bowl up. If a fish fork is used, it goes to the right.
5. At semiformal luncheons, you may have the dessert spoon or fork in place above the plate; or you may bring the silver when the dessert is served.
6. The water glass is placed at the tip of the knife, and the wine glass, if used, is placed to the right of the water glass.
7. Place forks to the left of the plate with tines up. It is not necessary to use a salad fork unless the salad is to be served as a separate course in the meal.
8. The bread and butter plate is placed at the tip of the fork. The butter spreader may be placed across the top of the plate, parallel to the edge of the table, or across the side of the plate in line with other silver.
9. Place the salad at the left of the cover near the tip of the fork.

10. The napkin is placed to the left of the fork. Open edges of the napkin are usually placed parallel to the edge of the table so that the open, lower corner is nearest the plate.

11. When cups are used, they are placed to the right of the knives.

12. The salt and pepper are placed where they can be easily reached yet give balance to the table.

ALTERING RECIPES

For several years health professionals have advised Americans to eat less fat, sugar, and salt and more fiber. The Food Pyramid eating plan reflects these recommendations.

Making these suggestions part of a daily eating pattern can involve several actions.

1. Eat fewer foods that are high in fat, sugar, and salt. Save foods like pastries, snack chips, cakes, cookies, and candies for special occasions.
2. Choose whole grain breads and cereals more often than highly processed cereals and breads.
3. Take smaller portions.
4. Modify recipes to decrease the amounts of fat, sugar, and salt, and to increase amounts of fiber.
5. Use more fresh fruits and vegetables.

Your plan depends on your current eating patterns, health status, and potential risk for health problems linked to diet. One of those actions may be to change some cooking methods. This section offers ways to make traditional recipes healthier.

Recipes Are Chemical Formulas

Recipes specify the ingredients, proportions, and methods necessary to produce a satisfactory product. Companies and publishers spend considerable time and money testing recipes for consumer use. Any change made in the recipe will produce a slightly different product from the one that was tested and published. You may or may not be satisfied with the result.

Some recipes, such as casseroles and soups, are more flexible than others. A cookie recipe is more adaptable than a cake recipe. Recipes for most baked products can be altered, but recipes for pickles, jellies, and most candies should not be changed.

Modifying a recipe may produce a product that does not meet traditional expectations. For example, a cake made with less fat will not have the same flavor or texture as the high-fat version. Cookies with less sugar or fat will still be acceptable but might not look or taste the same as those made by the original recipe. Substituting skim milk for whole milk in puddings, soups, and sauces will give a product that is less rich and creamy.

The main point to remember when altering recipes is that all changes are experiments. Some work very well; others are less satisfactory. However, it is up to you to decide when to change a recipe instead of serving it less frequently or in small portions.

Know Which Ingredients Can Be Changed

Food scientists have found that most people either do not notice much difference or accept the difference that results when the following kinds of changes are made.

Reduce sugar by one-third

Example: If a recipe calls for 1 cup, use ⅔ cup.

17

This works best in canned and frozen fruits and in making puddings and custards. In cookies and cakes, try using ½ cup sugar per cup of flour. For quick breads and muffins, use 1 tablespoon sugar per cup of flour. To enhance the flavor when sugar is reduced, add vanilla, cinnamon, or nutmeg.

Reduce fat by one-third

Example: If a recipe calls for ½ cup, use ⅓ cup.

This works best in gravies, sauces, puddings, and some cookies. For cakes and quick breads, use 2 tablespoons fat per cup of flour.

Omit salt or reduce by one-half

Example: If a recipe says ½ teaspoon, use ¼ teaspoon.

This may be more acceptable if you gradually reduce the amount each time you make the recipe. Herbs, spices, or salt-free seasoning mixes also can be used as flavor enhancers. Do not eliminate salt from yeast bread or rolls; it is essential for flavor and helps texture.

Substitute whole grain and bran flours

Whole wheat flour can replace from one-fourth to one-half of the all-purpose flour. Example: If a recipe calls for 3 cups all-purpose flour, use 1½ cups whole wheat flour and 1½ cups all-purpose flour.

Oat bran or oatmeal (that has been ground to flour consistency in a food processor or blender) can replace up to one-fourth of the all-purpose flour. Example: If a recipe calls for 3 cups all-purpose flour, use ¾ cup oat bran or ground oatmeal and 2¼ cups all-purpose flour.

Bran cereal flour is made by grinding a ready-to-eat cereal such as Bran Buds or 100% Bran in a blender or food processor for 60 to 90 seconds. It can replace up to one-fourth of the all-purpose flour. Example: If a recipe calls for 2 cups all-purpose flour, use ½ cup bran flour and 1½ cups all-purpose flour.

Find the Fat

. . . and when you do, you will know where to start making changes. All fats and oils are high in calories, but you can make a healthier choice by selecting those with less saturated fat. Likewise, when you use lower-fat milk products, you reduce fat, calories, and cholesterol.

Fat and Oil Comparison

Type of fat or oil	Cholesterol (mg/tbsp)	Saturated fat
Coconut oil	0	77%
Butter	33	54%
Palm oil	0	51%
Beef fat	14	51%
Lard	12	41%
Cottonseed oil	0	27%
Vegetable shortening (Crisco)	0	26%
Margarine	0	18%
Soybean oil	0	15%
Olive oil	0	14%
Peanut oil	0	13%
Corn oil	0	13%
Sunflower oil	0	11%
Safflower oil	0	9%
Canola oil	0	6%

From *Small Steps Make a Big Fat Difference,* Puritan Oil, Proctor and Gamble, 1989.

Can I Substitute Oil for Margarine or Shortening When Making Cookies?

All three ingredients are fats, but that does not make them interchangeable, as the examples show.

Example 1: Oil is 100 percent fat; margarine is an emulsion containing 80 percent fat and 20 percent water ("lite" margarine-type spreads contain a higher proportion of water). Substituting 1 cup oil for 1 cup margarine adds more fat than the recipe intended. Consequently, the cookies would feel and taste greasy.

Example 2: A well-textured cookie depends on thorough creaming of fat and sugar. Oil cannot be creamed, so substituting it for a solid shortening is likely to change both texture and volume.

Can I Substitute Lite Margarine-Type Spreads for Solid Shortening When Baking?

This is possible, but it cannot be a direct substitution. Since lite or diet margarines have more water, the amount of liquid in the recipe also must be reduced. Rather than substituting reduced fat margarine, try using less regular margarine. You will not have to alter the amount of liquid and you will save calories.

Dairy Product Comparison

(Values are approximations for general comparison; check labels for specific values.)

Dairy products (1 cup)	Calories	Fat(g)	Cholesterol(mg)
Whipping cream (heavy cream, fluid)	832	90	336
Medium cream (25% fat)	590	61	208
Light cream	470	46	159
Half and half (half milk, half cream)	315	28	89
Whole milk	150	8	33
2 percent milk	120	5	18
1 percent milk	100	3	10
Skim milk	85	trace	4
Evaporated whole milk	340	19	74
Evaporated skim milk	200	1	9

From *Food Values of Portions Commonly Used*, 15th edition. New York: Harper and Row, 1989.

Ingredient Substitutions for a Healthier Heart

By making a few substitutions and changes, you can still prepare your favorite recipes and reduce your intake of calories, fat, and cholesterol.

Instead of	Try	Best choice
Butter	60/40 margarine-butter blend	Margarine or reduced calorie margarine*
Sour cream	Lite sour cream	Mock Sour Cream**
Whole milk	2% milk	Skim milk
Cream	Evaporated milk	Evaporated skim milk
Cream cheese	Lite cream cheese or Neufchâtel	Yogurt Cheese**
Whipped cream or non-dairy whipped topping		Nonfat Whipped Topping**
Cheddar, Colby, Swiss cheese	Eat half the amount you usually eat	Select part-skim mozzarella, reduced fat natural cheese, farmer cheese, or low-fat processed cheese
Cottage cheese	Low-fat cottage cheese	Nonfat ricotta or cottage cheese
Baking chocolate (1 ounce)		3 tablespoons powdered cocoa plus 1 tablespoon cooking oil
Mayonnaise	Lite mayonnaise	Half cholesterol-free mayonnaise and half nonfat yogurt
Salad dressing	Reduced-fat dressing	Fat-free dressing
Chicken with skin	Remove skin *after* cooking	Remove skin *before* cooking
Regular ground beef	Lean ground beef	Use extra lean ground beef or lean ground turkey

*Not recommended for baking
**Recipes follow

Recipes for Reduced Fat Substitutes

You often can save money as well as calories by making your own low-fat substitutes using the recipes that follow.

No-fat Whipped Topping
1 tablespoon unflavored gelatin
2 tablespoons boiling water

½ cup nonfat dry milk powder
⅓ cup ice water
2 tablespoons lemon juice
3 tablespoons sugar
1 teaspoon vanilla

1. Dissolve gelatin in boiling water.
2. In a thoroughly chilled, small bowl, beat milk and ice water.
3. Beat in lemon juice.
4. Add sugar and vanilla and beat to soft peaks.
5. Add gelatin mixture and beat.
Yield: about 1½ cups
Calories: 12 per tablespoon

Homemade Egg Substitute
Because this recipe contains raw eggs, do not use it in uncooked products such as eggnog and ice cream.

¼ cup nonfat dry milk powder
6 egg whites
1 teaspoon vegetable oil

1. Combine all ingredients (using a blender or electric mixer) until mixture is smooth.
2. Store in covered container in refrigerator for up to 2 days. Or freeze in ¼ cup portions; thaw overnight in the refrigerator.
Yield: 1 cup; ¼ cup is equivalent to 1 egg

	Large egg	Homemade egg substitute (¼ cup)
Calories	79.0	70.0
Fat, grams	5.6	3.5
Cholesterol, mg	215.0	<1.0

From *The New American Diet*, 1986.

Casserole Sauce Mix
Use this instead of canned cream soups in casserole recipes. It has about one-third the calories.
2 cups nonfat dry milk powder
¾ cup cornstarch
¼ cup instant reduced sodium chicken or beef bouillon
½ teaspoon dried crushed thyme
½ teaspoon dried crushed basil
¼ teaspoon pepper

Combine all ingredients using blender or food processor. Store in an airtight container.
To prepare as substitute for one can of condensed cream soup in recipes, stir together ⅓ cup dry mix and 1¼ cups water in a saucepan. Cook and stir until thickened.
Yield: Equivalent to 9 cans condensed soup
Calories: 107 per ⅓ cup dry mix
Fat: 1 g

Mock Sour Cream
1 cup low-fat cottage cheese*
2 tablespoons skim milk
1 tablespoon lemon juice

Combine all ingredients using blender or food processor.
Yield: about 1 cup

	Sour cream	Mock sour cream
	(per tablespoon)	
Calories	26.0	14
Fat, grams	2.5	0
Cholesterol, mg	5.0	1

*Use nonfat cottage cheese if available.
Another option is to use a blender to combine equal amounts of low-fat or nonfat cottage cheese with low-fat or nonfat plain yogurt.

Yogurt Cheese
Use this as a substitute for cream cheese in spreads or in desserts and frostings. Make your own spreads by mixing with cinnamon, orange peel, dried fruit, jam, or herbs.

32 ounces plain nonfat or low-fat yogurt made without stabilizers or gelatin

1. Line a strainer with a double layer of cheesecloth or with a paper coffee filter; place over bowl.
2. Pour yogurt into lined strainer. Cover with plastic wrap and refrigerate.
3. Allow to drain for 8 to 24 hours until the liquid has drained into the bowl and the yogurt is thick and spreadable. The longer it drains, the more whey is expressed and the firmer the cheese.

4. Remove cheese from cloth and refrigerate in an airtight container.

Yield: 1½ cups

	Cream cheese	Yogurt cheese
		(per tablespoon)
Calories	49.0	5
Fat, grams	4.9	0
Cholesterol, mg	15.5	0

Lean Meat Cooking

Meat, poultry, and fish provide needed iron, protein, and B vitamins. Traditionally, they have been cooked with added fat. Your goal in altering meat recipes should be to choose cuts that have little fat and then cook and serve them without adding fat. Here are some tips to guide you.

some tips to guide you.

Pork's leanest picks*		Beef's skinniest six*	
Loin roast	196 Cal	Sirloin tip	162 Cal
Loin chops	196 Cal	Sirloin	177 Cal
Tenderloin	141 Cal	Tenderloin	174 Cal
Fresh ham	187 Cal	Top loin	172 Cal
Processed ham	140 Cal	Eye round	155 Cal
		Top round	162 Cal

*Per 3-ounce trimmed portion

Beef and Pork

1. Buy lean cuts.
   Beef: Top round, bottom round, eye of round, tip, arm chuck, sirloin, top loin, tenderloin, lean ground beef.
   Pork: Tenderloin, leg (fresh ham), loin chops, low-fat ham.
2. Trim all visible fat before cooking. Trim any separable fat before eating.
3. Bake, broil, or roast meat on a rack so fat can drip away.
4. Pan-broil steaks and chops on a rack without added fat instead of frying in fat. Limit use of oil or use nonstick spray coating for stir-fry.
5. When browning stew meat or roasts, do not coat with flour or add oil to the pan. Use a nonstick pan or nonstick spray coating. Remove any drippings.
6. Drain ground beef after browning; use a sieve and/or paper towels. (Fat content may be reduced more by rinsing cooked ground beef in a sieve under hot water.)
7. Whenever possible, prepare soups, stews, and spaghetti sauces ahead; chill and skim fat. Reheat for serving.
8. Use oil-free marinades.
9. Season with herbs and spices and serve meat juices unthickened, or make gravy only occasionally.
10. Learn to recognize a three-ounce serving of meat as similar in size to a deck of cards or the palm of your hand.

Poultry

1. Remove skin and visible fat.
2. Bake, roast, broil, or oven-fry instead of pan-frying.
3. Use nonstick spray coating instead of oil for stir-fry.
4. Use oil-free marinades.
5. Season with herbs and spices; make gravy only occasionally.
6. Whenever possible, prepare soups and stews ahead; chill and skim fat. Reheat for serving.
7. If using ground turkey, check label or ask butcher about fat content. Look for products that are made from meat only, not meat and skin.

Fish and Seafood

1. Learn to recognize low-fat choices such as cod, haddock, northern pike, perch, pollock, scallops, shrimp, snapper, sole, whiting. All have less than 2 grams fat per 3 ounces raw fish.
2. Bake, broil or oven-fry instead of pan-frying.
3. Use nonstick spray coating instead of oil for stir-fry.
4. Use oil-free marinades.
5. Season with herbs and spices.
6. Whenever possible, prepare soups and stews ahead; chill and skim fat. Reheat for serving.

How To Oven-Fry Chicken and Fish

Wash chicken or fish pieces; remove skin and visible fat from chicken. Dip pieces in skim milk, then in bread crumbs or crushed cornflakes seasoned with herbs and spices. Arrange on shallow baking pan that has been sprayed with nonstick spray coating. Lightly spray tops of coated fish or chicken pieces with nonstick spray coating. Bake at 375°F for 20 minutes (fish) to 45 minutes (chicken legs and thighs) or until done. For visual check, fish should flake easily with a fork; poultry juices should run clear.

Find the Sugar

At least 21 different forms of simple carbohydrates are identified as sugars. All provide calories, but few nutrients. Sugar is a necessary ingredient in many products because it provides sweetness and bulk. Specific reasons for using sugar in various products are included in "Guidelines for Modifying Recipes" section.

What Health Concerns Are Related to Sugar?

Health concerns about sugar consumption are not as strong as they were 20 years ago. The only health problem strongly linked to sugar is tooth decay. Studies have found that most people consume about the right proportion of sugar for a healthful diet.

Sugar is not "bad" in terms of being harmful. But its use should be monitored because it contains more calories than nutrients. Eating too many sugary foods can cause individuals to bypass more nutritious foods or to take in more calories than needed and thus lead to weight gain.

What about Sugar Substitutes?

Sugar substitutes have few calories and no nutrients. They provide sweetness but do not have the functional properties of sugar and are adversely affected by heat.

Fruit juices, honey, and molasses are offered as sugar substitutes for baking and cooking. However, the sugar they provide is no more nutritious than other forms of sugar. The amounts used are seldom enough to provide meaningful amounts of vitamins or minerals.

To reduce sugar:

- Try new recipes or adjust old ones by using one-third less sugar. To add flavor, use more vanilla or spice.
- Satisfy your longing for something sweet with fruits for snacks and desserts. Eat baked sweets and candies less frequently and/or in smaller portions.
- Read labels of commercially prepared products; many are high in sugar. Whenever possible, substitute home-prepared items made with less sugar.
- Recognize that the following are names of sugars: sucrose, sorbitol, maple syrup, corn syrup, high fructose corn syrup, glucose, fructose, mannitol, molasses, dextrose, maltose, honey, lactose.

Find the Fiber

Dietary fiber is the undigested material left after nutrients are absorbed from food. Both insoluble fibers—such as in wheat, fruits, and vegetables—and soluble fibers—such as in oats, legumes, apples, and citrus fruits—are important. This section identifies high-fiber choices, so you can use your imagination to find ways to include them more often.

Here are three general reminders.

1. Fruits, vegetables, and grains have fiber animal products do not.
2. The closer a fruit, vegetable, or grain is to its original, natural state, the more fiber it will have. An apple has more fiber than applesauce, which has more fiber than apple juice.
3. Whenever you can substitute a high-fiber food for a low-fiber one, you increase your daily fiber supply.

High-Fiber Substitutes

Instead of	Try	For
Chinese noodles canned onion rings croutons/bacon bits	bran cereal	casserole toppings
Cornflakes graham crackers bread crumbs	crushed bran cereal wheat or oat bran	dessert crusts and crumb toppings, in meat loaf, for chicken/fish coatings
White rice	brown rice barley, wheat kernels	casseroles, soup, stir-fry, side dishes
Chocolate chips	half chips and half raisins	cookies, bars

In addition, bran cereals, oat bran, and wheat bran all can be added to streusel toppings, chili, sloppy joes, sandwich spreads, and spaghetti sauce; or used as a topping for baked potatoes and salads.

Bran cereal flour can be substituted for up to one-fourth of all-purpose flour to increase fiber content. Bran cereals can contain 30 grams of fiber or more per cup. Check labels for exact amounts.

What You Should Know about Flours

When a recipe lists flour as an ingredient, we assume it means all-purpose flour. To increase your success rate when substituting other flours, we need to review why flour is used.

The gluten that is formed when protein from wheat flour is combined with liquid gives dough elasticity and baked products their structure. Flours from other grains have little or no gluten-forming protein.

Using specialty flours may result in a reduced volume and a "heavier" finished product; as well as changes in color, flavor, and nutritional value.

When using specialty flours:

- Stir whole grain flours with a spoon before measuring but do not sift. Spoon into measuring cup and level with a metal spatula.
- Decrease the oven temperature by 25°F and increase the baking time because the dough is likely to be more compact.
- For yeast breads, add all the specialty flour first, then work the all-purpose or bread flour into the dough. The doughs are mixed and kneaded for a shorter time because of the higher proportion of non-gluten-forming materials. The dough also requires a shorter rising time.

How Much Fiber Is in Flour?

All-purpose flour is a highly refined ingredient; consequently it has very little fiber. If you want to increase fiber in home baked products, you can substitute other flours in many products. Here is how some flour choices compare in fiber content:

Least fiber		to		Most fiber	
All-purpose flour	Medium Rye flour	Cornmeal		Oat flour	Whole Wheat flour

To make oat flour, put oatmeal in blender and blend about 60 seconds. Store in refrigerator or freezer because of high fat content.

To be sure you get whole wheat fiber—not caramel coloring or molasses—read the label on bread and cracker products. By law, a product labeled "whole wheat" must be made from 100 percent whole-wheat flour. "Wheat bread" may have varying proportions of enriched white flour and whole-wheat flour. The type of flour present in the largest amount is listed first on the ingredient label.

Find the Salt

Salt—the traditional seasoning of choice—has been linked to high blood pressure. As a result, many no-salt and low-salt seasoning mixes now are on the market. You also can make them at home using the recipes on the following pages.

Spices and herbs can be used to enhance the flavor of a fat-or sodium-reduced food. Experiment with small amounts to find an acceptable seasoning level. Powdered herbs are stronger than crumbled, and dried herbs are stronger than fresh herbs. If a recipe calls for ¼ teaspoon powdered herb, you can use ¾ to 1 teaspoon crumbled or flaked or 2 teaspoons fresh herb.

What Is the Difference?

Herb (ùrb,hùrb)n. leaves of plants and shrubs with nonwoody stems

Spice (spis)n. comes from bark, roots, fruit, seeds, or flowers of plants

When adding herbs or spices, take a tip from professional recipe developers. Start with 1 teaspoon of a mild herb (dried) or spice (such as oregano, basil, cumin, and cinnamon) per six servings. Use only ¼ teaspoon of a strong herb or spice (such as rosemary, cloves, nutmeg, ginger, mustard, allspice) per six servings.

Guide To Using Herbs and Spices

Beef (See also Meat Loaf): allspice, basil, bay leaf, caraway seed, chervil, chili powder, cloves, coriander, cumin, curry powder, dill, fennel, ginger, marjoram, oregano, paprika, pepper, rosemary, savory, tarragon

Breads: anise, caraway seed, cardamom, cinnamon, coriander, dill, fennel, nutmeg, parsley, poppy seed

Cheeses: basil, caraway seed, cayenne, celery seed, chervil, chives, coriander, cumin, dill, marjoram, oregano, parsley, pepper, sage, thyme

Dips: cayenne, chili powder, chives, curry powder, dill, oregano, parsley, pepper, sage

Eggs: basil, cayenne, celery seed, chervil, chili powder, chives, cumin, curry powder, dill, marjoram, mustard seed, oregano, paprika, parsley, pepper, rosemary, saffron, sage, savory, tarragon, thyme, turmeric

Fish: basil, bay leaf, cayenne, celery seed, chervil, cumin, curry powder, dill, ginger, marjoram, mustard seed, oregano, paprika, parsley, pepper, saffron, sage, savory, tarragon, thyme, turmeric

Fruits: allspice, anise, basil, cardamom, cinnamon, cloves, curry powder, fennel, ginger, mace, mint, nutmeg, rosemary

Grains: basil, celery seed, chili powder, cumin, curry powder, dill, marjoram, mint, oregano, parsley, pepper, rosemary, saffron, savory, thyme

Jams and Jellies: allspice, bay leaf, cardamom, cinnamon, mace, mint, nutmeg

Lamb: basil, bay leaf, chervil, cinnamon, cloves, cumin, curry powder, dill, marjoram, mint, nutmeg, oregano, parsley, pepper, rosemary, saffron, sage, savory, thyme

Lentils: basil, cinnamon, curry powder, dill, oregano, sage, savory, thyme

Liver: basil, bay leaf, caraway seed, chives, tarragon, thyme, turmeric

Marinades: allspice, bay leaf, cayenne, celery seed, chili powder, cloves, ginger, mustard seed, oregano, parsley, rosemary, tarragon, turmeric

Meat Loaf: chili powder, cumin, curry powder, marjoram, nutmeg, oregano, parsley, pepper, sage, savory, thyme

Pasta: basil, oregano, parsley, pepper, poppy seed

Pickled vegetables: allspice, bay leaf, cardamom, cinnamon, cloves, coriander, dill, ginger, mint, mustard seed, pepper, tarragon, tumeric

Pork: allspice, basil, bay leaf, caraway seed, chervil, cinnamon, cloves, coriander, fennel, ginger, marjoram, nutmeg, pepper, rosemary, sage, savory, thyme

Poultry: basil, bay leaf, chervil, coriander, curry powder, dill, ginger, marjoram, paprika, parsley, pepper, rosemary, saffron, sage, savory, tarragon, thyme, turmeric

Relishes: allspice, cayenne, chili powder, cloves, coriander, ginger, mace, tarragon

Salad Dressings: caraway seed, celery seed, chervil, chili powder, dill, ginger, mint, mustard seed, paprika, parsley, pepper, poppy seed, tarragon, turmeric

Shellfish: basil, bay leaf, cayenne, curry powder, marjoram, oregano, paprika, parsley, saffron, sage, savory, tarragon, thyme

Soups and Stews: allspice, basil, bay leaf, caraway seed, cayenne, celery seed, chervil, chili powder, chives, cloves, coriander, curry powder, dill, ginger, marjoram, oregano, paprika, parsley, pepper, rosemary, saffron, tarragon, thyme

Stuffing: basil, marjoram, oregano, pepper, rosemary, sage, savory, tarragon, thyme

Vegetables

Artichoke: bay leaf, coriander, parsley, savory, thyme

Asparagus: chives, marjoram, mustard seed, parsley, tarragon, thyme, turmeric

Beans, dried: allspice, bay leaf, celery seed, chili powder, cloves, cumin, mint, mustard seed, oregano, sage, savory, tarragon, turmeric

Beans, lima: cumin, dill, marjoram, nutmeg, oregano, sage, savory, tarragon, thyme

Beans, snap: basil, caraway seed, chili powder, dill, marjoram, mustard seed, oregano, sage, savory, tarragon, thyme

Beets: allspice, anise, bay leaf, caraway seed, cinnamon, dill, fennel, ginger, mustard seed, savory, tarragon, thyme

Broccoli: caraway seed, dill, mustard seed, oregano, tarragon

Brussels sprouts: basil, caraway seed, dill, mustard seed, sage, thyme

Cabbage: caraway seed, celery seed, cumin, dill, fennel, mustard seed, nutmeg, oregano, paprika, savory, tarragon, turmeric

Carrots: allspice, anise, bay leaf, caraway seed, cinnamon, cloves, dill, fennel, ginger, mace, marjoram, mint, nutmeg, parsley, rosemary, sage, thyme

Cauliflower: caraway seed, celery seed, coriander, dill, mace, nutmeg, paprika, parsley

Corn: chili powder, chives, oregano, parsley, sage, savory

Cucumber: basil, chives, cinnamon, cloves, dill, mint, parsley, pepper, tarragon

Eggplant: basil, marjoram, oregano, parsley, sage, thyme

Greens, dark leafy: allspice, basil, mace, marjoram, nutmeg, oregano, tarragon

Green, salad: basil, celery seed, chervil, chives, dill, marjoram, oregano, parsley, pepper, sage, savory, tarragon

Mushrooms: chives, dill, marjoram, parsley, tarragon, thyme

Onions: caraway seed, curry powder, mustard seed, nutmeg, oregano, parsley, sage, thyme, turmeric

Parsnips: chervil, dill, marjoram, parsley, rosemary, sage, thyme

Peas: allspice, basil, chervil, chives, dill, marjoram, mint, oregano, poppy seed, rosemary, sage, savory, tarragon, thyme

Potatoes, sweet: allspice, cardamom, cinnamon, cloves, ginger, mace, nutmeg

Potatoes, white: basil, bay leaf, caraway seed, celery seed, chives, dill, mustard seed, oregano, parsley, pepper, poppy seed, rosemary, savory, tarragon, thyme

Pumpkin: allspice, cardamom, cinnamon, cloves, ginger, mace, nutmeg

Squash, summer: chervil, marjoram, parsley, pepper, savory

Squash, winter: allspice, basil, cardamom, cinnamon, cloves, fennel, ginger, mace, mustard seed, nutmeg, rosemary

Squash, zucchini: marjoram, oregano, parsley

Tomatoes: basil, bay leaf, celery seed, chervil, chili powder, chives, curry powder, dill, oregano, parsley, sage, savory, tarragon, thyme

Turnips: allspice, dill, mace, nutmeg, paprika, thyme

Vegetable juices: basil, bay leaf, oregano, parsley, pepper, tarragon

No-salt seasoning recipes

Because 1 teaspoon of salt has about 2,000 mg sodium, you can substantially reduce your sodium intake by substituting any of these seasonings.

Zesty Herb Seasoning
Sodium: 47 mg per teaspoon

Grated peel of 1 lemon
2 tablespoons ground cinnamon
1 tablespoon ground mace
1 tablespoon dried basil leaves, crushed
1 tablespoon dried thyme leaves, crushed
1 tablespoon dried rosemary leaves,
    crushed
2 teaspoons paprika
1 teaspoon salt and potassium chloride
    mixture (a purchased product with
    half the sodium of table salt)
1 teaspoon pepper
1 teaspoon ground cloves
½ teaspoon ground nutmeg
½ teaspoon ground allspice

Combine all ingredients. Refrigerate in
covered container. Sprinkle as desired over
meat, poultry, or fish before broiling or baking.

Oriental Spice
Sodium: About 1.6 mg per teaspoon

1 teaspoon fresh grated lemon peel
¼ teaspoon anise seed, crushed
¼ teaspoon fennel seed, crushed
¼ teaspoon ground cinnamon
¼ teaspoon ground cloves
¼ teaspoon ground ginger

Combine all ingredients. Refrigerate in
covered container. To use, sprinkle as desired
over poultry or meat stir-fry dishes.

Herbed Seasoning
Sodium: 0.65 mg per teaspoon

2 tablespoons dried dill weed or basil
    leaves, crumbled
2 tablespoons onion powder
1 teaspoon dried oregano leaves,
    crumbled
1 teaspoon celery seed
¼ teaspoon grated dried lemon peel
Pinch freshly ground pepper

Combine all ingredients in small bowl and
blend well. Spoon into shaker and use with
poultry and fish. Store in cool, dry place.

Herb 'n' Lemon Seasoning
Sodium: 1 mg per teaspoon

Grated peel of ½ lemon
2 teaspoons dried parsley flakes
½ teaspoon garlic powder
½ teaspoon dried oregano or basil
    leaves, crushed
½ teaspoon dried marjoram leaves,
    crushed
¼ teaspoon ground allspice
¼ teaspoon pepper

Combine all ingredients. Refrigerate in
covered container. Sprinkle as desired over
meat, poultry, or fish before broiling or baking.

Shaker Spice Blend
Sodium: 1.78 mg per teaspoon

5 teaspoons onion powder
2½ teaspoons garlic powder
2½ teaspoons paprika
2½ teaspoons dry mustard
1¼ teaspoons thyme leaves,
    crushed
½ teaspoon ground white pepper
¼ teaspoon celery seed

Mix thoroughly and place in shaker for
use at table on main dishes, vegetables, soups,
or salads.

Spicy Blend
Sodium: 0.59 mg per teaspoon

2 tablespoons dried savory, crushed
1 tablespoon dry mustard
2½ teaspoons onion powder
1¾ teaspoons curry powder
1¼ teaspoons fresh ground white
    pepper
1¼ teaspoons ground cumin
½ teaspoon garlic powder

Mix thoroughly and place in shaker. Store
in cool, dry place. Use with main dishes.

Guidelines for Modifying Recipes

	Reason for ingredient	*Amount usually used*	*Result of reducing ingredient*
Candies			
Fat	Adds to rich flavor and helps prevent large crystals from forming	Amount varies widely	May result in a coarser texture
Sugar	Necessary for crystallization, proper consistency, texture, and flavor	About 3 cups sugar per cup liquid	**Do not change recipe.** May drastically affect the volume, texture, and consistency
Salt	Helps balance and round out the flavor	Amount varies widely	May change flavor
Cakes			
Fat	Contributes to tenderness, fine grain, and texture	2 to 4 tablespoons fat per cup of flour	May seem less moist and flavorful
Sugar	Contributes to tenderness, texture, moistness, browning, and flavor	½ to ¾ cup sugar per cup of flour	Flavor may be less sweet; may become stale faster. May have paler crust, less color, more open texture, more rounded top, and be drier
Salt	Adds flavor	Variable	Little effect
Canned and Frozen Fruit			
Sugar	Helps to preserve firm texture and bright color	½ to 1⅓ cups sugar per cup water for syrup; ¼ to ⅓ cup sugar per pint of frozen fruit (dry pack)	Texture may be less firm. Flavor may be less sweet. Color may be less bright
Canned Vegetables			
Salt	Adds flavor	1 teaspoon salt per quart	Flavor may change
Cooked Fruits			
Sugar	Helps retain fruit shape and texture during cooking. Increases transparency so brighter	½ cup sugar per cup cooking water (Too much sugar causes fruits to shrink and become firm)	Texture likely to be softer; color likely to be less bright; flavor will be less sweet
Cookies			
Fat	Increases tenderness	¼ to ½ cup fat per cup flour	May make cookies less tender
Sugar	Contributes to sweetness, browning, and tenderness. Melts during baking so cookie spreads out	⅓ to 1⅓ cups sugar per cup flour	Flavor will be less sweet; cookie will be tougher and paler. With less sugar to melt, cookie will not spread as much
Salt	Adds flavor	¼ to ½ teaspoon salt per cup flour	May alter flavor slightly
Custards and Puddings			
Sugar	Causes eggs to coagulate at higher temperature so consistency is softer	1½ to 3 tablespoons sugar per cup milk	Consistency will be firmer and baking time may be shorter
Salt	Adds flavor	⅛ teaspoon salt per cup milk	Flavor may change

	Reason for ingredient	*Amount usually used*	*Result of reducing ingredient*
Ice Cream			
Fat	Fat (in cream) helps make a smooth texture and aids incorporation of air during freezing; also gives a rich flavor	Liquid is usually about half milk and half cream	Using a milk product that is lower in fat reduces the richness, creaminess, and smoothness of the ice cream
Sugar	Lowers freezing point and lengthens freezing time so ice cream will be softer at a given temperature. Contributes to smooth texture. Adds sweetness	½ cup sugar to each cup of milk or cream	Texture may be coarser. Ice cream will be harder and less sweet. Freezing time will be shorter
Salt	Adds flavor	Amount varies	Little effect
Main Dishes			
Salt	Adds flavor	1 teaspoon salt per 4–6 servings; 1 teaspoon salt to each pound ground beef	Little effect
Pasta, Rice, Legumes			
Salt	Adds flavor	1 teaspoon salt to each cup of uncooked pasta, rice, legumes	May change flavor
Pickles			
Sugar	Contributes to crisp texture. May act as a preservative if enough is used	Highly variable	**Do not change recipe.** May cause texture changes and/or spoilage
Salt	Essential in brine to permit growth of desirable microorganisms which produce the acid needed to prevent spoilage	Highly variable	**Do not change recipe.** May cause texture changes and/or spoilage
Quick Breads			
Fat	Increases tenderness	1 to 4 tablespoons fat per cup of flour	May be less tender and less moist
Sugar	Contributes to sweetness, tenderness, browning, moistness, and volume	1 to 4 tablespoons sugar per cup of flour	May result in a less sweet, less tender product with a greater tendency to dry out
Salt	Adds flavor	¼ to ½ teaspoon salt per cup of flour	May affect flavor slightly
Sauces and Gravies			
Fat	Separates the flour or starch granules to prevent lumpiness	1 to 3 tablespoons fat per cup liquid	Smooth sauces can be made with less fat. If no fat is used, blend starch or flour with cold liquid. Flavor will be milder
Salt	Adds flavor	¼ teaspoon salt per cup liquid	Little effect

	Reason for ingredient	Amount usually used	Result of reducing ingredient
Sweet Spreads (Jellies, Jams, Preserves, Butters)			
Sugar	Essential for jelling and protecting against spoilage	Highly variable	Never change recipes for sweet spreads unless they are to be frozen or refrigerated. They are carefully balanced to produce a high quality product that will not spoil
Yeast Breads and Rolls			
Fat	Increases tenderness and enhances keeping quality. Large amounts decrease volume	1 to 3 teaspoons fat per cup of flour in bread; 1 to 4 tablespoons fat per cup flour in rolls	May reduce keeping quality
Sugar	Contributes to a soft texture, sweet flavor, and brown crust. Provides food for yeast during fermentation. Small amounts of sugar increase the rate of fermentation; large amounts of sugar depress yeast action	Up to 1 tablespoon sugar per cup flour in bread; ½ to 2 tablespoons sugar per cup flour in rolls	May affect rate of fermentation. May not be as tender or moist. Rolls may not brown as quickly
Salt	Inhibits yeast fermentation. Improves texture. Adds flavor. Has a slight toughening effect on the gluten	¼ to ½ teaspoon salt per cup flour	May cause yeast to grow too rapidly, resulting in a poor texture. Satisfactory bread needs some salt

Helpful Information and Tips

Health professionals recommend a daily sodium intake below 2,400 mg. About one-third of the average daily intake of sodium comes from salt added to food during cooking or at the table.

The amount of saturated fat in the diet has a much greater effect on blood cholesterol than does the amount of cholesterol in the diet.

You can use reduced fat sour cream, low-fat or nonfat yogurt, or cottage cheese instead of regular sour cream in sauces and dips. Skim milk can be used instead of whole milk in most recipes. Evaporated milk can be substituted for whipping cream, and evaporated skim milk can be substituted for regular evaporated milk in some recipes.

Comparing numbers—of calories and grams of fat or fiber, for example—is one way to decide which foods to choose to eat. But specific numbers do not reflect flavor, cost, or individual nutritional status. Healthy eating means learning to balance both the variety and quantity of foods eaten over several days.

When using a regular—not lite or microwave—brownie or cake mix, you can substitute ½ cup plain nonfat yogurt for the 2 eggs and ½ cup oil.

The information in this section is taken from North Central Regional Extension Publication 473, ALTERING RECIPES, written by Patricia Redlinger, Iowa State University extension food science specialist, and Diane Nelson, Iowa State University extension communication specialist. Information used by permission.

APPETIZERS, BEVERAGES, AND DIPS

APPETIZERS

Artichoke Appetizer

1 3-ounce can Parmesan cheese
1 14-ounce can artichoke hearts, chopped and drained
8 ounces mayonnaise
1 package party rye bread

In bowl, combine cheese, mayonnaise, and artichokes. Place 1 tablespoon of cheese mixture onto party rye bread slices. Broil slices until they become light brown. Serves 20.

Nutritional analysis per serving: 105 cal, 0 g fiber, 10 g fat, 10 mg chol, 185 mg sodium

Asparagus Fingers

1 large loaf fresh, sliced white bread
1 8-ounce package cream cheese
salt and pepper, to taste
1 bottle Italian dressing
1 10.5-ounce can asparagus pieces, drained

Trim crust from bread. Flatten trimmed bread with rolling pin and set aside. In mixing bowl, combine cream cheese, salt, pepper, and enough salad dressing to make mixture spreadable. Spread mixture evenly onto bread slices and place asparagus pieces along one end. Roll into finger sandwiches. Chill. Serves 30.

Nutritional analysis per serving: 95 cal, 0 g fiber, 6.7 g fat, 8.6 mg chol, 116 mg sodium

Asparagus Sandwich ★

1 large bell pepper, chopped fine
1 large onion, grated
1 large pimento, drained and mashed fine
2 tablespoons mayonnaise
1 15-ounce can asparagus spears
12 slices sandwich bread, crusts trimmed
1 tablespoon butter, melted
paprika

Combine bell pepper, onion, pimento, and mayonnaise. With rolling pin, roll each slice of bread flat. Spread mayonnaise mixture evenly on flattened bread slices. Place 1 asparagus spear on each slice of bread, and roll bread around asparagus spear. Fasten with toothpick. Brush bread with butter. Sprinkle with paprika. Brown under broiler. Serves 12.

Nutritional analysis per serving: 34 cal, 0.12 g fiber, 3 g fat, 4 mg chol, 143 mg sodium

Baked Popcorn Crunch

½ cup butter
½ cup brown sugar
3 quarts popped corn
1 cup peanuts

Mix butter and sugar until fluffy. Combine popcorn and peanuts. Stir in butter and sugar mixture. Place in baking dish. Bake at 350°F for 8 minutes. Pour into bowl to serve. Serves 24.

Nutritional analysis per serving: 95.2 cal, 0.75 g fiber, 6.8 g fat, 10.4 mg chol, 66.2 mg sodium

Cheese Ball

1 pound extra sharp Cheddar cheese, finely grated
3 ounces cream cheese, at room temperature
1 4-ounce jar chopped pimento, undrained
2 teaspoons Worcestershire sauce
1 teaspoon minced garlic
1 cup chopped pecans

Mix together all ingredients except nuts. Roll cheese mixture into ball. Roll ball in nuts. Serves 24.

Nutritional analysis per serving: 118 cal, 0 g fiber, 10.5 g fat, 23.5 mg chol, 136 mg sodium

Cheese Hors d'Oeuvres

4 8-ounce jars cheese spread
1 pound butter or margarine, at room temperature
1 teaspoon pepper sauce
1½ teaspoons beau monde seasoning
dash of cayenne pepper
2 teaspoons dill weed
½ teaspoon dill seed
2 large loaves stale sandwich bread, crusts trimmed

In large bowl, combine all ingredients except bread and mix well. Spread light, even layer of cheese mixture over 2 slices and top with third slice of bread. Cut stack into fourths. Ice each square stack with cheese mixture (as icing a cake). Place stacks on cookie sheet, being sure they do not touch each other. Place cookie sheet in freezer. Once stacks are frozen, transfer into freezer containers, seal, and keep frozen until ready to use. To serve: Place frozen squares on cookie sheet and bake at 350°F for 15 to 20 minutes, or until bubbly and lightly brown. Serve hot. Do not allow squares to thaw before baking as cheese icing will puddle. Serves 68.

Nutritional analysis per serving: 80 cal, 0 g fiber, 5 g fat, 5 mg chol, 238 mg sodium

Cheese Straws

1 stick (½ cup) margarine, at room temperature
1 pound sharp Cheddar cheese, grated fine
2 cups plus 2 tablespoons sifted all-purpose flour
⅛ teaspoon ground cayenne, if desired

Cream margarine. Add cheese and cream with electric mixer until smooth. Add flour slowly and mix until smooth. Add cayenne, if desired. Fill large cookie press with mixture. Form straws on ungreased cookie sheet, making each straw about 2 inches long. Bake at 375°F for 8 to 15 minutes, until golden brown. Serves 25.

Nutritional analysis per serving: 141 cal, 0 g fiber, 10 g fat, 19 mg chol, 154 mg sodium

Cheese Straws √

1 cup sharp Cheddar cheese
1 cup all-purpose flour
½ tablespoon red pepper
1 stick butter, softened
40 drained olives (optional)

Sift flour and pepper into cheese. Add softened butter and mix well. Mixture will be stiff. Shape into straws using star-shaped disc on cookie press, or shape into ball about size of marble. Indent center and place well-drained olive in center of dough. Pull dough up around sides of olive until enclosed. Bake in preheated 350°F oven until light brown, about 12 to 15 minutes. Makes about four dozen straws or olive crackers. Serves 12.

Nutritional analysis per serving: 157 cal, 1 g fiber, 13 g fat, 31 mg chol, 406 mg sodium

Cheese Wafers

2 cups Cheddar cheese, grated
1 stick margarine, at room temperature
1½ cups all-purpose flour
¾ teaspoon salt
¾ teaspoon paprika
½ cup finely chopped nuts

Preheat oven to 300°F. Combine all ingredients in large mixing bowl. Divide mixture into halves. Make two 6-inch long rolls from mixture and wrap in waxed paper. Place rolls in refrigerator for at least 1 hour. Remove rolls from refrigerator and slice into ¼-inch wafers. Bake 10 minutes, or until lightly brown. Serves 48.

Nutritional analysis per serving: 45.5 cal, 0 g fiber, 3 g fat, 5 mg chol, 74.3 mg sodium

Clemson Bleu Cheese Balls

½ stick margarine
½ cup Bleu cheese, crumbled
½ cup flour
⅔ cup pecans, chopped

Cream margarine and cheese well. Add flour and blend well. Add pecans and roll into walnut-size balls. Bake in preheated 350°F oven 15 minutes. Serves 4.

Nutritional analysis per serving: 336 cal, 0 g fiber, 28 g fat, 13 mg chol, 508 mg sodium

Corned Beef Cheese Rolls

1 15-ounce can corned beef, chopped fine
½ pound grated cheese
½ cup mustard
1 stick (½ cup) butter, at room temperature
40 slices day-old bread, crust trimmed

Preheat oven to 350°F. Combine corned beef, cheese, mustard, and butter. Mix well. Spread 2 tablespoons of beef mixture on each slice of bread. Roll bread and fasten with toothpick. Place in single layer on cookie sheet. Bake 10 minutes or until brown. Serves 40.

Nutritional analysis per serving: 126 cal, 0 g fiber, 5.6 g fat, 19 mg chol, 27.5 mg sodium

Corned Beef Cracker Spread

1 15-ounce can corned beef
1 large onion, quartered
3 hard-cooked eggs, peeled
1 small sweet pickle
½ cup mayonnaise

1 tablespoon lemon juice
salt and pepper, to taste

In food processor, combine corned beef, onion, eggs, and pickle. Process until uniform. Add mayonnaise and lemon juice. Season to taste. Process until blended. Store in refrigerator. Serves 5.

Nutritional analysis per serving: 555 cal, 0.13 g fiber, 45.6 g fat, 421 mg chol, 1148 mg sodium

Crab Topping or Dip √

2 cups crab meat
8 ounces cream cheese
1 tablespoon mayonnaise
2 teaspoons horseradish
1 teaspoon grated onion
¼ cup grated sharp cheese
dash of salt and pepper
dash of garlic powder

Mix all ingredients. Serve as dip cold or spread on top of crackers and place under broiler until bubbly. Serves 12. (May reduce calories and fat by using low-fat and/or lite cheeses.)

Nutritional analysis per serving: 103 cal, 0 g fiber, 8 g fat, 46 mg chol, 200 mg sodium

Cracker Snack Mix

2 cups small pretzels
1 cup bite-size Cheddar cheese crackers
2 cups goldfish-shaped crackers
1 cup crispy rice cereal squares
3 tablespoons butter or margarine, melted
2 teaspoons Worcestershire sauce
½ teaspoon seasoning salt

Combine first four ingredients in large bowl. Combine butter, Worcestershire sauce, and seasoning salt; pour over mixture, tossing to coat. Spread mixture in 15 × 10 × 1-inch jellyroll pan. Bake at 250°F for 30 minutes, stirring twice. Let cool, and store in airtight container. Serves 24.

Nutritional analysis per serving: 53 cal, 0.2 fiber, 3 g fat, 2 mg chol, 178 mg sodium

Gorp

1 12-ounce can unsalted dry roasted
  peanuts
1½ cups raisins
1 cup chocolate chips

Mix together peanuts, raisins, and chocolate chips in medium-size bowl. Store in covered container. Serves 14.

Nutritional analysis per serving: 245 cal, 3 g fiber, 15 g fat, 0 mg chol, 4 mg sodium

Holiday Appetizer Pie

8 ounces cream cheese, at room
  temperature
2 tablespoons milk
½ cup sour cream
1 2.5-ounce jar sliced dried beef,
  chopped fine
2 tablespoons dried minced onion
2 tablespoons minced bell pepper
⅛ teaspoon black pepper
¼ cup coarsely chopped pecans or
  walnuts

Preheat oven to 350°F. Blend cream cheese and milk in mixing bowl. Stir in sour cream. Add beef, onion, green pepper, and black pepper and stir well. Spoon mixture into shallow 9-inch pie pan. Sprinkle nuts on top. Bake for 15 minutes. Serve warm with assorted crackers. Serves 12.

Nutritional analysis per serving: 112 cal, 0.2 g fiber, 11 g fat, 27.4 mg chol, 99 mg sodium

Mexican Appetizers

2 4-ounce cans green chilies, chopped
8 ounces sharp Cheddar cheese, grated
2 eggs
2 tablespoons milk

Preheat oven to 350°F. Lightly grease 9-inch pie pan with butter or margarine. Place chilies in pan. Sprinkle grated cheese over chilies. Blend eggs and milk. Pour over cheese. Bake for 30 minutes. Serve with crackers. Serves 16.

Nutritional analysis per serving: 42 cal, 0 g fiber, 3 g fat, 42 mg chol, 153 mg sodium

Peanut Butter Sticks

1 loaf white sandwich bread
1 cup smooth peanut butter
½ cup vegetable oil
bread crumbs

Remove crust from bread. Slice bread into strips. Place strips of bread onto large cookie sheet. Put into 175°F oven for 60 minutes to dry bread. In saucepan, melt peanut butter with oil over low heat. Drop sticks of bread into peanut butter mixture. Remove sticks and roll in bread crumbs. Store coated sticks in metal tins. Serves 100.

Nutritional analysis per serving: 42 cal, 0 g fiber, 2.6 g fat, 0.2 mg chol, 43.7 mg sodium

Sausage-Cheese Roll Ups

1 can Pillsbury French Bread
½ pound bulk sausage, fried and drained
1 cup sharp cheese, shredded

Unroll french bread dough. Spread sausage and cheese over whole surface, leaving 1-inch rim around edges. Roll into log. Seal edges and ends. Place on cookie sheet with seam side down. Bake in preheated 350°F oven for 25–30 minutes. If browning too quickly, cover with sheet of aluminum foil after about first 15 minutes. Cool slightly and slice into rounds to serve. Serves 10.

Nutritional analysis per serving: 177 cal, 1 g fiber, 11 g fat, 31 mg chol, 386 mg sodium

Shrimp-Cheese Ball

8 ounces cream cheese, at room
  temperature
1 4.5-ounce can shrimp, drained and
  chopped
6 to 8 drops hot sauce
1½ tablespoons minced onion
parsley flakes, for color

Mix cream cheese, shrimp, hot sauce, and onion together. Form mixture into ball and roll ball in parsley. Chill. Serves 12.

Nutritional analysis per serving: 76 cal, 0.01 g fiber, 7 g fat, 35 mg chol, 69.3 mg sodium

BEVERAGES

Banana Crush ★

3 cups water
4 cups pineapple juice
2½ cups orange juice
½ cup lemon juice
5 bananas, mashed
64-ounce bottle lemon-lime carbonated
   soda, chilled

Mix water, juices, and bananas together. Pour into freezer container and freeze. When ready to serve, thaw slightly, pour into punch bowl, pour soda over, and break frozen mixture into chunks with fork. Serves 22.

Nutritional analysis per serving: 239 cal, 0.4 g fiber, 0.2 g fat, 0 mg chol, 11.3 mg sodium

Banana Punch +

4 large ripe bananas
3 cups pineapple juice
2 cups frozen orange juice
6 cups water
4 cups sugar
juice of 2 lemons
5 12-ounce cans ginger ale or lemon-
   lime drink (low-calorie ginger ale may
   be used)

Liquefy bananas in pineapple juice in blender. Combine remaining ingredients, except ginger ale. Freeze at least 24 hours. Remove from freezer 1 to 1½ hours before serving. Mash with potato masher and pour ginger ale over. Serves 50.

Nutritional analysis per serving: 96 cal, 0 g fiber, 0 g fat, 0 mg chol, 4 mg sodium

Combination Punch + ★

1 46-ounce can pineapple juice
1 46-ounce can orange juice
1 46-ounce can apple juice
2 quarts ginger ale

Mix juices. Let stand 1 to 2 hours for flavors to blend. Pour in ginger ale before serving.

Have all ingredients very cold, but may need some crushed ice. Serves 50.

Nutritional analysis per serving: 65 cal, 0 g fiber, 0 g fat, 0 g chol, 5 mg sodium

Concord Punch +

1 12-ounce can undiluted frozen
   concentrate Concord grape drink (or
   juice)
1 12-ounce can undiluted frozen
   concentrate pink lemonade
6 cups cold water
½ gallon orange sherbet
2 quarts cold orange-flavored soda

Combine grape and lemonade concentrates. Add water and stir until dissolved. Just before serving, drop scoops of sherbet on top; last, pour orange drink over all. Note: If desired, add sherbet to juice mixture. Mix with electric mixer. Add orange drink and stir. Serves 40.

Nutritional analysis per serving: 97 cal, 0 g fiber, 1 g fat, 3 mg chol, 27 mg sodium

Extra Special Punch +

6 quarts Ice Cream Parlor Lemon Peel
   Sherbet
12 quarts Catawba grape juice

Allow sherbet to soften and pour grape juice over it. Since this flavor of sherbet is not available at all times, you may substitute any lemon or pineapple sherbet. This punch is expensive, but it's extra special. Serves 100.

Nutritional analysis per serving: 126 cal, 0 g fiber, 1 g fat, 3 mg chol, 21 mg sodium

Frosty Geechie Tea ★

1 cup hot American Classic Tea
2 cups crushed ice
⅓ cup sugar
1 cup strawberries, washed and
   quartered
juice of ⅛ lemon
2 firm kiwi, peeled and quartered

Blend first three ingredients. Add strawberries, lemon juice, and kiwi. Blend 30 seconds. Serve in frosted parfait glasses and garnish with kiwi slice, strawberry, lemon, or mint leaf. Serves 4.

Nutritional analysis per serving: 83 cal, 1 g fiber, 0 g fat, 0 mg chol, 2 mg sodium

Fruit Punch ★

    1 46-ounce can pineapple juice
    1 6-ounce can frozen orange juice
        concentrate
    1 6-ounce can frozen lemonade
        concentrate
    1 quart cold water
    2 quarts ginger ale

Mix juice and concentrates together. Chill. When ready to serve, stir in water and ginger ale. Serves 30.

Nutritional analysis per serving: 116 cal, 0 g fiber, 0.06 g fat, 0 mg chol, 5.5 mg sodium

Fruit Punch + ★

    1 6-ounce can frozen orange juice
    1 6-ounce can frozen lemonade
    2 6-ounce cans frozen limeade
    1 1-pound, 14-ounce can pineapple juice
    1 pint cranberry juice cocktail
    2 to 4 cups cold water
    2 quarts ginger ale, chilled
    1 quart plain soda water, chilled
    fruit; mint for garnish

Empty frozen juices, pineapple, and cranberry juice cocktail into large container or bowl; add water. Thaw; stir well. Pour mixture into punch bowl. Add ice cubes. Just before serving, gently pour in ginger ale and soda water. Top with Fruit Ice Ring and sprigs of mint or other fruit garnish. Serves 30.

Fruit Ice Ring: Use any combination of lime, lemon, or orange slices. Arrange in pattern in bottom of 8-inch ring mold. Add water to cover fruit. Freeze. To unmold, loosen ring by dipping into warm water. Float on top of punch. Garnish with mint leaves and, if available, fresh strawberry slices.

Nutritional analysis per serving: 68 cal, 0 g fiber, 0 g fat, 0 g chol, 8 mg sodium

Grandma's Hot Chocolate

    1 25-ounce package dry milk
    1 pound powdered sugar
    1 pound powdered chocolate milk
    1 12-ounce jar powdered dairy creamer

Combine all ingredients in airtight container for storage. Use 2 heaping tablespoons of powder to 8-ounce cup of hot water. Serves 72.

Nutritional analysis per serving: 85 cal, 0 g fiber, 2.4 g fat, 5.5 mg chol, 39 mg sodium

Hot Apple Punch ★

    2 quarts unsweetened apple juice
    ½ cup red hot cinnamon hearts

Cook apple juice and cinnamon hearts over medium heat until the candies melt. Serve hot. Serves 12.

Nutritional analysis per serving: 10 cal, 0 g fiber, 0.02 fat, 0 mg chol, 0.6 mg sodium

Hot Cranberry Punch +

    1 cup dark brown sugar, packed
    1 cup water
    ½ teaspoon ground cinnamon
    ¼ teaspoon ground nutmeg
    ½ teaspoon ground cloves
    ¼ teaspoon ground allspice
    2 16-ounce cans cranberry sauce
    4 cups water
    7 cups apple juice
    butter
    cinnamon sticks

Combine sugar, 1 cup water, and spices in large kettle. Heat to boiling; then simmer. Put cranberry sauce and small amount of water in blender and liquefy. Add additional water then add apple juice and cranberry mixture to spices. Heat to simmer. Pour into mugs; put a pat of butter on each; and garnish with cinnamon sticks. Serves 24.

Nutritional analysis per serving: 126 cal, 1 g fiber, 0 g fat, 0 mg chol, 17 mg sodium

Mocha Punch +

1 cup instant coffee
6 cups cold water
1 cup chocolate syrup
4 pints chocolate ice cream
4 cups milk
2 teaspoons almond extract

Add cold water to coffee and stir until coffee is dissolved. Blend in remaining ingredients. Serves 32.

Nutritional analysis per serving: 70 cal, 0 g fiber, 2 g fat, 6 mg chol, 44 mg sodium

Orange Julius

½ cup sugar
1 cup milk
1 cup water
6 ice cubes
1 6-ounce can orange juice concentrate
½ teaspoon vanilla extract

Combine all ingredients in blender until ice is crushed. Serve immediately. Serves 4.

Nutritional analysis per serving: 155 cal, 0 g fiber, 2 g fat, 8.3 mg chol, 31 mg sodium

Peach Shake ★

1 cup low-fat milk
1 ripe peach, peeled and sliced
¼ teaspoon artificial sweetener, optional

Blend ingredients together for 30 seconds or until smooth. Serves 1.

Nutritional analysis per serving: 175 cal, 1 g fiber, 3 g fat, 10 mg chol, 123 mg sodium

Perked Punch

2 cups unsweetened pineapple juice
2 cups cranberry juice cocktail
1¾ cups water
¾ cup light brown sugar
1¼ teaspoons whole cloves
½ stick cinnamon

Use 6-cup or larger percolator. In bottom of percolator, put pineapple juice, cranberry juice, and water. In basket, put sugar, cloves, and cinnamon. Allow to perk until appliance stops. Remove basket that contains spices. Keep warm. To use coffee maker instead of percolator, put juices in carafe. Put water in usual section. Put spices and sugar in coffee basket. Brew until finished. Remove basket that contains spices. Keep warm. Serves 6.

Nutritional analysis per serving: 198 cal, 0 g fiber, 0.2 g fat, 0 mg chol, 11 mg sodium

Perky Cinnamon-Apple Juice ★

1 gallon apple juice
1 33.8-ounce bottle ginger ale
1 teaspoon whole cloves
2 3-inch sticks cinnamon, broken
¾ cup cinnamon candies

Pour apple juice and ginger ale into 30-cup electric percolator, place spices and candy in percolator basket. Perk through complete cycle. Serves 30.

Nutritional analysis per serving: 79 cal, 0 g fiber, 0 g fat, 0 mg chol, 7 mg sodium

Pineapple-Cranberry Punch ★

2 cups pineapple juice
1 32-ounce bottle cranberry juice, chilled
1 12-ounce can frozen orange juice
   concentrate, thawed
½ cup sugar
1 28-ounce bottle ginger ale, chilled
orange slices, to garnish

Combine all ingredients except ginger ale in pitcher. Refrigerate until ready to serve. When ready to serve, add ginger ale. Pour into ice-filled glasses and garnish with orange slices. Serves 10.

Nutritional analysis per serving: 170 cal, 0 g fiber, 0.2 g fat, 0 mg chol, 9 mg sodium

Punch +

6 large cans pineapple juice
2 large cans Hawaiian punch
2 large cans frozen lemonade
1 small can frozen lemon juice

4 large bottles ginger ale
2 gallons pineapple sherbet

Mix all ingredients. Serves 100.
Nutritional analysis per serving: 210 cal, 0 g fiber, 1 g fat, 4 mg chol, 44 mg sodium

Quick Punch ★

2 liters cherry-flavored carbonated
 drink, chilled
1 46-ounce can pineapple juice, chilled

Mix together just before serving. Serves 12.
Nutritional analysis per serving: 134.3 cal, 0 g fiber, 0.3 g fat, 0 mg chol, 17.6 mg sodium

Russian Tea Mix ★

2 7-ounce jars sugar-free powdered
 orange drink mix
¾ cup instant sugar-free tea mix
1 teaspoon ground cinnamon
½ teaspoon ground cloves

Combine all ingredients and mix well. Store in airtight container. To serve: Stir 2 teaspoons of mix into cup of hot water. Serves 72.
Nutritional analysis per serving: 5 cal, 0 g fiber, 0 g fat, 0 mg chol, 7 mg sodium

Simple Fruit Punch ★

1 5.5-ounce package lemonade-flavored
 drink mix
1 48-ounce can unsweetened pineapple
 juice, chilled
1 33.8-ounce bottle ginger ale, chilled
 liquid red food coloring, optional

Prepare drink mix according to package directions; chill. Just before serving, stir in juice and ginger ale; add a few drops of food coloring, if desired. Serves 18.
Nutritional analysis per serving: 100 cal, 0 g fiber, 0 g fat, 0 mg chol, 8 mg sodium

Spiced Coffee Mix ★

½ cup instant coffee granules
¼ cup firmly packed brown sugar
¼ teaspoon ground cinnamon

¼ teaspoon ground cloves
¼ teaspoon ground nutmeg

Combine all ingredients, stirring well. Store at room temperature in airtight container. Combine 1 tablespoon coffee mix and 1 cup boiling water. Serves 12.
Nutritional analysis per serving: 18 cal, 0 g fiber, 0 g fat, 0 mg chol, 2 mg sodium

Tazzy Tea ★

½ cup instant sugar-free lemon-flavored
 ice tea mix
1 16-ounce can frozen lemonade
 concentrate, thawed
2¾ quarts water
1 liter sugar-free lemon-lime soda

Combine all ingredients in large pitcher. Serves 16.
Nutritional analysis per serving: 11 cal, 0 g fiber, 0.01 g fat, 0 mg chol, 30 mg sodium

Teaberry Punch + ★

4 cups cold water
12 cups unsweetened tea
1 6-ounce can lemonade frozen
 concentrate
1 6-ounce can limeade frozen
 concentrate
1 cup cranberry juice cocktail
1 28-ounce bottle ginger ale

Mix all ingredients except ginger ale. Pour over crushed ice and add ginger ale last. Serves 25.
Nutritional analysis per serving: 43 cal, 0 g fiber, 0 g fat, 0 mg chol, 4 mg sodium

Wassail + ★

4 quarts apple juice
1 cup firmly packed dark brown sugar
1 6-ounce can frozen lemon juice
 concentrate
1 6-ounce can frozen orange juice
 concentrate
6 whole cloves
6 allspice berries

24 cinnamon sticks
1 tablespoon ground nutmeg

Combine apple juice, sugar, and undiluted juices. Tie spices in bag and drop in apple juice mixture. Cover and simmer 15–20 minutes. Remove spice bag. Serve hot in mugs, with a cinnamon stick in each. Serves 24.

Nutritional analysis per serving: 134 cal, 1 g fiber, 0 g fat, 0 mg chol, 7 mg sodium

Wassail Beverage ★

1 gallon apple cider or apple juice
1 6-ounce can frozen lemonade
   concentrate
1 6-ounce can frozen orange juice
   concentrate
4 sticks cinnamon
½ teaspoon ground allspice
1 tablespoon whole cloves

Pour apple cider and concentrates in large pot. Tie spices together in cheesecloth bag and add to pot. Simmer on medium heat until flavors are blended. Remove spices. Serve warm. Serves 24.

Nutritional analysis per serving: 98 cal, 0 g fiber, 0.2 g fat, 0 mg chol, 5.4 mg sodium

DIPS

Crab Dip

8 ounces cream cheese, at room
   temperature
⅓ cup mayonnaise
1 teaspoon horseradish
½ teaspoon seasoned salt
1 tablespoon parsley
dash of garlic powder
1½ tablespoons minced onion
1 6-ounce can crab meat

Combine all ingredients. Stir well. Refrigerate until ready to use. Serve with crackers. Serves 16. (May reduce calories and fat by using low-fat and/or lite cream cheese and mayonnaise.)

Nutritional analysis per serving: 92 cal, 0 g fiber, 8.6 g fat, 27.5 mg chol, 103 mg sodium

Hot Chicken Dip +

2 10.75-ounce cans mushroom soup,
   undiluted
2 8-ounce packages cream cheese
2 5-ounce cans chunk white chicken
2 2.75-ounce packages slivered almonds
2 2-ounce cans mushrooms, drained and
   sliced
1 teaspoon Worcestershire sauce
¼ teaspoon garlic powder
¼ teaspoon pepper

Combine all ingredients in 1-quart sauce pan or fondue pot. Cook over medium heat, stirring often, until blended and heated thoroughly. Serve dip hot with chips. Serves 14.

Nutritional analysis per serving: 261 cal, 2 g fiber, 23 g fat, 36 mg chol, 545 mg sodium

Mex Tex Dip

8 ounces sour cream
½ cup mayonnaise
1 package taco seasoning
hot sauce (optional)
2 8-ounce cans bean dip
1 cup onion, diced
3 tomatoes, chopped
1 15-ounce can ripe olives, chopped
8 ounces sharp Cheddar cheese, grated
tortilla chips

In mixing bowl, combine sour cream, mayonnaise, and taco mix. Mix well. Add hot sauce to taste, if desired. Divide sour cream mixture between two 9-inch pie pans. Cover sour cream with layer of bean dip. Top layers with remaining ingredients in following order: onions, tomatoes, olives, and cheese. Serve with tortilla chips. Serves 16. (May reduce calories and/or fat by using low-fat and/or lite sour cream, cheese, and mayonnaise.)

Nutritional analysis per serving: 199 cal, 0.3 g fiber, 16.5 g fat, 18 mg chol, 424 mg sodium

Nacho Chip Dip

8 ounces cream cheese, at room
   temperature
1 medium onion, chopped

1 16-ounce can chili with beans
8 ounces Monterey Jack cheese with
  jalapeño, grated

Spread cream cheese into bottom of 9-inch square casserole dish. Cover with onions. Pour chili over onions. Sprinkle grated cheese evenly over top. Heat in microwave on high for 10 minutes or place in 350°F oven until cheese melts, about 10 minutes. Serve with tortilla or nacho chips. Serves 35.

Nutritional analysis per serving: 63.3 cal, 0.02 g fiber, 5 g fat, 15.2 mg chol, 130 mg sodium

Nacho Dip

1 pound ground beef
1 pound Cheddar cheese, grated
1 2-ounce can jalapeño relish

In skillet, brown ground beef. Drain fat. Melt cheese into beef. Add relish. Transfer mixture to Crock-Pot and set heat on low. Serve with nacho chips. Serves 10.

Nutritional analysis per serving: 165 cal, 0 g fiber, 12 g fat, 52.4 mg chol, 207 mg sodium

Simple Crab Dip

1 6-ounce can white crab meat
8 ounces cream cheese
1 stick (½ cup) butter

Combine crab meat, cream cheese, and butter in saucepan. Heat thoroughly over low heat, stirring constantly. Transfer mixture to hot chafing dish. Serve with crackers. Serves 32. (May reduce calories and fat by using low-fat and/or lite butter and cream cheese.)

Nutritional analysis per serving: 55 cal, 0 g fiber, 5.4 g fat, 20.2 mg chol, 68 mg sodium

Spinach Dip +

2 10-ounce packages frozen chopped
  spinach
2 cups mayonnaise
2 cups commercial sour cream
2 medium onions, chopped
2 8-ounce cans water chestnuts, chopped

2 15/8-ounce packages vegetable soup
  mix

Thaw spinach; place on paper towels and press until barely moist. Combine spinach, mayonnaise, sour cream, onion, water chestnuts, and vegetable soup mix; stir well. Cover and chill mixture several hours. Serve dip with crackers or raw vegetables. Serves 12.

Nutritional analysis per serving: 269 cal, 1 g fiber, 22 g fat, 17 mg chol, 380 mg sodium

Vegetable Garden Dip ★

½ cup 2% cottage cheese
1 cup plain low-fat yogurt
1 tablespoon diced green pepper
1 tablespoon grated carrot
1 tablespoon minced onion
¼ teaspoon garlic powder
1 teaspoon lemon juice

Combine all ingredients and stir well. Refrigerate until ready to serve. Serve with raw vegetables and crackers. Serves 12.

Nutritional analysis per serving: 20 cal, 0.02 g fiber, 0.4 g fat, 1.6 mg chol, 52 mg sodium

Vegetable Dip

1 medium onion, chopped
2 cups small-curd cottage cheese
¼ teaspoon pepper sauce
1 teaspoon black pepper
½ teaspoon seasoned salt
1 teaspoon dill weed
½ teaspoon garlic powder
1 teaspoon beau monde seasoning
½ teaspoon celery seed
1½ tablespoons Worcestershire sauce
1 teaspoon dry mustard
2 cups low-calorie mayonnaise

Blend onion and cottage cheese together. Add all remaining spices and mix well. Stir in mayonnaise. Place mixture in refrigerator to chill. Serve with raw vegetables. This dip can also be used as salad dressing. Serves 32.

Nutritional analysis per serving: 37 cal, 0.02 g fiber, 2.6 g fat, 9.8 mg chol, 90.3 mg sodium

SOUPS AND SALADS

PICKLES AND RELISHES

Basic Cranberry Relish

4 medium oranges
4 medium apples, unpeeled and cored
2 pounds fresh cranberries
4 cups sugar

Peel colored rind from oranges and save. Peel off and discard white skin (pith). Put orange rind, orange pulp (seeds removed), cranberries, and apples through food grinder. Add sugar to ground mixture. Mix well. Cover and refrigerate. Serve chilled. To preserve, pour into pint containers, leaving half-inch headspace. Seal and freeze. Thaw in refrigerator. Serves 16.

Nutritional analysis per serving: 231 cal, 0.6 g fiber, 0.3 g fat, 0 mg chol, 1.4 mg sodium

Cranberry Relish

1 pound tart apples (Winesaps or
   Jonathans are good)
1 16-ounce package whole fresh
   cranberries
1 cup sugar, or to taste

Core apples; do not peel, unless skins are tough. Grind apples and cranberries. Add sugar and mix well. Refrigerate covered. Allow to marinate at least 24 hours, stirring several times. Serves 16.

Nutritional analysis per serving: 98.4 cal, 0.7 g fiber, 0.2 g fat, 0 mg chol, 0.3 mg sodium

Jerusalem Artichoke Pickles √

4 quarts artichoke roots
4 large onions
3 pints vinegar
1 tablespoon turmeric
2 tablespoons white mustard seed
2½ cups brown sugar
3 tablespoons salt

Wash and scrape artichokes. Put artichoke and onion through food chopper. While grinding vegetables, have other ingredients cooking. Combine all and let boil slowly for 30 minutes. Pour into hot sterile jars and seal while hot. Makes 6 pints.

Nutritional analysis per serving: 22 cal, 0 g fiber, 0 g fat, 0 mg chol, 101 mg sodium

Piccalilli √

2 quarts chopped green tomatoes
1 pint chopped green peppers
1 pint thinly sliced carrots
2 ounces mustard seed
2 pounds sugar
2 quarts white vinegar
1 pint chopped onion
1 quart shredded cabbage
1 pint chopped celery
1 teaspoon turmeric
4 tablespoons salt

Place all ingredients in large pot. Mix well and cook slowly for 1 hour, stirring occasionally. Pour into hot, sterilized jars and seal.

Nutritional analysis per serving: 12 cal, 0 g fiber, 0 g fat, 0 mg chol, 69 mg sodium

Refrigerator Pickles

8 cups unpeeled, unwaxed cucumber
  slices
3 medium onions, sliced
2 tablespoons salt
4 cups sugar
4 cups vinegar
1 tablespoon pickling spices

Place cucumber slices with onions in glass gallon jar. Sprinkle with salt. In saucepan heat sugar, vinegar, and spices to boiling. Remove from heat. Pour liquid over pickles and cool. Refrigerate for 7 days prior to using to develop flavor. Store in refrigerator. Serves 64.

Nutritional analysis per serving: 54.2 cal, 0.13 g fiber, 0.04 g fat, 0 mg chol, 0.7 mg sodium

Sweet Crisp Dill Pickles

1 46-ounce jar whole dill pickles (not
  kosher)
2 cups granulated sugar
1 tablespoon whole cloves

Drain pickles and slice into strips or slices. Place layer of pickles in jar and sprinkle with layer of sugar, then cloves. Repeat process until all ingredients are used. Screw top onto jar and shake well. Allow jar to sit at room temperature until sugar dissolves. Refrigerate. Serves 46.

Nutritional analysis per serving: 37.2 cal, 0 g fiber, 0.1 g fat, 0 mg chol, 420 mg sodium

Watermelon Rind Pickles √

4 pounds watermelon rind
2 quarts cold water
1 tablespoon slake lime
6 sticks cinnamon
2 tablespoons whole allspice
1 quart vinegar
1 quart water
3½ pounds sugar

Remove all pink pulp and peel green skin from melon. Weigh white rind. Cut into 1-inch cubes to get 4 pounds. Combine cold wa-

ter and lime; pour over rind. Let stand 1 hour. Drain. Cover with fresh cold water. Simmer 1 hour or until tender. Drain. Tie spices in cheesecloth. Combine vinegar, remaining water, and sugar. Heat until sugar dissolves. Add spice bag and rind. Simmer gently 2 hours. Add green vegetable color if desired. Pack rind in hot sterile jars. Fill with boiling syrup. Seal and process for 10 minutes in boiling water bath. Yield: approximately 12 half pints.

Nutritional analysis per serving: 41 cal, 0 g fiber, 0 g fat, 0 mg chol, 328 mg sodium

SALADS

Apple and Pecan Salad

2 large, tart red apples, peeled, cored,
  chopped
1 teaspoon lemon juice
½ cup celery, diced thin
1 cup pecans, chopped
¼ cup mayonnaise
¼ teaspoon salt
½ cup heavy cream, whipped

In mixing bowl combine apples, lemon juice, celery, pecans, mayonnaise, and salt. Stir until just combined. Cover and refrigerate until hour before serving. Fold in whipped cream. Return salad to refrigerator until ready to serve. Serves 4.

Nutritional analysis per serving: 615 cal, 1.6 g fiber, 58.8 g fat, 48.9 chol, 236.4 mg sodium

Apple Salad

1 6-serving package strawberry-flavored
  gelatin
¼ teaspoon ground cinnamon
1¾ cups boiling water
1½ cups apple juice
1 cup apples, peeled, cored, and
  chopped
½ cup finely chopped celery
½ cup finely chopped pecans

In large bowl, combine gelatin, cinnamon, and boiling water. Dissolve gelatin, stirring

41

constantly. Stir in apple juice. Chill until thickened (about 1 hour). Add remaining ingredients. Chill until set. Serves 10.

Nutritional analysis per serving: 129.3 cal, 0.5 g fiber, 3.8 g fat, 0 mg chol, 61.5 mg sodium

Best Ever Fruit Salad ★

1 pint fresh strawberries, halved
1 cup white grapes, halved
4 peaches, sliced
4 apples, sliced
2 tablespoons sugarless instant orange drink
2 tablespoons lemon juice
3 large bananas, sliced

Gently mix strawberries, grapes, peaches, apples, orange drink, and lemon juice together. Chill for up to 3 hours. Mix in bananas just before serving. Serves 8.

Nutritional analysis per serving: 133.3 cal, 3.4 g fiber, 0.8 g fat, 0 mg chol, 4.8 mg sodium

Black-Eyed Pea Salad + ★

6 15-ounce cans black-eyed peas, drained
1½ cups green pepper, chopped
1½ cups red onion, chopped
1½ cloves garlic
¾ cup vinegar
¾ cup vegetable oil
dash of pepper
¾ cup sugar
1½ teaspoons salt
dash of hot sauce

Combine first four ingredients; toss lightly. Combine remaining ingredients; mix well and pour over pea mixture. Cover and refrigerate at least 12 hours. Remove garlic before serving. Serves 24.

Nutritional analysis per serving: 215 cal, 4 g fiber, 12 g fat, 0 mg chol, 456 mg sodium

Blender Lime Congealed Salad

2 cups boiling water
1 6-serving package lime-flavored gelatin
8 ounces cream cheese
1 15-ounce can crushed pineapple
4 tablespoons nondairy whipped topping
½ cup chopped nuts

Combine boiling water and gelatin. Stir until dissolved. Pour gelatin, cream cheese, crushed pineapple, and whipped topping into blender, and blend until well mixed. Pour into 9 × 13-inch dish. Stir in nuts. Refrigerate overnight, or until firm. Cut into squares when firm. Serves 18.

Nutritional analysis per serving: 98 cal, 4.5 g fiber, 4.5 g fat, 13.7 mg chol, 69 mg sodium

Carrot-Apple Salad

1 cup chopped red delicious apples
1 tablespoon lemon juice
2 cups grated carrots
½ cup raisins
½ cup chopped nuts
1 8-ounce can pineapple chunks, drained
3 tablespoons mayonnaise

In large bowl toss apples and lemon juice together. Add carrots, raisins, nuts, pineapple, and mayonnaise. Stir until well combined. Serves 8.

Nutritional analysis per serving: 139.2 cal, 0.93 g fiber, 7.6 g fat, 2 mg chol, 31.4 mg sodium

Christmas Salad

1 20-ounce can crushed pineapple, juice reserved
1 6-serving package lemon gelatin
6 ounces cream cheese, at room temperature
1 2-ounce jar chopped pimento, drained
4 tablespoons mayonnaise
1 cup chopped nuts
2 cups finely chopped celery

Combine pineapple juice with water to make gelatin, following package directions. Allow gelatin to partially congeal. Add cream cheese, pimento, mayonnaise, nuts, celery, and pineapple. Stir until well mixed. Pour into 9 × 13-inch pan. Refrigerate overnight or until set. Serves 10.

Nutritional analysis per serving: 353 cal, 0.7 g fiber, 25 g fat, 22 mg chol, 158 mg sodium

Cornbread-Vegetable Layer Salad

1 1-ounce package Hidden Valley Ranch Dry Salad Dressing Mix
1 cup sour cream
1 cup mayonnaise
1 pan cornbread (Jiffy/crumbled)
2 16-ounce cans kidney beans
3 large tomatoes, chopped
½ cup green peppers, chopped
½ cup onions, chopped
2 cups Cheddar cheese, shredded
10 slices bacon, cooked and crumbled
2 17-ounce whole kernel sweet corn, drained

Combine salad dressing mix, sour cream, and mayonnaise. Set aside. Place half of crumbled cornbread in bottom of large serving bowl. Top with 1 can of beans. In medium bowl, combine tomatoes, peppers, and onions; layer half of mixture over beans. Layer half of cheese, half of bacon, 1 can corn, and half of reserved salad dressing mix. Repeat layers, using remaining ingredients. Garnish as desired. Cover and chill 2 to 3 hours before serving. For fewer calories and less fat, use low-cal or nonfat sour cream, mayonnaise, and salad dressing mix. Also, use bacon bits. Serves 12.

Nutritional analysis per serving: 438 cal, 6 g fiber, 23 g fat, 33 mg chol, 1077 mg sodium

Cranberry Salad

1 20-ounce can crushed pineapple, drained, juice reserved
2 4-serving packages red gelatin
2 cups jellied cranberry sauce
1 cup chopped celery
1 cup chopped nuts

Add enough water to pineapple juice to make 2 cups liquid. Bring liquid to boil and dissolve gelatin in it. Stir in cranberry sauce, celery, nuts, and crushed pineapple. Chill until firm (2 hours or longer). Serves 5.

Nutritional analysis per serving: 514 cal, 0.22 g fiber, 15 g fat, 0 mg chol, 192.4 mg sodium

Cranberry Salad

1 6-serving package cherry-flavored gelatin
2 cups boiling water
2 tablespoons sugar
1 20-ounce can crushed pineapple
2 apples, peeled and chopped
1 10.5-ounce can whole berry cranberry sauce
1 cup chopped nuts
1 cup chopped celery

Mix together gelatin, water, and sugar. Refrigerate until almost firm (about an hour). Stir in remaining ingredients, pour into a 9 × 13-inch dish, and refrigerate overnight or until firm. Serves 12.

Nutritional analysis per serving: 207 cal, 0.53 g fiber, 6.3 g fat, 0 mg chol, 71 mg sodium

Cranberry Salad

1 4-serving package raspberry-flavored gelatin
1 4-serving package orange-flavored gelatin
1 cup boiling water
1 16-ounce can crushed pineapple
1 16-ounce can jellied cranberry sauce, mashed
1 cup chopped walnuts

Dissolve gelatins in boiling water. Stir in remaining ingredients. Pour into lightly oiled 6-cup mold. Chill overnight or until firm. Serves 12.

Nutritional analysis per serving: 230 cal, 0.31 g fiber, 6.3 g fat, 0 mg chol, 76 mg sodium

Cranberry Salad ★

1 16-ounce package fresh cranberries
2 apples, peeled, cored, and quartered
2 oranges, quartered and seeds removed,
   peel from ½ orange
1¾ cups sugar
2 4-serving packages cherry-flavored
   gelatin
1½ cups boiling water

Grind together cranberries, apples, and oranges. Add sugar and mix thoroughly. In separate bowl dissolve gelatin in boiling water. Allow gelatin to partially congeal (about an hour) and add to blended fruit mixture. Chill overnight, or until firm. Serve on lettuce with mayonnaise garnish, if desired. Serves 10.

Nutritional analysis per serving: 236.3 cal, 0.6 g fiber, 0.2 g fat, 0 mg chol, 56 mg sodium

Creamy Potato Salad +

18 medium potatoes
6 eggs, hard-cooked
1⅓ cups mayonnaise
2 teaspoons prepared mustard
1½ cups commercial sour cream
2 teaspoons salt
½ teaspoon pepper
22 slices bacon
½ cup green onions, chopped
1 cup celery, chopped
½ cup commercial Italian salad dressing

Cook potatoes in boiling, salted water about 30 minutes, or until tender. Drain well and cool slightly. Peel and cut potatoes into ¾-inch cubes. Remove yolks from eggs and mash; set whites aside. Stir mayonnaise, mustard, sour cream, salt, and pepper into yolks; set aside. Cook bacon until crisp; drain on paper towels and crumble. Chop egg whites; add bacon, potatoes, onion, celery, and Italian dressing. Fold in mayonnaise mixture; chill at least 2 hours. Serves 24.

Nutritional analysis per serving: 254 cal, 2 g fiber, 19 g fat, 39 mg chol, 441 mg sodium

Crunchy Hot Chicken Salad +

9 cups chicken, cooked and diced
2 tablespoons onion, chopped
3 10.75-ounce cans cream of chicken
   soup, undiluted
1½ teaspoons salt
3 cups celery, finely chopped
1½ cups sliced almonds
4½ cups rice, cooked
3 tablespoons lemon juice
¾ teaspoon pepper
2¼ cups mayonnaise
¾ cup water
9 eggs, hard-cooked and sliced
6 cups potato chips, crushed
2¼ cups Cheddar cheese, shredded

Combine first nine ingredients; toss gently and set aside. Combine mayonnaise and water; beat with wire whisk until smooth. Pour over chicken mixture; stir well. Add eggs and toss gently. Spoon into greased, shallow steam table pan; cover and refrigerate 8 hours or overnight. Bake at 450°F for 10 to 15 minutes or until thoroughly heated. Sprinkle with potato chips and cheese; bake an additional 5 minutes. Serves 24.

Nutritional analysis per serving: 366 cal, 1 g fiber, 25 g fat, 130 mg chol, 1041 mg sodium

Cucumber Combination Salad +

20–24 medium-sized cucumbers
salt
6 onions, sliced thin
1½ cups white vinegar
½ cup salad oil
6–8 fresh tomatoes, diced
1 cup sugar

Peel and slice cucumbers into cold, salted water; use about 1½ teaspoons salt for each quart of water, and have enough water to cover them. Chill for 2 or 3 hours. When ready to prepare salad, drain and rinse cucumbers and combine with all other ingredients. Toss lightly. Lift salad out of liquid and serve in lettuce cup in small bowls garnished with lettuce. Variations: Omit oil and vinegar dressing and substitute 1 quart of mayonnaise or sour cream. To make Cauliflower Combination Salad, omit cucumbers and substitute 8 pounds fresh, crisp cauliflower. Serves 50.

Nutritional analysis per serving: 47 cal, 2 g fiber, 1 g fat, 0 mg chol, 4 mg sodium

Cucumber Salad √ ★

    8 to 10 cucumbers, sliced
    3 to 4 sliced onions
    1 cup vinegar
    2 cups water
    1 cup sugar
    3 tablespoons salt
    1 clove garlic, minced

Place sliced onions and cucumbers in quart jar. Bring vinegar, water, sugar, salt, and garlic to boil. Pour over cucumber mixture. Seal jar. Let marinate 3 or 4 days in refrigerator before using. Serve cold. Serves 16.

Nutritional analysis per serving: 67 cal, 1 g fiber, 0 g fat, 0 mg chol, 1204 mg sodium

D and M Italian Salad

    1 head romaine lettuce, cleaned and torn
        into bite-size pieces
    1 head iceberg lettuce, cleaned and torn
        into bite-size pieces
    1 10-ounce can artichoke hearts, drained
        and halved
    1 4-ounce jar pimento, drained and
        chopped
    ½ cup (1½ ounces) freshly grated
        Parmesan cheese
    salt and pepper, to taste
    ⅓ cup vinegar
    ½ cup salad oil

Combine lettuces, artichokes, and pimento in large salad bowl. Mix together cheese, seasoning, and vinegar. When salt has dissolved, add oil and mix thoroughly. Pour over salad and toss before serving. Serves 12.

Nutritional analysis per serving: 136.5 cal, 0.4 g fiber, 12 g fat, 7.4 mg chol, 221 mg sodium

Delicious Congealed Salad

    1 cup boiling water
    1 4-serving package lemon-flavored
        gelatin
    1 cup (4 ounces) grated sharp Cheddar
        cheese
    1 tablespoon lemon juice
    1 15-ounce can crushed pineapple
    1 8-ounce container nondairy whipped
        topping

In large bowl combine boiling water and gelatin. Stir until gelatin is dissolved. Let cool until mixture begins to gel. Stir in cheese, lemon juice, pineapple, and whipped topping. Lightly spray 5-cup mold with nonstick vegetable spray. Pour mixture into mold, and chill overnight or until set. Serves 10.

Nutritional analysis per serving: 124 cal, 0.4 g fiber, 5 g fat, 12 mg chol, 107 mg sodium

Delight Spaghetti Salad

    1 pound vermicelli spaghetti, cooked
    ½ cup celery, chopped
    ½ cup cucumber, peeled and chopped
    ½ jar salad delight
    1 tomato, diced (garnish)
    ½ cup onion, diced
    ½ cup green bell pepper, chopped fine
    1 bottle Italian salad dressing, or oil and
        vinegar

Combine spaghetti with all remaining ingredients. Toss gently. Marinate in refrigerator for 12 to 24 hours. Serves 6.

Nutritional analysis per serving: 470 cal, 0.5 g fiber, 20 g fat, 0 mg chol, 322 mg sodium

Five Bean Salad ★

    1 16-ounce can green lima beans,
        drained
    1 16-ounce can green beans, drained
    1 16-ounce can kidney beans, drained
    1 16-ounce can yellow wax beans,
        drained
    1 16-ounce can English peas, drained
    ½ cup onion, diced

1 8-ounce jar pimento, chopped and drained
½ cup salad oil
1 cup sugar
1 cup vinegar

Combine beans, peas, onion, pimento, and oil. In separate bowl, stir sugar and vinegar until sugar is dissolved. Pour vinegar mixture over vegetables and toss until well combined. Refrigerate overnight to blend flavors. Serves 20.

Nutritional analysis per serving: 145.3 cal, 1 g fiber, 5.7 g fat, 0 mg chol, 270 mg sodium

Fresh Fruit Salad with Dressing √ ★

1 large box vanilla pudding (not instant)
2 cans Mandarin orange slices (reserve juice)
1 can sliced peaches, drained
1 can fruit cocktail, drained
4 or 5 sliced ripe bananas
2 cups red seedless grapes, sliced
1 can pears, drained
1 cup sliced strawberries
1 jar cherries, sliced

Place vanilla pudding in pot, add juice from mandarin oranges, and cook over medium heat until pudding looks clear and shiny. Pour over drained fruit and toss. Chill. Serve alone or with pound cake. Flavor develops as it chills. Better if made day before serving. Serves 12.

Juice from peaches, pears and fruit cocktail may be frozen in ice cube tray and used in fruit drinks or iced tea.

Nutritional analysis per serving: 339 cal, 3 g fiber, 1 g fat, 0 mg chol, 449 mg sodium

Frozen Fruit Salad

1 pint sour cream
⅓ cup sugar
15 maraschino cherries, chopped
2 small bananas, mashed
1 10-ounce can crushed pineapple
¼ cup chopped pecans

Combine all ingredients. Mix well. Pour mixture into 8-inch square pan. Freeze overnight or until firm. Cut into squares for serving. Serves 10.

Nutritional analysis per serving: 190 cal, 0.6 g fiber, 11.6 g fat, 20.4 mg chol, 25.5 mg sodium

Fruited Chicken Salad

2 cups cooked, diced chicken
2 cups diced celery
2 cups unpeeled, diced red apples
½ cup plumped raisins
½ cup chopped nuts
½ cup cubed sweet pickles
2 tablespoons mayonnaise

Combine all ingredients in a serving bowl. Refrigerate. Serve chilled. Serves 4.

Nutritional analysis per serving: 392 cal, 1.7 g fiber, 18 g fat, 58 mg chol, 328 mg sodium

Fruity Frozen Salad +

1 16-ounce container whipped topping
2 tablespoons lemon juice
2 cups sour cream
1¼ cups sugar
12 bananas, mashed
⅔ cup maraschino cherries
2 cups crushed pineapple, drained
1 cup pecans

Mix first four ingredients together. Add last four ingredients. Put into a large chafing pan and freeze. Remove from freezer 10–15 minutes before serving. Serves 32.

Nutritional analysis per serving: 170 cal, 1 g fiber, 9 g fat, 6 mg chol, 12 mg sodium

Funny Bunny Salad ★

shredded lettuce
1 pear half
1 marshmallow
½ maraschino cherry
2 raisins
2 blanched almonds

Arrange nest of lettuce. On it, place drained pear half, cut-side down. With marshmallow, make tail at larger end of pear. The smaller end is the head. Make mouth with cherry and eyes with raisins. Long upright ears are made with blanched almonds. Serves 1.

Nutritional analysis per serving: 172 cal, 3 g fiber, 617 g fat, 0 mg chol, 18 mg sodium

Grated Sweet Potato Salad √

1 large can pineapple chunks
½ cup sugar
3 large raw sweet potatoes (peeled and grated)

Bring pineapple chunks (with liquid) and sugar to boil. Pour over raw sweet potato and toss well. Bake in 350°F oven for 25 minutes. Serve hot as vegetable or cold as salad. Serves 4.

Nutritional analysis per serving: 205 cal, 3 g fiber, 0 g fat, 0 mg chol, 10 mg sodium

Green Bean and Mushroom Salad

1 quart water
1 pound green beans, trimmed
½ pound fresh mushrooms
1 tablespoon Dijon mustard
2 tablespoons red wine vinegar
½ teaspoon chopped garlic
1 teaspoon salt
freshly ground pepper—4 turns
4 tablespoons olive oil
¼ cup fresh parsley, chopped
¼ cup green onions, sliced

Bring water to boil and cook green beans, uncovered, for 8 to 10 minutes. Drain and cool. Wash and dry mushrooms; slice thinly. Prepare sauce by whisking together mustard, vinegar, garlic, salt, and pepper. Slowly add olive oil while whisking. Put green beans, parsley, and onions in a bowl. Pour sauce over vegetables and toss gently. Serves 6.

Nutritional analysis per serving: 141 cal, 2 g fiber, 11 g fat, 0 mg chol, 784 mg sodium

Knox Blox + ★

4 envelopes Knox unflavored gelatin
3 3-ounce packages flavored gelatin
4 cups boiling water

In medium bowl, combine Knox unflavored gelatin and fruit-flavored gelatin. Add boiling water and stir until gelatin is completely dissolved. Pour into 8-inch square baking pan. Chill until firm. To serve, cut into 1-inch squares. Serves 72.

Nutritional analysis per serving: 13 cal, 0 g fiber, 0 g fat, 0 mg chol, 10 mg sodium

Macaroni Salad

1 8-ounce box macaroni, cooked and drained
¾ cup mayonnaise
2 teaspoons Dijon mustard
2 tablespoons vinegar
½ cup sugar
2 tablespoons sweet pickles, chopped
2 hard-cooked eggs, finely chopped
1 medium green bell pepper, finely chopped
1 medium onion, finely chopped
2 tablespoons pimento
½ cup finely chopped celery
salt and pepper, to taste

Combine all ingredients. Allow salad to marinate 12 to 24 hours in refrigerator before serving. Serves 10.

Nutritional analysis per serving: 267 cal, 0.2 g fiber, 14.6 g fat, 64.5 mg chol, 135.2 mg sodium

Mama's Cherry Salad

2½ cups boiling water
1 6-serving package wild cherry-flavored gelatin
1 15.5-ounce can crushed pineapple
1 10-ounce can sour pie cherries, drained
8 ounces cream cheese, at room temperature
1 cup sour cream

½ cup sugar
1 teaspoon vanilla extract
1 cup chopped pecans

Dissolve gelatin in boiling water, stirring constantly. Add pineapple and cherries. Pour gelatin mixture into 9 × 13-inch dish and refrigerate until firm. In separate bowl, beat together cream cheese and sour cream. Gradually add sugar and vanilla extract. Spread cream cheese mixture on top of firm gelatin. Sprinkle with pecans. Serves 12.

Nutritional analysis per serving: 279 cal, 0.2 g fiber, 15 g fat, 24 mg chol, 99.3 mg sodium

Mexican Chef Salad

1 pound lean ground beef
1 15-ounce can kidney beans, drained
1 package taco seasoning mix
1 head lettuce, washed and shredded
1 onion, chopped
1 tomato, chopped
1 cup (4 ounces) shredded cheese (Jack or Cheddar)
1 8-ounce package of tortilla chips, crushed

Brown beef in large skillet. Drain excess fat. Add beans and seasoning mix. Stir until well mixed. Simmer for 10 minutes. In separate dish combine lettuce, onion, tomato, cheese, and tortilla chips. Add beef mixture and toss lightly. Serve with salad dressing, if desired. Serves 6.

Nutritional analysis per serving: 499 cal, 1.1 g fiber, 28.6 g fat, 65 mg chol, 992.2 mg sodium

Old-Fashioned Potato Salad

1½ cups water
½ cup skim milk
2 tablespoons margarine
1 package instant potatoes
1 hard-boiled egg, chopped fine
1 small onion, diced
⅓ to 1 cup mayonnaise
1 to 2 tablespoons mustard, to taste

In saucepan bring water, milk, and margarine to boil. Remove from heat. Add potato mix to liquid. Mix until stiff. Add egg, onion, mayonnaise, and mustard. Mix until well combined. Refrigerate until ready to serve. Serves 8.

Nutritional analysis per serving: 204 cal, 0.08 g fiber, 20 g fat, 46.3 mg chol, 241 mg sodium

Phillips Pea Salad

1 16-ounce can English peas
1 boiled egg, chopped
1 green onion, chopped
pepper, to taste
1 tablespoon pimento
½ cup cheese, cubed
½ cup mayonnaise
natural seasoning salt, to taste

In large bowl combine all ingredients. Stir until well mixed. Chill for 1 hour. Serves 6.

Nutritional analysis per serving: 219 cal, 1.34 g fiber, 18.8 g fat, 66.3 mg chol, 378.8 mg sodium

Pickled Shrimp √

1 pound shrimp cooked and cleaned
2 tablespoons salad oil
1 cup apple cider vinegar
¼ cup Worcestershire sauce
2 tablespoons water
1 teaspoon sugar
¼ cup chopped onion
¼ teaspoon cayenne pepper
8 whole cloves

Drizzle oil over shrimp. Bring rest of ingredients to boil and pour over oiled shrimp. Cool and refrigerate at least overnight. Serves 8.

Nutritional analysis per serving: 73 cal, 0 g fiber, 2 g fat, 85 mg chol, 469 mg sodium

Pineapple-Chicken Salad Pie +

4 20-ounce cans pineapple chunks, drained
4 cups celery, chopped
8 tablespoons lemon juice

1 cup cashew nuts, chopped
12 cups chicken, cooked and diced
1 cup green onion, finely chopped
6–8 teaspoons seasoned salt
2 cups mayonnaise
3 9-inch pastry shells, baked and cooled

Combine half of pineapple chunks and next seven ingredients. Stir well. Spoon salad into pastry shells, pressing firmly. Garnish with remaining pineapple chunks; chill before serving. Note: Pastry shell may be omitted; salad may be served on lettuce leaves if desired. Serves 24.

Nutritional analysis per serving: 395 cal, 2 g fiber, 25 g fat, 73 mg chol, 913 mg sodium

Pineapple Salad

1 20-ounce can crushed pineapple
1 6-serving box orange-flavored gelatin
1 cup chopped nuts
1 cup shredded coconut
2 cups buttermilk
1 12-ounce container nondairy topping

Bring pineapple to boil. Dissolve gelatin in pineapple, stirring constantly. Stir in nuts, coconut, and buttermilk. Add whipped topping, stirring until combined. Spoon mixture into glass bowl. Refrigerate overnight or until set. Serves 16.

Nutritional analysis per serving: 201 cal, 0.4 g fiber, 12 g fat, 1.1 mg chol, 84.3 mg sodium

Sauerkraut Salad ★

½ cup vinegar
½ cup water
1 16-ounce sauerkraut, drained and chopped
1 large green bell pepper, chopped
½ cup onion, chopped
1 4-ounce jar pimento
1 8-ounce can bean sprouts, drained
1 5.5-ounce can water chestnuts, drained and chopped
½ cup celery, chopped
2 cups sugar

Boil vinegar and water for 5 minutes. Combine remaining ingredients in large jar. Pour vinegar and water over ingredients. Marinate for 24 hours. Serves 12.

Nutritional analysis per serving: 110.3 cal, 0 g fiber, .8 g fat, 1.8 mg chol, 12.2 mg sodium

Seafood Pasta Salad

1 8-ounce box colored rotini, cooked according to package
1 pound imitation crabmeat, cut into 1-inch pieces
1 medium onion, chopped
¾ cup olives
¾ cup diced carrots
¾ cup chopped celery
¼ cup peas, fresh or frozen
½ cup mayonnaise
salt and pepper, to taste

Put cooked pasta into large mixing bowl. Add remaining ingredients. Toss gently until well combined. Refrigerate for at least an hour before serving. Serves 8.

Nutritional analysis per serving: 270 cal, 0.5 g fiber, 10.3 g fat, 15 mg chol, 751.7 mg sodium

Shrimp Salad ★

1½ pounds boiled shrimp, peeled and deveined
½ cup chopped celery
1 small can crushed pineapple, drained
fat-free salad dressing, any type

Cut shrimp into bite-size pieces. Combine shrimp with celery and pineapple. Add desired salad dressing. Serve chilled. Serves 6.

Nutritional analysis per serving: 150 cal, 0.5 g fiber, 2 g fat, 170 mg chol, 175 mg sodium

Shrimp Rice Salad ★

½ pounds cleaned raw shrimp
2 tablespoons vegetable shortening
1 cup uncooked rice
2 stalks celery, chopped
1 small bell pepper, chopped

2 green onions, chopped
¼ cup pimentos, chopped
4 tablespoons mayonnaise
½ teaspoon seasoning
tomato and lettuce to garnish
¼ cup stuffed olives
2 tablespoons horseradish

Sauté cleaned shrimp in vegetable shortening on high, stirring constantly until done. Remove from pan onto paper towel and into container to place in refrigerator to cool overnight. Prepare rice. Place in refrigerator overnight. Place chopped celery, onion, and bell pepper on bottom of container. Place chopped olives and pimentos with a little vinegar over vegetables and place in refrigerator over night. Combine all ingredients and mix well. Place firmly into a container to mold. When ready to serve, unmold and garnish with tomatoes and lettuce. Serves 10.

Nutritional analysis per serving: 167 cal, 1 g fiber, 7 g fat, 103 mg chol, 336 mg sodium

Spiced Apple Salad +

50 cooking apples, peeled, cored, and
    cut in half crosswise
1 cup vinegar
2 ounces stick cinnamon
8 pounds granulated sugar
4 quarts water
2 teaspoons red coloring

Place apples in flat pan. Combine remainder of ingredients and boil 1 minute. Pour over apples. Bake at 375°F 1 hour. Watch closely so apples do not become mushy. Turn apples over after removing from oven if syrup has not covered them completely. Refrigerate overnight in syrup. Serve chilled rings on green leafy lettuce. Dot with mayonnaise. Serves 100.

Nutritional analysis per serving: 356 cal, 13 g fiber, 2 g fat, 0 mg chol, 65 mg sodium

Strawberry Pretzel Salad

2 cups crushed pretzels
¾ cup margarine, melted
4 teaspoons sugar

Mix above ingredients and press in bottom of 9 × 13-inch pan or baking dish. Bake for 10 minutes at 350° and let cool.

1 8-ounce package cream cheese,
    softened
1 cup whipped topping
1 cup sugar

Mix above ingredients and spread over crust.

1 6-ounce package strawberry flavored
    gelatin
2 10-ounce packages frozen
    strawberries, thawed and drained
    (can use 2–3 cups fresh strawberries,
    washed and sliced)
2 cups hot water

Mix topping ingredients and refrigerate until thickened. Pour over top. Refrigerate until set. Serves 12.

Nutritional analysis per serving: 233 cal, 1.5 g fiber, 18.6 g fat, 20.9 mg chol, 398.7 mg sodium

Sunset Salad + ★

3½ cups lemon gelatin
2 teaspoons salt
1 gallon hot water
½ cup vinegar
2½ quarts grated carrots
1 quart can crushed pineapple
1 cup nuts, chopped

Dissolve gelatin and salt in hot water. Add vinegar and chill until slightly thickened. Fold in carrots, pineapple, and pecans. Pour into individual molds, shallow pans, or two 3-quart molds. Chill until formed. Remove from molds or cut into squares. Serve on crisp lettuce with mayonnaise, if desired. Note: Chill large molds 8 hours or overnight. Serves 48.

Nutritional analysis per serving: 92 cal, 1 g fiber, 2 g fat, 0 mg chol, 544 mg sodium

Sunshine Congealed Salad

1 4-serving box lemon-flavored gelatin
1 4-serving box orange-flavored gelatin
2 cups boiling water
2 cups cold water
2 cups grated carrots
¼ teaspoon salt

Dissolve gelatins in boiling water, stirring constantly. Mix in cold water, carrots, and salt. Pour mixture into 9 × 13-inch dish. Chill until set. Serves 8.

Nutritional analysis per serving: 91.4 cal, 0.4 g fiber, 0.2 g fat, 0 mg chol, 127.4 sodium

Sunshine Delight Salad

1 3-ounce package lemon gelatin
1 3-ounce package orange gelatin
2 cups hot water
1½ cups cold water
1 15-ounce can crushed pineapple
4 bananas, sliced
1 cup miniature marshmallows
1 egg, beaten
1 tablespoon butter
1 tablespoon all-purpose flour
½ cup sugar
1 8-ounce container nondairy whipped
   topping

In mixing bowl, dissolve gelatins in hot water, then add cold water. Drain pineapple and reserve juice. Add pineapple to gelatin. Add bananas and marshmallows and stir to combine. Chill until jelled. Add water to reserved pineapple juice to make 1 cup of liquid. Combine juice, egg, butter, flour, and sugar in saucepan. Cook over medium heat, stirring constantly, until thick. Once mixture is thick, remove from heat and allow to cool completely. Add nondairy topping to cooled mixture. Spread topping onto gelatin salad and chill. Serves 16.

Nutritional analysis per serving: 128 cal, 0.4 g fiber, 0.8 g fat, 18 mg chol, 43 mg sodium

Sweet-Sour Cole Slaw √ ★

3 cups cabbage, shredded
¼ cup bell pepper, chopped
Dressing:
3 tablespoons salad oil
½ cup vinegar
½ cup grated onion
1 tablespoon sugar
½ teaspoon dry mustard
¼ teaspoon celery seed
1 teaspoon salt
pepper to taste

Shake dressing ingredients together; pour over cabbage and bell pepper. Place in covered container in refrigerator. Keeps well over a week. Serves 8.

Nutritional analysis per serving: 71 cal, 2 g fiber, 4 g fat, 0 mg chol, 278 mg sodium

Tropical Ambrosia + ★

3½ cups orange gelatin
3¼ quarts hot water
1½ quarts orange sections, drained
2 cups flaked coconut
1 teaspoon salt
2 tablespoons orange rind, grated
1½ quarts crushed pineapple

Dissolve gelatin and salt in hot water. Chill until slightly thickened. Add remaining ingredients. Pour into individual molds, shallow pans, or two 3-quart molds. Chill until firm. Remove from molds, or cut into squares. Serve as a salad with salad dressing or as a dessert with custard sauce, if desired. Serves 48.

Nutritional analysis per serving: 193 cal, 1 g fiber, 6 g fat, 0 mg chol, 117 mg sodium

Under the Sea Salad + ★

2 pounds canned pears, drained and
   diced
1 9-ounce package lime gelatin
1 teaspoon salt
1 pint boiling water
2 tablespoons vinegar
2 pints pear syrup

½ teaspoon ground ginger
2 pounds cottage cheese
Salad greens as needed

Retain drained syrup from pears for part of liquid in recipe. Dissolve gelatin and salt in boiling water; stir until gelatin is thoroughly dissolved. Add vinegar and pear syrup to gelatin. Fill individual molds or shallow pan half full of gelatin; refrigerate until firm. Chill remaining gelatin until partially thickened. Add ginger, cottage cheese, and diced pears to partially thickened gelatin. Spread cheese and gelatin mixture over firm gelatin in individual molds or shallow pan. Chill until completely firm. Remove from molds and place on crisp salad greens. Garnish with canned sliced pear, cottage cheese, rosettes of mayonnaise, and maraschino cherries. Serves 20.

Nutritional analysis per serving: 93 cal, 1 g fiber, 0 g fat, 5 mg chol, 201 mg sodium

Vegetable Salad ★

2 cups small shell macaroni, cooked and drained
1 10-ounce can English peas, drained
1 10-ounce can whole kernel corn, drained
1 small onion, finely chopped
1 cup finely chopped celery
1 cup (8 ounces) nonfat creamy ranch-style salad dressing
salt and pepper, to taste

Combine all ingredients. Toss until well mixed. Refrigerate until ready to serve. Serves 16.

Nutritional analysis per serving: 82 cal, 0.4 g fiber, 0.6 g fat, 0 mg chol, 286 mg sodium

Vegetable Bars √

2 packages Crescent Rolls
2 8-ounce packages cream cheese
1 package dry Ranch Dressing mix
1 cup salad dressing
¾ cups each finely chopped tomatoes, broccoli, carrots, cauliflower, squash, and bell pepper
2 cups shredded sharp cheese

Press Crescent Rolls into jelly roll pan and bake 10 minutes. Cool. Mix cream cheese, ranch dressing mix, and salad dressing. Spread over crust. Sprinkle vegetables over mixture. Top with shredded cheese. Chill several hours. Cut into slices. Serves 10.

(May reduce calories and fat by using low fat and/or lite cheeses.)

Nutritional analysis per serving: 474 cal, 2 g fiber, 39 g fat, 81 mg chol, 1047 mg sodium

Vegetable Vinaigrette √ ★

2 medium tomatoes, quartered
2 medium yellow squash, sliced
2 cups sliced mushrooms
2 medium cucumbers, sliced
1 cup sliced green onion
2 bell peppers, sliced
¼ cup safflower oil
¼ teaspoon tarragon
⅛ teaspoon pepper
1 teaspoon sugar
½ cup vinegar
⅛ teaspoon crumbled bay leaf
¼ teaspoon celery seed
shredded lettuce

Alternate layers of vegetables in deep glass bowl. Combine oil, vinegar, and seasonings. Mix well. Pour over vegetables. Cover and chill 6–8 hours or overnight. Serve drained vegetables over shredded lettuce. Serves 10.

Nutritional analysis per serving: 113 cal, 3 g fiber, 6 g fat, 0 mg chol, 8 mg sodium

SAUCES AND DRESSINGS

Barbecue Sauce + ★

2 pounds onions, chopped
1 pint vegetable oil
½ cup flour
1 cup prepared mustard
2½ tablespoons salt
2 teaspoons pepper
¾ cup brown sugar

1 quart chicken broth
2 1 pound, 13 ounce-cans tomato puree
1 quart vinegar
2 14-ounce bottles ketchup
1 cup Worcestershire sauce

Sauté onions lightly in oil in heavy skillet. Combine flour, mustard, salt, pepper, and sugar. Stir into onions. Add remaining ingredients; heat to boiling, stirring constantly. Serves 50.

Nutritional analysis per serving: 144 cal, 1 g fiber, 9 g fat, 0 mg chol, 664 mg sodium

Italian Cooking Sauce + ★

2 14.5-ounce cans stewed tomatoes, pureed
2 cups water
2 tablespoons instant onion
3 teaspoons salt
4 teaspoons green pepper flakes
3 teaspoons sugar
2 16-ounce cans tomato sauce
2 6-ounce cans tomato paste
2 tablespoons parsley flakes
2 tablespoons cornstarch
1 teaspoon instant minced garlic
1½ teaspoons Italian seasoning

Combine all ingredients in large pot. Simmer for 1 hour over low to medium heat. Cool and transfer to three 1-quart or six 1-pint freezer containers. Fill containers leaving a 1-inch headspace. Freeze until ready to use. Thaw overnight in refrigerator or remove top, cover with waxed paper, and thaw in microwave oven. Serves 16.

Nutritional analysis per serving: 110 cal, 0 g fiber, 3.3 g fat, 0 mg chol, 872.3 mg sodium

Parmesan Cheese Sauce +

4 tablespoons butter or margarine
4 tablespoons all-purpose flour
2 cups milk
8 tablespoons Parmesan cheese, grated

1 teaspoon dry mustard
½ teaspoon salt
dash red pepper
dash of pepper

Melt butter in small, heavy saucepan over low heat. Add flour, stirring until smooth. Cook 1 minute, stirring constantly. Gradually add milk; cook over medium heat, stirring constantly until thickened and bubbly. Stir in cheese, mustard, salt, and pepper; cook, stirring constantly until cheese is melted. Serves 8.

Nutritional analysis per serving: 115 cal, 0 g fiber, 8 g fat, 6 mg chol, 357 mg sodium

Simple Barbecue Sauce

1 small onion, chopped fine
2 cups catsup
2 tablespoons Worcestershire sauce
¼ cup sugar
¼ teaspoon salt
½ teaspoon pepper

Mix all ingredients together in saucepan. Heat sauce until it begins to boil. Use within hour or refrigerate. Serves 8.

Nutritional analysis per serving: 52 cal, 0 g fiber, 0.2 g fat, 0 mg chol, 475 mg sodium

Southern Tomato Topping
for Vegetables ★

1 14.5-ounce can whole tomatoes
½ cup sugar
¼ cup vinegar
salt and pepper, to taste

In saucepan, cook tomatoes until they fall apart. Mash tomatoes with potato masher. Add sugar, vinegar, salt, and pepper. Cook until mixture thickens. Use hot as sauce for corn, dried peas, or beans. Pour leftover into 1-pint jar. Store in refrigerator. Makes 1 pint.

Nutritional analysis per serving: 15 cal, 0.01 g fiber, 0.03 g fat, 0 mg chol, 22.2 mg sodium

SOUPS

Brunswick Stew + ★

1 6–8 pound chicken, cut up
5 quarts tomatoes, peeled and sliced
2 quarts butter beans
2 quarts freshly cut corn
1 quart diced potatoes
2 medium onions, chopped
¼ teaspoon ground red pepper or 1
    medium pepper pod
salt and pepper, to taste

Place chicken in heavy kettle and cover with water. Cook until meat falls away from bone, adding more water if necessary. Add vegetables and seasonings. Simmer slowly until tender and mixture is thick and well blended. Remove pepper pod, if used. Serve hot. Freezes well. Serves 20.

Nutritional analysis per serving: 530 cal, 12 g fiber, 11 g fat, 74 mg chol, 212 mg sodium

Brunswick Stew √

1 pound pork, ground
1 pound beef, ground
2 medium onions
1 boiled chicken, deboned and finely
    chopped
2 cans corn, drained
2 cans lima beans, drained
2 cans tomatoes
2 cans okra
1 tablespoon vinegar
2 cups V-8 juice
salt and pepper to taste
1 cup barbecue sauce

Brown pork, beef, and onions. Add chicken, onions, and vegetables. Cook slowly about 30 minutes. Add vinegar, juice, barbecue sauce, and salt and pepper and simmer for another 30 minutes. May remove about half and puree in blender, then add back to stew. Delicious with corn muffins and salad. Serves 12.

Nutritional analysis per serving: 455 cal, 3 g fiber, 24 g fat, 100 mg chol, 731 mg sodium

Carolina Stew √

4 cups water
1 cube chicken bouillon
1 cube beef bouillon
1 cup white rice
1 medium onion, chopped
2 cloves garlic, chopped
2 carrots, sliced thin
1 can whole corn
1 can butterbeans
2 cans tomatoes
1 can okra
4 chicken breasts, boned
½ teaspoon seasoned salt
pepper to taste
1 pound Kielbasa sausage, sliced

Bring water and bouillon cubes to boil. Add rice, onion, garlic, and carrots. Cook 15 minutes. Add other vegetables, chicken, salt, and pepper. Reduce heat and simmer covered for 1½ hours. Microwave sausage and drain well. Remove lid from pot, add sausage, and simmer uncovered additional 30 minutes. Stew should be thick. Serves 8.

Nutritional analysis per serving: 535 cal, 7 g fiber, 22 g fat, 112 mg chol, 2037 mg sodium

Catfish Stew √

½ pound bacon
4 pounds catfish
3 pounds white potatoes, diced
2 pounds onions, diced
1 cup hot water
1 10.75-ounce can condensed tomato
    soup
4 tablespoons butter, melted
hot sauce, to taste
salt and pepper, to taste

Fry bacon in large, heavy pot until brown. Remove bacon, leaving fat in pot. Add in layers catfish, potatoes, and onion, using about 2 layers of each. Add hot water, cover, and cook for 1½ hours without stirring. Mix together tomato soup, butter, hot sauce, salt, and pepper. Add to stew. Thin with additional water, if desired. Serve hot. Serves 12.

Nutritional analysis per serving: 367 cal, .6 g fiber, 12.3 g fat, 100 mg chol, 394 mg sodium

Chicken Bog √

> 1 hen (5–7 pounds)
> ½ gallon water
> 1 pound hot pork sausage
> 1 large onion
> 3 cups raw rice
> 6 cups chicken broth
> salt and pepper, to taste

Cut hen into pieces; add salt and pepper to taste. Boil until tender in ½ gallon of water. Remove skin and bones. Save broth. Brown pork sausage and onion. Pour off grease. Mix rice, chicken broth, chicken, sausage, salt, and pepper in heavy pot. Bring to boil and boil vigorously about 3 minutes. Turn heat down and simmer 30 minutes to 1 hour. Serves 12.

Nutritional analysis per serving: 478 cal, 0 g fiber, 21 g fat, 139 mg chol, 973 mg sodium

Chicken Stew

> 2 8-ounce packages extra wide egg
>   noodles
> 2 10-ounce cans clear chicken broth
> 2 cups water
> 1 hard-boiled egg, peeled
> 1 6-ounce can white chicken meat
> 2 10-ounce cans cream of chicken soup
> ½ cup milk
> 2 tablespoons butter
> ½ cup grated cheese

In 2-quart saucepan, boil noodles in chicken broth and water. Cook for 8 to 10 minutes until noodles are tender. Drain liquid. Chop boiled egg and chicken. Add egg and chicken to noodles. Add soup and milk. Mix to just combine. Simmer mixture over medium

heat for 20 minutes. Add butter and grated cheese. Cover pan and continue simmering until cheese melts. Mix well prior to serving. Serves 4.

Nutritional analysis per serving: 930.5 cal, 0 g fiber, 37 g fat, 272.7 mg chol, 3100 mg sodium

Chicken Stew

> 2 large potatoes, peeled and diced
> 1 large onion, chopped
> 1 5-ounce can chunky chicken
> 1 8-ounce can cream-style corn
> salt and pepper, to taste
> ¼ teaspoon herb seasoning
> 1 cup milk

In saucepan, combine potatoes and onion. Cover with 1 inch of water. Cook over medium heat until potatoes are tender when pierced with fork. Add chicken. Cook for 5 minutes. Add corn and seasonings. Reduce heat to low, and simmer for a few minutes until hot. Add milk, stirring gently. Cook until stew is thoroughly heated, but do not boil. Serves 4.

Nutritional analysis per serving: 188 cal, 0.16 g fiber, 2.9 g fat, 28.6 mg chol, 238.2 mg sodium

Chili and Beans ★

> 2 tablespoons vegetable oil
> 1 pound ground turkey meat
> 1 onion, chopped
> 1 cup catsup
> 1 tablespoon mustard
> 1 tablespoon chili powder
> 2 16-ounce cans tomato sauce
> 1 15-ounce can pinto beans, drained

In large skillet, heat oil and brown ground turkey and onion. Drain excess oil. Add catsup, mustard, chili powder, and tomato sauce. Simmer for 5 minutes. Add pinto beans and continue to simmer for 20 minutes, stirring frequently. Serves 8.

Nutritional analysis per serving: 246 cal, 0.1 g fiber, 7.3 g fat, 31.2 mg chol, 1587 mg sodium

Chili Con Carne +

8 cups dry kidney beans (4 pounds) or 2 6-pound, 12-ounce cans kidney beans
4 cups onions, chopped
¼ cup oil
2 cloves garlic crushed (optional)
20 pounds ground beef
4 pounds ground fresh pork
12 quarts cooked or canned tomatoes
5 tablespoons chili powder
⅔ cup salt
1 teaspoon pepper
½ cup sugar

If using dry beans, wash beans and soak overnight in water to cover. Drain, but do not season. Cover with fresh-drawn water and simmer until tender. Brown onion slightly in hot oil in heavy skillet; add garlic. Add ground beef and pork and cook until browned, stirring occasionally with fork to break up meat. Add drained kidney beans. Stir in tomatoes, chili powder, salt, pepper, and sugar. Simmer 1½ hours to blend flavors. Note: If chili needs to be thinned, add 8 beef bouillon cubes dissolved in 2 quarts boiling water.

To make this into an Italian Spaghetti Supper, leave beans out of Chili Con Carne and serve over spaghetti using 18 quarts water, 9 tablespoons salt, and 6 pounds thin spaghetti. Bring water to boil; add salt. Gradually add spaghetti; cook uncovered, stirring occasionally, until tender. Drain in colander; rinse. Note: If kettles will not hold 18 quarts of water, cook 2 pounds of spaghetti at a time in 6 quarts boiling water, using 3 tablespoons salt for each 2 pounds of spaghetti. Serves 50.

Nutritional analysis per serving: 529 cal, 4 g fiber, 32 g fat, 131 mg chol, 1849 mg sodium

Cucumber Soup √

3 medium white potatoes
1 pint milk
1 medium onion, chopped
1 cup clear chicken broth
salt and pepper to taste
2 medium cucumbers
1 cup cream, whipped
chopped parsley

Peel potatoes and boil in just enough water to cover. When done, drain and mash through strainer or place in blender. Bring milk, onion, and chicken broth to a boil. Season with salt and pepper. Cool. Add finely chopped cucumbers. Chill thoroughly. Serve with a teaspoon of whipped cream on top sprinkled with parsley. Serves 6.

Nutritional analysis per serving: 170 cal, 4 g fiber, 1 g fat, 2 mg chol, 179 mg sodium

Gazpacho Soup ★

1 small sweet onion, quartered
½ medium cucumber, halved lengthwise and cut in 1-inch pieces
1 stalk of celery, cut in 1-inch pieces
4 medium tomatoes, peeled and quartered
½ medium green pepper, cut in six pieces
4 cups tomato juice
2 tablespoons olive oil/veg oil
2 tablespoons wine vinegar
1½ teaspoons salt
dash of pepper

Using blender or food processor, chop vegetables a few at a time with small amount of tomato juice. Pour into large pitcher. Repeat until all vegetables have been chopped. Add remaining tomato juice, olive oil, vinegar, salt, and pepper, and stir well. Cover and chill thoroughly before serving. Garnish with seasoned croutons, if desired. Serves 8.

Nutritional analysis per serving: 70 cal, 3 g fiber, 4 g fat, 0 mg chol, 854 mg sodium

Hamburger Vegetable Soup ★

1 pound ground beef
1 medium onion, chopped
2 10.75-ounce cans condensed vegetable
  soup
2 10.75-ounce cans water
1 teaspoon chili powder
black pepper, to taste

In large saucepan, brown beef and onion. Drain excess fat. Add soup and water. Add chili powder and pepper. Simmer until soup is heated thoroughly. Serve over rice. Serves 10.

Nutritional analysis per serving: 167.3 cal, 0.06 fiber, 11.4 fat, 28.5 mg chol, 421.8 mg sodium

Health Soup ★

4–5 cloves garlic
1 cup chopped onion
2 tablespoons olive oil
1 cup sliced carrots
1 cup chopped celery
1 cup chopped broccoli
1 cup chopped spinach
1 teaspoon black pepper
1 teaspoon dried basil
1 teaspoon oregano
½ teaspoon salt
1 cup chopped green pepper
4 cups water or broth
2 cups tomato puree
1 can dark red kidney beans
1 cup stewed tomatoes
1 cup large shell macaroni

Sauté garlic (finely chopped) and onion in olive oil. Add carrots, celery, broccoli, spinach, black pepper, basil, oregano, salt, green pepper, and water or broth. Allow mixture to reach boiling point and reduce heat. Simmer covered for 10 minutes. Add tomato puree, red kidney beans, tomatoes, and macaroni. Return mixture to boil and reduce heat; simmer until pasta is tender. Serve hot. Serves 12.

Nutritional analysis per serving: 100 cal, 3 g fiber, 3 g fat, 0 mg chol, 169 mg sodium

Helen's Broccoli Soup ★

1 10-ounce package frozen chopped
  broccoli
1 large onion, chopped
1 10.75-ounce can condensed cream of
  chicken soup
⅔ cup (5-ounce can) evaporated milk
½ cup water

Cook broccoli and onion together until tender. Drain. Combine broccoli, onion, soup, milk, and water together in blender until well mixed. Cook over low heat until hot, stirring frequently. Serves 6.

Nutritional analysis per serving: 104 cal, 1 g fiber, 3.2 g fat, 5.9 mg chol, 469.5 mg sodium

New Year's Day Chili ★

1 16-ounce package dried kidney beans
1 tablespoon instant minced onion
2 teaspoons beef-flavored bouillon
  granules
1 teaspoon salt
½ teaspoon garlic powder
1 pound ground beef, cooked and
  drained
1 8-ounce can tomato sauce
1 1-ounce can tomato paste
2½ teaspoons chili powder
1 teaspoon dried whole oregano
¼ teaspoon red pepper
1 small bay leaf

Sort and wash beans. Place in large Dutch oven. Cover with water 2 inches above beans and let soak 8 hours. Drain. Combine beans, minced onion, bouillon, salt, garlic powder, and 7 cups of water in large Dutch oven. Bring to boil, cover, reduce heat, and simmer 1 hour, stirring occasionally. Stir in ground beef, tomato sauce, tomato paste, chili powder, oregano, red pepper, and bay leaf. Bring to boil; reduce heat and simmer, uncovered, 30 minutes, stirring occasionally. Remove bay leaf. Serves 11.

Nutritional analysis per serving: 61 cal, 3 g fiber, 1 g fat, 0 mg chol, 291 mg sodium

Okra and Tomato Gumbo ★

4–5 strips bacon
2 quarts peeled red-ripe tomatoes
1 cup fresh corn (optional)
1 teaspoon sugar
salt and pepper to taste
1 quart sliced okra
1 onion, sliced

Brown bacon in saucepan. Add other ingredients and let simmer for 1 hour or longer. Delicious served over rice or cornbread. Serves 6.

Nutritional analysis per serving: 153 cal, 5 g fiber 4 g fat, 4 mg chol, 700 mg sodium

Okra Soup √ ★

1 pound lean ground beef
2 quarts water
1 large onion, chopped
2 pounds fresh okra, chopped
2 16-ounce cans tomatoes, mashed
salt and pepper to taste
1 teaspoon sugar
1 can creamed corn (optional)

Brown ground beef. Add water and onion and simmer for 1 hour. Add okra and cook 30 minutes. Add tomatoes, salt and pepper, and sugar. Simmer for at least 1 hour more. Add more water if desired. A can of creamed corn added during last few minutes of simmering changes flavor of soup. Be sure to stir often during simmering. Serves 12.

Nutritional analysis per serving: 166 cal, 3 g fiber, 7 g fat, 25 mg chol, 136 mg sodium

Quick Chili ★

½ of a medium onion, chopped
½ of a green bell pepper, chopped
1 pound lean ground beef
1 16-ounce can tomato sauce
1 16-ounce can whole tomatoes, drained and coarsely chopped
1 16-ounce can kidney beans, drained and rinsed
1 teaspoon salt
½ teaspoon red pepper
¼ teaspoon black pepper
¼ teaspoon cumin
2 tablespoons chili powder

In large skillet, cook onion, pepper, and ground beef over medium heat, stirring frequently until meat is brown. Add tomato sauce, tomatoes, kidney beans, salt, peppers, cumin, and chili powder. Simmer for 15–30 minutes, stirring occasionally. Serves 8.

Nutritional analysis per serving: 206.5 cal, 0.5 g fiber, 9.4 g fat, 40.3 mg chol, 1010 mg sodium

Quick Chili +

1 pound ground round beef
½ teaspoon salt
½ cup onions, chopped
2 teaspoons chili powder
2 cups water
⅛ teaspoon pepper
2 tablespoons Worcestershire sauce

In large saucepan, combine all ingredients. Cook over medium heat, stirring constantly to separate meat. Bring chili to boil. Reduce heat and simmer for 30 to 45 minutes or until chili thickens. Serves 16.

Nutritional analysis per serving: 53.1 cal, 0.05 g fiber, 3.3 g fat, 17 mg chol, 169 mg sodium

Salmon Stew ★

1 quart milk
4 medium potatoes, peeled, cubed, and boiled
1 small onion, chopped
1 16-ounce can salmon
salt and pepper, to taste
ground red pepper, optional

Pour milk into large pot. Cook over low heat; do not allow milk to boil. Add potatoes, onions, salmon, and seasonings. Simmer mixture for 5 minutes. Serve hot. Serves 4.

Nutritional analysis per serving: 429.4 cal, 0.2 g fiber, . 15.2 g fat, 95 mg chol, 757 mg sodium

Sea Garden Chowder ★

1 pound skinless fish fillets, fresh or
  frozen (thawed)
½ cup chopped onion
2 tablespoons vegetable oil
2 cups potatoes, diced into small pieces
1 cup water
¾ teaspoon salt
pepper, to taste
2 cups milk
1 8-ounce can cream-style yellow corn

Cut fish into 1-inch pieces. In large, deep skillet, fry onion in vegetable oil until it becomes transparent. Add potatoes, water, salt, pepper, and fish. Cover and simmer over low heat for 15 minutes, or until potatoes are cooked. Add milk and corn. Cook until chowder is thoroughly heated. Serves 4.

Nutritional analysis per serving: 362.2 cal, 0.2 g fiber, 13.9 g fat, 106.6 mg chol, 712.3 mg sodium

Seafood Gumbo √ ★

3 tablespoons oil
3 cups okra, sliced
¾ cup celery, chopped
2 cloves garlic, chopped
1 green pepper, chopped
2 bunches green onions, chopped
2 tablespoons parsley, chopped
1 No. 2 can tomatoes
1 can tomato sauce
1 bay leaf
½ teaspoon thyme
salt and pepper, to taste
3 quarts hot water
2 cups raw shrimp, cleaned
1½ cups crab meat

Place oil in large, heavy pot. Add okra and sauté. Add celery, garlic, and pepper. Cook until light brown. Add onions and parsley. Cook about 2 minutes longer. Add tomatoes and sauce, bay leaf, thyme, salt, and pepper. Cook 5 minutes. Add 1 quart of water and cook 20 minutes. Add shrimp and crab meat and another quart of water. Cook 30 minutes.

Add remaining quart of water. Cook 1 hour. Serve over rice in soup bowl. Serves 12.

Nutritional analysis per serving: 140 cal, 3 g fiber, 5 g fat, 75 mg chol, 174 mg sodium

Shrimp-Okra Gumbo √

2 tablespoons oil
2 medium onions, chopped
2 pounds okra, sliced
1 gallon hot water
¾ cup tomatoes, canned
salt and pepper to taste
½ clove garlic
½ teaspoon cayenne pepper
4 pounds shrimp

Heat oil in heavy saucepan. Add onions and okra and fry until brown around edges. Cook on low heat, stirring occasionally, until okra does not stick to pan (about 1 hour). Add water gradually, about 1 cup every few minutes. Add tomatoes. Add salt and pepper to taste. Add garlic and cayenne pepper. Add peeled shrimp and cook 15 minutes longer. Serve in soup bowl over heaping servings of rice. Serves 8.

Nutritional analysis per serving: 311 cal, 1 g fiber, 8 g fat, 344 mg chol, 420 mg sodium

Slumgullion ★

1½ pounds lean ground beef
1 16-ounce can whole tomatoes
1½ cups chopped green bell pepper
1½ cups chopped onion
1 cup catsup
3 teaspoons oregano
2 teaspoons Italian seasoning
1 teaspoon garlic powder
1 teaspoon chili powder
1 teaspoon paprika
1 teaspoon marjoram
salt and pepper, to taste
2 cups cooked white rice

In large pot, brown ground beef. Drain excess fat. Add remaining ingredients (except rice) to pot and cook over low heat for 45 minutes. Spread cooked rice evenly in 9 × 13-inch lightly greased baking pan. Cover with sauce. Allow mixture to sit for 15 minutes before serving. Serves 18.

Nutritional analysis per serving: 135.4 cal, 0.3 g fiber, 7.5 g fat, 23.4 mg chol, 276.2 mg sodium

Turkey and Cabbage Stew ★

2 tablespoons vegetable oil
1 pound ground turkey
½ cup chopped celery
½ cup chopped onions
½ cup chopped green bell pepper
1 16-ounce can crushed tomatoes
2 teaspoons chili powder
salt and pepper, to taste
½ small cabbage, chopped

In large saucepan, add oil and brown ground turkey. Add celery, onions, and peppers. Cook until almost tender. Add tomatoes and spices. Mix well. Add cabbage and cook until tender but crisp. Serves 8.

Nutritional analysis per serving: 121.5 cal, 0.4 g fiber, 4.7 g fat, 24.2 mg chol, 280.7 mg sodium

Venison Hash ★

1 quart prepackaged ground venison roast (see below)
1 onion, chopped
1 tablespoon margarine
¼ cup cider vinegar
1 teaspoon salt
¼ teaspoon pepper
3 to 4 cups water
2 tablespoons mustard
1 tablespoon Worcestershire sauce
¼ teaspoon seasoning salt

To prepare ground venison roast: roast venison at 350°F to internal temperature of 185°F. Once venison is cooked, remove meat from bones and refrigerate until cold. Grind venison with large raw onions, to taste. Package ground venison in 1-quart freezer bags. Freeze until ready to make hash. To make hash: combine prepared venison, onion, margarine, vinegar, salt, pepper, water, mustard, Worcestershire sauce, and seasoning salt in saucepan. Mix well. Cook mixture over low heat for 30 minutes, stirring frequently. Serves 8.

Nutritional analysis per serving: 166.3 cal, 0.1 g fiber, 6.1 g fat, 76 mg chol, 475 mg sodium

BREADS

BISCUITS AND ROLLS

Feather Biscuits +

1 package dry yeast
2 tablespoons warm water (105 to 115°F)
2 cups buttermilk
5 cups self-rising flour
¼ cup sugar
1 cup shortening

Dissolve yeast in warm water. Stir yeast mixture into buttermilk; mix well and set aside. Combine flour and sugar; cut in shortening until mixture resembles coarse meal. Add buttermilk mixture; stir until dry ingredients are moistened. Cover and let rise in warm place until doubled or cover bowl tightly and store in refrigerator until needed (may be stored up to three days). Punch dough down; turn dough out on a lightly floured surface. Knead lightly three to four times. Roll dough to ½-inch thickness; cut with 2-inch biscuit cutter. Place biscuits on lightly greased baking sheets; bake at 450°F for 10 to 12 minutes or until lightly browned. Serves 36.

Nutritional analysis per serving: 124 cal, 1 g fiber, 6 g fat, 1 mg chol, 235 mg sodium

Luvenia's Angel Biscuits

5 cups all-purpose flour
3 teaspoons baking powder
1½ teaspoons salt
2 tablespoons sugar
1 cup vegetable shortening
1 tablespoon active dry yeast
2 tablespoons warm water
2 cups buttermilk

In large bowl, combine flour, baking powder, salt, and sugar. Cut shortening into flour mixture. In separate bowl, dissolve yeast in warm water. Add buttermilk to yeast and stir. Gradually add flour mixture to yeast and buttermilk. Mix until well combined. Shape dough into large ball and place in large bowl. Brush top of dough with melted margarine. Place bowl in refrigerator for 45 minutes. Remove from refrigerator and shape into biscuits. Place biscuits on baking sheet and allow to rise for 45 minutes. Bake at 400°F for 12 to 15 minutes. Serves 24.

Nutritional analysis per serving: 188 cal, 0 g fiber, 9.6 g fat, 2.9 mg chol, 216 mg sodium

Pineapple Upside Down Breakfast Rolls

½ cup brown sugar, packed
½ cup butter or margarine
¾ cup crushed pineapple, drained
1 teaspoon ground cinnamon
½ cup pecans or walnuts, chopped
1 18.6-ounce can refrigerator biscuits

Preheat oven to 425°F. Melt brown sugar in butter over medium heat. Remove from heat and add pineapple, cinnamon, and nuts. Mix well. Pour mixture into 8-inch square baking pan. Place separated biscuits on top of mixture. Bake for 10 minutes. Invert biscuits onto serving plate and add remaining mixture on top. Serves 6.

Nutritional analysis per serving: 557 cal, 0.24 g fiber, 37.2 g fat, 0.6 mg chol, 554 mg sodium

Pronto Pecan Rolls

½ cup butter or margarine
⅓ cup brown sugar
½ cup chopped pecans
1 can (18.6-ounce) refrigerator dinner
  rolls

In saucepan over low heat, melt butter. Reserve 1 tablespoon of melted butter. Add brown sugar and stir until dissolved. Stir in nuts. Pour mixture into 9-inch cake pan. Place rolls in pan and brush lightly with reserved butter. Bake at 425°F for 15 to 20 minutes or until golden brown. Invert on serving platter and spoon remaining mixture on top. Serves 6.

Nutritional analysis per serving: 490 cal, 0 g fiber, 30 g fat, 2.8 mg chol, 422 mg sodium

Quick Doughnuts √

2 packages canned biscuits
hot oil, for frying
granulated or confectioners' sugar

Punch hole in center of each biscuit. Drop into deep, hot oil. Do not let oil get too hot. Brown about 1 minute on each side. Drain, and shake in bag of granulated or confectioners' sugar. Cinnamon may be mixed with sugar, if desired. Serves 16.

Nutritional analysis per serving: 205 cal, 1.1 g fiber, 11.2 g fat, 13 mg chol, 117. mg sodium

Refrigerator Rolls

1 cup shortening
1 cup sugar
1½ teaspoons salt
1 cup boiling water
2 eggs, beaten
2 packages active dry yeast
1 cup lukewarm water
6 cups unsifted all-purpose flour

In large bowl, combine shortening, sugar, and salt. Pour boiling water over mixture. Add beaten eggs and mix ingredients until combined. Dissolve yeast in lukewarm water. Add yeast to first mixture. Gradually add flour and mix well. Refrigerate batter for at least 4 hours or overnight. Remove from refrigerator and form dough into small rolls. Place rolls onto greased cookie sheet. Allow rolls to rise for 3 hours. Bake at 425°F for 10–12 minutes, or until golden brown. Serves 30.

Nutritional analysis per serving: 193 cal, 0 g fiber, 7.5 g fat, 18.3 mg chol, 112 mg sodium

Refrigerator Rolls ★

½ cup lukewarm water
2 packages active dry yeast
2 teaspoons sugar
1 tablespoon salt
6 tablespoons sugar
1 stick (½ cup) margarine
1 cup boiling water
1 cup scalded milk
1 egg, beaten
6 cups all-purpose flour

Using warm bowl, combine lukewarm water, yeast, and 2 teaspoons sugar. Stir with spoon until dissolved. In separate large bowl, combine salt, 6 tablespoons sugar, margarine, water, and milk. Mix with spoon until combined. Allow mixture to cool. Add yeast mixture and egg. Gradually add flour. Mix well. Cover batter and place in refrigerator for at least four hours or overnight. Remove from refrigerator and form dough into oblong rolls that are about 2 inches long. Place rolls on greased baking sheet. Allow to rise for 3 hours. Bake at 450°F for 10 minutes, or until golden brown. Serves 72.

Nutritional analysis per serving: 58 cal, 0 g fiber, 1.6 g fat, 4.3 mg chol, 107 mg sodium

Simply Sensational Cinnamon Rolls

Dough:
2 packages dry yeast
1 cup shortening
1½ teaspoons salt

2 eggs, beaten
1 cup warm water (105–115°F)
½ cup sugar
1 cup boiling water
6–7 cups all-purpose flour
Filling:
½ cup margarine, softened
½ cup brown sugar
½ cup sugar
1 teaspoon cinnamon
Icing:
2 cups confectioners' sugar
1 teaspoon vanilla
3–4 tablespoons milk

Dissolve yeast in 1 cup warm water. Set aside. Combine shortening, sugar, and salt in large mixing bowl. Add boiling water, stirring until shortening melts. Cool to 105°F. Add yeast mixture and eggs. Mix well. Gradually beat in half of flour. Add remainder of flour, stirring in by hand, to make soft dough. Turn dough onto floured surface and knead about 3–5 minutes. Place dough in well-greased bowl, turning to grease top of dough. Cover tightly and store in refrigerator. Using half of dough at a time, roll out in large rectangle with rolling pin. Spread dough with half of softened margarine. Mix sugars and cinnamon and sprinkle half of mixture on dough. Roll up dough in jelly-roll fashion. Cut into ¾-inch slices and place 8 slices in slightly greased round 9-inch cake pan, leaving room to rise. (Half of dough should fill two pans.) Continue same method for other half of dough. Cover and let rise in warm place (85°F) about 1 hour or until doubled in size. Bake in 400°F preheated oven for 12–15 minutes. Mix icing ingredients together and spread or drizzle onto rolls when taken from oven. Cool slightly and serve. Serves 32.

Nutritional analysis per serving: 242.6 cal, 1.1 g fiber, 9.7 g fat, 13.4 mg chol, 143.5 mg sodium

Yeast Rolls ★

½ cup vegetable shortening
4 cups self-rising flour
½ cup sugar
¼ teaspoon salt
1 package active dry yeast
1 cup warm water—not hot
1 egg
1 tablespoon vegetable oil

Cut shortening into flour. Add sugar and salt to flour mixture. Dissolve yeast in warm water. Add yeast to flour mixture. Beat egg and add to dough; mix well. Work dough just until well formed. Add vegetable oil to large bowl and spread around bottom. Place dough into bowl in shape of ball. Cover bowl with cloth and allow to rise 12 to 24 hours. Remove dough from bowl and roll out until ¼ inch thick. Cut dough with biscuit cutter. Add small pat of margarine to cut piece and fold over dough. Place folded piece of dough onto greased baking pan. Allow folded pieces to rise for 4 hours. Bake rolls at 400°F for 15 to 20 minutes, or until golden brown. Serves 36.

Nutritional analysis per serving: 80 cal, 0 g fiber, 3.5 g fat, 7.6 mg chol, 167 mg sodium

BREADS

Banana Bread ★

1½ cups all purpose-flour
½ cup whole wheat flour
½ cup sugar
2 teaspoons baking powder
½ teaspoon salt
¾ teaspoon baking soda
3 bananas, mashed
3 tablespoons canola oil
⅓ cup skim milk
1 egg plus 1 egg white
vegetable cooking spray

Combine first six ingredients; add bananas, oil, milk, and eggs until well blended. Pour into 8 × 5-inch loaf pan coated with cooking spray. Bake at 350°F for 50 minutes or until toothpick inserted in center comes out clean. Cool 10 minutes; remove from pan. Wrap tightly; slice the next day. Serves 15.

Nutritional analysis per serving: 149 cal, 2 g fiber, 3 g fat, 6 mg chol, 178 mg sodium

Banana Nut Bread

2 eggs
1 cup sugar
¼ cup cooking oil
4 large bananas, mashed
2 cups all-purpose flour
¼ teaspoon salt
1 teaspoon baking soda
½ teaspoon vanilla extract
1 cup chopped nuts

Preheat oven to 325°F. Lightly grease and flour one 9 × 5 × 3-inch loaf pan. In large bowl beat eggs, sugar, and oil together until smooth. Add mashed bananas. Stir in flour, salt, baking soda, vanilla, and nuts. Pour batter into pan and bake for 60 minutes, or until golden brown. Allow bread to cool in pan for 15 minutes, then turn onto wire racks to complete cooling. Serves 9.

Nutritional analysis per serving: 397 cal, 1.5 g fiber, 16 g fat, 61 mg chol, 77.6 g sodium

Banana-Pineapple Bread

½ cup butter or margarine, at room
    temperature
1½ cups sugar
2 eggs
1 teaspoon vanilla extract
2 cups all-purpose flour
1 teaspoon baking soda
½ cup buttermilk
3 large bananas, mashed
1 cup crushed pineapple, drained

Preheat oven to 325°F. Lightly grease and flour two 8 × 5-inch loaf pans. In large bowl, cream butter and sugar. Add eggs and vanilla to creamed mixture, and beat until smooth. In separate bowl, sift flour and baking soda together. Alternately add flour and buttermilk to creamed mixture. Stir in banana and pineapple. Divide batter evenly between loaf pans. Bake for 60 to 75 minutes, or until toothpick inserted into center comes out clean. Allow

bread to cool in pan for 15 minutes, then turn onto wire racks to complete cooling. Serves 18.

Nutritional analysis per serving: 198 cal, 0.4 g fiber, 6 g fat, 31 mg chol, 75 mg sodium

Broccoli Corn Bread ★

10 ounces chopped broccoli
⅔ cup yellow corn meal
⅔ cup all-purpose flour
2 tablespoons sugar
2 teaspoons baking powder
½ teaspoon salt
2 teaspoons butter-flavor flakes
½ cup skim milk *or* fat-free cottage
    cheese
2 egg whites
2 tablespoons canola oil
⅓ cup chopped onion
vegetable cooking spray

Thaw broccoli if frozen; steam 5 minutes if fresh. Combine dry ingredients. Mix remaining ingredients together and stir into others until moistened. Spread into 8-inch or 9-inch square pan coated with cooking spray. Bake at 400°F 25 minutes or until lightly browned. Cut into 9 squares. Serves 9.

Nutritional analysis per serving: 130 cal, 1 g fiber, 4 g fat, 0.2 mg chol, 222 mg sodium

Broccoli Corn Bread

½ stick (¼ cup) butter or margarine,
    melted
12 ounces cottage cheese
4 eggs
1 10-ounce package frozen broccoli,
    thawed and chopped
1 medium onion, chopped
½ teaspoon salt
1½ cups self-rising corn meal
1½ cups (6 ounces) grated sharp
    Cheddar cheese

Preheat oven to 375°F. Lightly grease 9 × 13-inch baking pan and dust with cornmeal. In large mixing bowl, combine butter, cottage cheese, and eggs. Mix together well. Add chopped broccoli, onion, and salt. Stir in cornmeal. Spread batter into prepared pan. Sprinkle cheese evenly on top. Bake for 25 to 30 minutes. Serves 12.

Nutritional analysis per serving: 252.5 cal, 0.7 g fiber, 15.7 g fat, 110.3 mg chol, 654 mg sodium

Brown Bread ★

    1 cup raisins
    2 cups boiling water
    1 cup sugar
    1 egg, beaten
    1 tablespoon melted shortening or
      cooking oil
    2¾ cups all-purpose flour
    1 teaspoon salt
    2 teaspoons baking soda

Three No. 2 cans are needed for round loaves or 9-inch loaf pan for standard loaf. Lightly grease and flour pans. Preheat oven to 350°F. Add raisins to boiling water and soak for 12 to 24 hours. In large mixing bowl, combine raisins (undrained) with sugar, egg, and oil. Mix well. In separate bowl, sift together flour, salt, and baking soda. Add flour mixture to wet ingredients. Mix until combined. Fill each can ⅔ full of batter or pour all of batter into single 9-inch loaf pan. Bake for 60 minutes, or until toothpick inserted into center of bread comes out clean. Serves 16.

Nutritional analysis per serving: 170 cal, 0 g fiber, 1.5 g fat, 17 mg chol, 183 mg sodium

Earth Bread

    3 eggs, beaten
    1 cup cooking oil
    2 teaspoons vanilla extract
    1½ cups sugar
    3 cups all-purpose flour
    1 teaspoon salt
    1 teaspoon baking soda
    1½ teaspoons cinnamon
    ½ cup mashed ripe banana
    ½ cup nuts, chopped (optional)
    ¼ cup raw grated carrots

Preheat oven to 350°F. Grease and flour two 9 × 5-inch loaf pans. In large bowl, combine eggs, oil, vanilla, and sugar; mix thoroughly. Gradually add flour, salt, soda, and cinnamon; mix. Add fruit, nuts, and vegetables. Pour batter into prepared pans. Bake at 350°F for 1 hour or until bread springs back when lightly touched. Cool in pans for 10 minutes. Remove from pans and allow to cool completely before storing. Makes 2 loaves or 20 slices.

Nutritional analysis per slice: 259 cal, 0.1 g fiber, 14 g fat, 41 mg chol, 12 mg sodium

Grandma's Hoe Cake √ ★

    2 cups whole wheat flour
    1 teaspoon salt
    2 cups plain flour
    2 tablespoons clarified butter
    1½ cups cold water

Sift together dry ingredients. Mix in butter and add enough of water to make very stiff dough. Cover bowl and let stand at leastan hour in warm place. Knead well. Pour into large preheated frying pan to bake large "pone," or may divide into 8 pieces, form into balls, and flatten into circles about ½-inch thick and bake in medium hot skillet. Be sure to turn and cook on other side until hoe cake is done through (takes about 30 minutes). Eat while hot with soups or stew. Serves 8.

This recipe reportedly was used while working in the fields and baked on a shovel placed on top of the hot coals in a fire.

Nutritional analysis per serving: 222 cal, 5 g fiber, 2 g fat, 0 mg chol, 317 mg sodium

Grits Spoon Bread √ ★

    2½ cups milk, scalded
    1 cup grits
    4 eggs (separated)
    1 teaspoon salt
    2 tablespoons butter, melted
    1 teaspoon baking powder

Add grits and egg yolks to scalded milk and cook over hot water in double boiler until thick. Add salt and butter. Cool slightly. Beat egg whites until stiff. Fold egg whites and baking powder into grits. Place in 2-quart buttered baking dish. Bake at 350°F for 45 minutes. Serves 8.

Nutritional analysis per serving: 163 cal, 2 g fiber, 6 g fat, 116 mg chol, 399 mg sodium

Healthful Date Nut Bread ★

    1½ cups dates
    1¼ cups water
    3 cups all-purpose flour
    1 teaspoon baking soda
    2 teaspoons baking powder
    ⅓ cup mashed banana
    3 egg whites
    ½ cup margarine, at room temperature
    1 teaspoon vanilla extract
    ⅓ cup chopped almonds

Preheat oven to 350°F. Grease 9 × 13-inch baking pan. Combine dates and water in small bowl. Allow to sit for 15 to 30 minutes. In large mixing bowl, combine flour, baking soda, and baking powder. Add date mixture to flour mixture. Add banana, egg whites, margarine, vanilla, and nuts. Mix until well combined. Pour batter into prepared pan and bake for 20 to 25 minutes, or until golden brown. Serves 16.

Nutritional analysis per serving: 173 cal, 0.2 g fiber, 3.8 g fat, 0 mg chol, 98.3 mg sodium

Hearty Whole Wheat-Bran Bread

    3 packages dry yeast
    4 cups warm water, divided
    1¼ cups + 2 tablespoons sugar, divided
    ⅓ cup cooking oil
    4 teaspoons salt
    4 cups wheat bran
    7 to 8 cups whole wheat flour (up to
        4 pounds)

Dissolve yeast in 2 cups warm water and 2 tablespoons sugar. In large bowl, mix remaining 2 cups water and 1¼ cups sugar, oil, and salt. Add yeast mixture, wheat bran, and 4 cups of flour. Mix well. Gradually add 3 to 4 more cups of flour, until dough is consistency for kneading (stiff but pliable). Divide dough into thirds and knead thoroughly (about 10 minutes). Place dough in three greased loaf pans and lightly grease tops. Allow to rise in warm place until doubled in size (an hour or longer). Bake at 350°F for 45 minutes. Turn out of loaf pans and allow to cool on wire rack. For softer crust, lightly butter top and sides while still hot. Serves 24.

Nutritional analysis per serving: 324 cal, 4 g fiber, 13.2 g fat, 0 mg chol, 443 mg sodium

Herb Bread ★

    1 package active dry yeast
    ¼ cup lukewarm water
    1 cup cottage cheese
    1 tablespoon margarine
    2 tablespoons sugar
    1 tablespoon minced onion
    2 teaspoons dill seed
    1 teaspoon salt
    ¼ teaspoon baking soda
    1 egg, well beaten
    2½ cups all-purpose flour

Dissolve yeast in lukewarm water and set aside. In saucepan or microwave oven, heat cottage cheese to lukewarm and remove it from heat. In large bowl, combine cottage cheese, margarine, sugar, onion, dill seed, salt, baking soda, egg, and yeast mixture. Mix until well combined. Slowly add flour, stirring to form soft dough. Dough should be soft and smooth. Place dough in clean and lightly oiled large mixing bowl. Flip dough ball over to coat all sides with oil. Cover bowl and allow dough to rise until doubled in bulk (about 1 hour). Punch dough down and form into loaf. Transfer to lightly greased 9-inch loaf pan. Allow dough to rise until double in bulk (about an hour). Bake at 350°F for 30–40 minutes, or until golden brown. Serves 16.

Nutritional analysis per serving: 77 cal, 0 g fiber, 1.8 g fat, 19 mg chol, 200 mg sodium

Hush Puppies √

½ cup sifted flour
1 cup cornmeal
1 minced onion
1½ teaspoons baking powder
1 egg
1 teaspoon salt
1 teaspoon sugar
milk as needed

Mix all ingredients with just enough milk to moisten dough to stiff consistency, but soft enough to spoon. Drop by tablespoonfuls into deep fat (350°F). Cook until golden brown. Serves 18.

Nutritional analysis per serving: 51 cal, 1 g fiber, 10 g fat, 12 mg chol, 146 mg sodium

Mexican Corn Bread

1 cup self-rising cornmeal
½ cup self-rising flour
⅓ cup cooking oil
1 8-ounce can cream-style corn
2 eggs
1 teaspoon sugar
1 small onion, chopped
1 to 3 jalapeño peppers, seeded and
  chopped
¼ cup (1 ounce) grated cheese
1 10-ounce can whole kernel corn,
  drained
5 ounces water

Preheat oven to 425°F. Lightly grease 9-inch square baking pan with cooking oil and warm in oven while preparing batter. In large mixing bowl, combine all ingredients in order listed. Mix well. Pour mixture into hot pan and bake for 20 minutes, or until golden brown. Serves 9.

Nutritional analysis per serving: 235.3 cal, 0.1 g fiber, 11 g fat, 64 mg chol, 538 mg sodium

"Old South" Spoon Bread

½ cup self-rising cornmeal
1 cup cold water

½ teaspoon salt
½ cup milk
1 egg
1 tablespoon butter, melted
½ cup cheese, grated (optional)

Preheat oven to 375°F. Grease 9-inch square pan with margarine. In saucepan, combine cornmeal, water, and salt. Boil for 5 minutes, stirring constantly. Remove from heat and allow to cool until warm. Stir milk into mixture. Add egg, cheese, and melted butter. Pour batter into prepared pan and place in oven. Bake for 35 to 40 minutes, or until golden brown. Serves 4.

Nutritional analysis per serving: 109 cal, 0 g fiber, 3.6 g fat, 75 mg chol, 552 mg sodium

Peach Bread

1½ cups sugar
½ cup cooking oil
2 eggs
2¼ cups fresh peach puree
1 teaspoon vanilla extract
2 cups all-purpose flour
1 teaspoon cinnamon
1 teaspoon baking soda
1 teaspoon baking powder
¼ teaspoon salt
1 cup finely chopped walnuts or
  almonds

Preheat oven to 325°F. Lightly grease and flour two 9-inch loaf pans. In large mixing bowl, mix sugar with oil. Add eggs, peach puree, and vanilla extract. Mix well. Sift together the dry ingredients. Add dry ingredients to peach mixture and mix until just combined. Fold in nuts. Divide batter evenly between prepared loaf pans. Bake for 55 to 60 minutes, or until toothpick inserted in center of loaf comes out clean. Allow bread to cool in pan for 15 minutes, then turn onto wire racks to complete cooling. Serves 18.

Nutritional analysis per serving: 232 cal, 0.5 g fiber, 10.3 g fat, 0 mg chol, 82 mg sodium

Poppy Seed Bread

3 cups all-purpose flour
2¾ cups sugar, divided
1½ teaspoons salt
1½ teaspoons baking powder
2 tablespoons poppy seeds
3 eggs
1½ cups milk
1⅛ cup cooking oil
2 teaspoons vanilla extract, divided
2 teaspoons butter flavoring, divided
2 teaspoons almond extract, divided
¼ cup orange juice

Preheat oven to 325°F. Lightly grease two 9-inch loaf pans. In large bowl, combine flour, 2¼ cups sugar, salt, baking powder, poppy seeds, eggs, milk, oil, and 1½ teaspoons each vanilla extract, butter flavoring, and almond extract. Mix well. Divide batter evenly between loaf pans. Bake for 60 minutes, or until golden brown. Remove from oven and cool for 10 minutes while making glaze. To make glaze: Combine orange juice, ½ cup sugar, and ½ teaspoon each vanilla extract, butter flavoring, and almond extract. Mix until sugar dissolves. While still warm, pierce loaves with toothpick. Pour half of glaze over top of each loaf. Allow to cool completely before removing bread from pans. Serves 19.

Nutritional analysis per serving: 330 cal, 0 g fiber, 16.2 g fat, 48.4 mg chol, 233 mg sodium

Sally Lund Bread

2 cups milk
1 package active dry yeast
2 tablespoons sugar
2 eggs, beaten
4 tablespoons margarine or butter
5½ cups all-purpose flour
1½ teaspoons salt

Heat milk until tiny bubbles begin to form on sides. Pour milk into large bowl and allow to cool to lukewarm. Add yeast and stir until dissolved. Add remaining ingredients and mix well. Allow dough to rise for 4 hours, until almost doubled in bulk. Punch down dough and knead for few minutes. Grease tube pan with margarine. Place dough into greased pan and allow to rise again for 2 hours. Bake at 375°F for 45 minutes, or until golden brown. Serves 12.

Nutritional analysis per serving: 290 cal, 0 g fiber, 6.7 g fat, 51.2 mg chol, 344 mg sodium

Sally Lund √ ★

1 envelope yeast
½ cup lukewarm water
1½ cups milk
½ cup shortening
½ cup sugar
3 eggs
4 cups plain flour
1 teaspoon salt
1 heaping teaspoon baking powder

Dissolve yeast in warm water. Scald milk. While hot, melt shortening in milk and add sugar. Beat eggs until light. When milk mixture is cool, add eggs and yeast. Sift flour with salt and baking powder. Add to milk mixture to make very stiff batter. Beat until smooth. Place in well-greased cake pan. Allow to rise 1 hour in warm place. Bake in slow oven (325°F) for 1 hour. While hot, cut in wedges and put butter between wedges. If any left over, makes delicious toast. Serves 8.

Nutritional analysis per serving: 433 cal, 2 g fiber 15 g fat, 81 mg chol, 356 mg sodium

Sour Cream Corn Bread

1 cup self-rising cornmeal
1 8.75-ounce can cream-style corn
½ cup vegetable oil
2 eggs
1 cup sour cream
¼ cup onion, chopped

Preheat oven to 400°F. Grease 9-inch square baking pan. In large mixing bowl, combine all ingredients and mix well. Pour batter into prepared pan and place in oven.

Bake for 20 to 30 minutes, or until golden brown. Serves 9.

Nutritional analysis per serving: 256 cal, 0.04 g fiber, 19 g fat, 72 mg chol, 326.4 mg sodium

Sour Dough Bread ★

Starter: Use a glass jar—cover with foil

⅔ cup sugar
2 cups warm water
6 tablespoons instant potatoes
1 package dry yeast

Mix well with a plastic spoon. Let the mixture sit out for 24 hours covered loosely with foil. You may then make your first batch of bread or the mixture may be stored in the refrigerator.

Feeding: Remove from refrigerator. Add:

⅓ cup sugar
1 cup warm water
3 tablespoons instant potatoes

After feeding, let stand in warm place overnight (8 to 10 hours). Mixture will be bubbly. Take out 1 cup to make bread or return to refrigerator and feed again in 3 to 5 days. Do not go over 10 days without feeding. If you cannot bake at that time, you may refrigerate and feed again in 3 to 5 days, or you may give cup of starter to a friend. Feed starter mixture no more than 2 to 3 times before using to bake, give away, or throw away 1 cupful. Otherwise, starter will not work.

To Bake Bread: (makes 3 loaves)

¼ cup sugar
1 teaspoon salt
1½ cups warm water
1 cup starter
½ cup vegetable oil
6 cups bread flour**

Mix ingredients together until dry ingredients are absorbed. Form ball. Place in large greased bowl. Turn dough over so greased side is up. Cover lightly with sheet of greased aluminum foil. Put in warm place. Let rise 6 to 8 hours (overnight or all day is alright). Punch dough down and knead on lightly floured surface 1 to 2 minutes. Divide dough into three parts and place in well-greased loaf pans. Cover loosely with greased aluminum foil. Let rise 4 to 5 hours (all day or overnight is alright). Dough will double in bulk. Bake in preheated 350°F degree oven for 30 to 45 minutes. Remove and brush with butter. Cool on rack (will cut better after cool). May be wrapped and frozen.

**May use 2 cups whole wheat flour and 4 cups white bread flour or all 6 cups of whole wheat flour or any mixture that you desire.

Alternates: When ready to place in pan to bake, you may pull dough wide and fill with cheese, jelly, jam, cinnamon-sugar-nuts, or any other filling you desire. Work dough back together, form into loaf shape, and place in pan to bake as above.

Nutritional analysis per serving: 140 cal, 1 g fiber, 4 g fat, 0 g chol, 340 mg sodium

Southern Cracklin' Corn Bread +

4 cups cornmeal
2 teaspoons soda
1½ teaspoons salt
4 eggs, beaten
4 cups buttermilk
⅓ cup butter
1 cup crumbled bacon

Combine cornmeal, soda, and salt; stir in eggs and buttermilk. Heat butter in a 9 × 13 × 2-inch baking pan until very hot; add butter and bacon to batter, mixing well. Pour batter into hot pan; bake at 450°F for 25 minutes or until bread is golden. Cut into squares. Serves 20.

Nutritional analysis per serving: 184 cal, 2 g fiber, 6 g fat, 53 mg chol, 470 mg sodium

Southern Spoon Bread √ ★

1 cup cornmeal
3 cups milk
2 tablespoons butter
1 teaspoon salt
1 teaspoon baking powder
2 eggs, beaten

Combine cornmeal and milk in double boiler and cook for about half hour or until mixture is mush. Stir in butter, salt, and baking powder. Slowly add this to beaten eggs while beating. Fold into greased casserole dish. Bake 30 minutes at 375°F. Serves 8.

Nutritional analysis per serving: 132 cal, 2 g fiber, 5 g fat, 63 mg chol, 397 mg sodium

Strawberry Bread

3 cups all-purpose flour
1 teaspoon baking soda
½ teaspoon salt
½ teaspoon ground cinnamon
2 cups sugar
3 eggs
1 cup cooking oil
2 10-ounce packages frozen sliced
   strawberries, thawed

Preheat oven to 350°F. Lightly grease and flour two 9 × 5 × 3-inch loaf pans. In large bowl, combine flour, baking soda, salt, cinnamon, and sugar. Mix well. In separate bowl, combine eggs, oil, and strawberries with syrup. Add wet ingredients to dry ingredients. Mix until just moistened. Divide batter evenly between two loaf pans and bake for 60 minutes, or until golden brown. Allow bread to cool in pans for 15 minutes, then turn onto wire racks to complete cooling. Serves 18.

Nutritional analysis per serving: 293 cal, 0 g fiber, 13.3 g fat, 45.7 mg chol, 72 mg sodium

Virginia Spoon Bread +

6 cups white cornmeal
4 quarts milk
2 dozen eggs
½ cup butter or margarine
3 tablespoons salt

Put cornmeal in large kettle; add milk. Mix thoroughly and cook over medium heat until mixture thickens, stirring constantly. Remove from heat. Separate eggs. Beat whites until stiff; then beat yolks until thick and lemon-colored. Add yolks to cornmeal mixture; add butter and salt. Blend well; fold in egg whites. Pour into four ungreased 9 × 13 × 2¼-inch pans. Bake in moderate oven (350°F) 45 to 55 minutes. Serves 50.

Nutritional analysis per serving: 140 cal, 1 g fiber, 5 g fat, 104 mg chol, 479 mg sodium

Zucchini Bread

3 eggs
1 cup cooking oil
1½ cups sugar
3 teaspoons vanilla extract
2 cups grated zucchini squash
2 cups all-purpose flour
1 cup whole wheat flour
2 teaspoons baking soda
2 teaspoons cinnamon
1 cup chopped nuts
1 cup raisins

Preheat oven to 350°F. Lightly grease and flour two 9 × 5 × 3-inch loaf pans. In large bowl, beat together eggs, oil, sugar, vanilla extract, and zucchini. In separate bowl, sift together flour, baking soda, and cinnamon. Add flour mixture and remaining ingredients to egg mixture. Mix well. Divide batter evenly between two loaf pans and bake for 55–60 minutes, or until golden brown. Allow bread to cool in pans for 15 minutes, then turn onto wire racks to complete cooling. Serves 18.

Nutritional analysis per serving: 368 cal, 0.11 g fiber, 21.5 g fat, 45.6 mg chol, 14 mg sodium

Zucchini-Orange Bread

4 eggs
1½ cups sugar
¾ cup cooking oil
1 cup orange juice, divided
2 teaspoons grated orange peel
2 cups shredded zucchini
3¼ cups all-purpose flour
1½ teaspoons baking powder
1½ teaspoons baking soda
1 teaspoon salt
2½ teaspoons cinnamon
½ teaspoon cloves

½ teaspoon allspice
½ cup chopped nuts
1 cup 4X sugar

Preheat oven to 350°F. Lightly grease and flour bottoms only of two 9 × 5 × 3-inch loaf pans. In large mixing bowl, beat eggs until thick and lemon-colored. Gradually add sugar while beating. Stir in oil, ⅔ cup orange juice, orange peel, and zucchini. In separate mixing bowl, mix together flour, baking powder, baking soda, salt, and spices. Add flour mixture to egg mixture. Mix well. Stir in nuts. Divide batter evenly between two loaf pans and bake for 45–55 minutes, or until toothpick inserted into center comes out clean. Allow bread to cool in pans for 15 minutes, then turn onto wire racks to glaze and complete cooling.

To make glaze: Combine 4X sugar with remaining orange juice. Mix until sugar dissolves. Spread glaze over warm loaves. Store cooled loaves in refrigerator. Serves 18.

Nutritional analysis per serving: 240 cal, 0.11 g fiber, 14.5 g fat, 61 mg chol, 165.5 mg sodium

MUFFINS

Angel Muffins

1 package active dry yeast
2 cups warm water
¼ cup sugar
¾ cup vegetable oil
1 egg
4 cups self-rising flour

In large mixing bowl, combine yeast with 2 tablespoons of warm water. Stir until dissolved. Add remaining water, sugar, oil, and egg. Gradually add in flour. Stir until well combined. Place batter in covered bowl and put in refrigerator until ready to use. Mixture will be thin. When ready to use, grease muffin tin and fill each tin ½ full of thin dough. Bake at 425°F for 12 to 15 minutes, or until golden brown. Serves 24.

Nutritional analysis per serving: 144 cal, 0 g fiber, 7 g fat, 0 mg chol, 229 mg sodium

Apple Muffins

¾ cup cooking oil
1 cup sugar
2 eggs
1 teaspoon black walnut extract
1½ cups all-purpose flour
½ teaspoon salt
½ teaspoon baking soda
½ cup chopped nuts
1 cup chopped, peeled apple
1 cup shredded coconut

Preheat oven to 350°F. Lightly grease muffin tin with margarine. In large mixing bowl, combine oil, sugar, eggs, and black walnut extract. In separate bowl, sift together flour, salt, and baking soda. Gently mix wet and dry ingredients together, just until flour is moistened. Fold in nuts, apple, and coconut. Fill prepared muffin cups ⅔ full of batter and bake for 20 to 25 minutes, or until golden brown. Serves 12.

Nutritional analysis per serving: 346 cal, 0.2 g fiber, 23 g fat, 46 mg chol, 102.3 mg sodium

Apple-Graham Muffins

2 cups graham cracker crumbs
½ cup all-purpose flour
¼ cup sugar
1 teaspoon baking powder
½ teaspoon baking soda
2 eggs, beaten
8 ounces plain yogurt
½ cup cooking oil
1 cup chopped, peeled apple

Preheat oven to 400°F. Lightly grease muffin tin with margarine. In large bowl, mix together dry ingredients. In separate bowl, combine wet ingredients. Gently mix wet and dry ingredients together, just until flour is moistened. Fold in apple. Fill prepared muffin cups ⅔ full of batter and bake for 20 to 25 minutes, or until golden brown. Serves 12.

Nutritional analysis per serving: 200 cal, 0.2 g fiber, 12 g fat, 48 mg chol, 144.4 mg sodium

Basic Breakfast Muffins

2 cups all-purpose flour
4 teaspoons baking powder
¼ teaspoon salt
⅓ cup butter or margarine, at room
    temperature
¼ cup sugar
1 egg, beaten
¾ cup milk

Preheat oven to 350°F. Lightly grease muffin tin with margarine. In large bowl, sift together flour, baking powder, and salt. In separate bowl, cream butter with sugar. Add egg to creamed mixture. Mix well. Alternately add flour and milk to creamed mixture. Mix only until flour is moistened. Fill each muffin cup ⅔ full of batter and bake for 20 to 25 minutes, or until golden brown. Serves 12.

Nutritional analysis per serving: 153.4 cal, 0 g fiber, 6.2 g fat, 25 mg chol, 233 mg sodium

Bran Muffins ★

1 cup whole wheat flour
1 cup 100% bran cereal
2 teaspoons baking powder
½ teaspoon salt
2 eggs, beaten
¼ cup oil
1¼ cup honey
1½ cups milk
½ cup raisins

Preheat oven to 400°F. Lightly grease muffin tin with margarine. In large mixing bowl, combine all dry ingredients. In separate bowl, combine wet ingredients. Gently mix wet and dry ingredients together, just until flour is moistened. Fill each cup ⅔ full of batter and bake for 15 to 20 minutes, or until golden brown. Serves 12.

Nutritional analysis per serving: 120 cal, 1.6 g fiber, 2.5 g fat, 50 mg chol, 155 mg sodium

Cornmeal Muffins ★

1 cup cornmeal
1 cup flour
½ teaspoon salt

1 tablespoon sugar
4 teaspoons baking powder
1 cup milk
2 large eggs, beaten
2 tablespoons melted shortening or
    salad oil

Preheat oven to 400–425°F. Mix and sift dry ingredients into mixing bowl. Add milk and mix well. Add eggs and melted shortening or oil. Pour into well-greased and heated muffin tins and bake 20 to 25 minutes or until brown. Butter and serve. Serves 10.

Nutritional analysis per serving: 140 cal, 1 g fiber, 3 g fat, 17 mg chol, 237 mg sodium

Oatmeal Muffins √ ★

2 large egg whites
3 tablespoons fresh orange juice
⅓ cup maple syrup
1 cup skim milk
1 tablespoon vanilla extract
1 teaspoon cinnamon
1 teaspoon allspice
1 teaspoon cloves
1 teaspoon nutmeg
1 teaspoon orange zest
1½ cups rolled oats
1 cup whole wheat flour
1 teaspoon baking powder
¼ cup pecans, chopped
¼ cup drained cranberries

Preheat oven to 350°F. Spray 12-muffin tin with vegetable spray. Place egg whites in large bowl and whisk until frothy. Add maple syrup, orange juice, and milk. Add vanilla, spices, and orange zest. Blend. Stir in oats, flour, and baking powder. Fold in pecans and cranberries. Fill muffin tin about ⅔ full. Bake 20 minutes, until muffins are firm in center. Serves 12.

Nutritional analysis per serving: 126 cal, 2 g fiber, 2 g fat, 0 mg chol, 43 mg sodium

Orange Minicakes

2½ cups sugar, divided
1 cup shortening
2 eggs

3 cups all-purpose flour
1 teaspoon baking soda
½ teaspoon salt
¾ cup buttermilk
1 teaspoon orange flavoring
1 teaspoon lemon flavoring
1¾ cup orange juice, divided
1 cup seedless raisins

Cream together 1 cup of sugar with shortening. Add eggs and beat well. Sift together flour, soda, and salt. Combine buttermilk, flavorings, ¼ cup orange juice, and raisins. Alternately add milk mixture and flour mixture to creamed mixture. Drop 1 tablespoon of batter into each greased miniature muffin cup and bake at 325°F for 12 to 15 minutes or until lightly browned. Cool in pan for 1 or 2 minutes, then remove. Combine remaining 1½ cups sugar and 1½ cups orange juice in small saucepan over medium heat. Stir constantly until sugar dissolves. Dip warm muffins into glaze and place on waxed paper to cool. Makes 80 small muffins.

Nutritional analysis per serving: 80 cal, 0 g fiber, 3 g fat, 8.4 mg chol, 6 mg sodium

Sassy Cinnamon Muffins

½ cup all-purpose flour
¼ cup sugar
¼ cup brown sugar, packed
2 teaspoons baking powder
½ teaspoon salt
1 teaspoon cinnamon
1 egg, beaten
½ cup cooking oil
½ cup milk
½ cup chopped pecans

Preheat oven to 400°F. Lightly grease muffin tin with margarine. In large bowl, mix together dry ingredients. In separate bowl, combine wet ingredients. Gently mix wet and dry ingredients together, just until flour is moistened. Fold in nuts. Fill prepared muffin cups ⅔ full of batter and bake for 20 to 25 minutes, or until golden brown. Serves 12.

Nutritional analysis per serving: 246.4 cal, 0 g fiber, 16.2 g fat, 24.2 mg chol, 71 mg sodium

Sugar-Top Date Muffins +

3 cups shortening
3 cups white sugar
1½ cups brown sugar
12 eggs
¾ cup milk
2¾ pounds flour
¼ cup baking powder
1 tablespoon salt
1 pint reconstituted lemon juice
4 pounds diced dates
½ cup white sugar
½ cup brown sugar
2 tablespoons cinnamon

Beat shortening, 3 cups white sugar, and 1½ cups brown sugar together in mixing bowl at medium speed until fluffy and creamy. Add eggs and milk and continue beating for 2 minutes. Sift flour, baking powder, and salt together. Add to sugar-egg mixture; beat. Add lemon juice and beat well for about 2 minutes at low speed. Scrape bottom of bowl and sides and beat again until blended. Fold in diced dates. Scale into well-greased muffin pans about ⅔ full. Combine ½ cup white sugar, ½ cup brown sugar, and cinnamon. Sprinkle over muffin tops. Bake at 375°F for 12 to 15 minutes or until well done. Serves 100.

Nutritional analysis per serving: 204 cal, 1 g fiber, 7 g fat, 26 mg chol, 107 mg sodium

Very Blueberry Muffins ★

1⅓ cups all-purpose flour
1 cup oats (quick or old-fashioned)
¼ cup brown sugar
1 tablespoon baking powder
½ teaspoon salt (optional)
½ teaspoon cinnamon
vegetable cooking spray
1 cup skim milk
2 egg whites
3 tablespoons canola oil
1 teaspoon vanilla
1 cup blueberries
2 tablespoons sugar

Coat muffin tin with cooking spray and preheat oven to 425°F. In large bowl, combine first six ingredients. Add milk, egg whites, oil, and vanilla. Stir just until dry ingredients are moist. Fold in blueberries; fill muffin cups ⅔ full. Sprinkle tops with sugar. Bake 20 minutes or until golden brown. Serves 12.

Nutritional analysis per serving: 172 cal, 2 g fiber, 5 g fat, 0.4 mg chol, 179 mg sodium

PANCAKES AND WAFFLES

Animal Pancakes ★

2 beaten eggs
2 cups buttermilk
2 tablespoons liquid shortening
2 cups all-purpose flour
1 teaspoon salt
2 teaspoons baking powder
2 tablespoons sugar
½ teaspoon soda

Combine eggs, milk, and shortening. Add flour sifted with salt, baking powder, and sugar; stir until well mixed. Bake on ungreased griddle in animal shapes—a big spoonful for the body and small spoonfuls for head, legs, ears, etc. Turtles and rabbits are easy to do. Have fun! Serves 4.

Nutritional analysis per serving: 396.3 cal, 1.9 g fiber, 0.6 g fat, 111 mg chol, 926.6 mg sodium

Pancakes ★

2 eggs, separated
2 tablespoons sugar
2 cups self-rising flour
1½ cups milk
2 tablespoons margarine

In large mixing bowl, combine egg yolks with sugar. Mix well. Add flour to egg yolks, alternating with milk. Add melted margarine. Blend well. In separate bowl, beat egg whites until stiff. Fold egg whites into batter. Spoon batter onto hot, greased frying pan or griddle. Cook until pancake is golden brown on both sides. Serves 4.

Nutritional analysis per serving: 389.5 cal, 0 g fiber, 12 g fat, 149.3 mg chol, 820.4 mg sodium

Pumpkin Pancakes ★

2 cups all-purpose flour
2 tablespoons light brown sugar
1 tablespoon baking powder
1 teaspoon ground cinnamon
1 teaspoon ground nutmeg
2 egg whites
1½ cups skim milk
½ cup canned pumpkin
1 teaspoon oil

Combine flour, sugar, baking powder, cinnamon, and nutmeg in mixing bowl. In separate bowl, beat egg whites until stiff. Combine milk and pumpkin in large measuring cup. Add milk and pumpkin mixture to dry ingredients, mixing well. Fold egg whites into flour mixture. Heat griddle to medium and brush lightly with oil. Pour ¼-cup batter onto griddle for each pancake. Cook until tops are bubbly, then turn and cook until remaining side is golden brown. Makes 16 4-inch cakes. Serve pancakes with applesauce, if desired.

Nutritional analysis per serving: 76.5 cal, 0 g fiber, 0.2 g fat, 0.4 mg chol, 37.4 mg sodium

Waffles ★

2 cups all-purpose flour
4 teaspoons baking powder
¼ teaspoon salt
2 tablespoons sugar
2 eggs
1¼ cups milk
6 tablespoons margarine, melted

In large mixing bowl, combine flour, baking powder, salt, and sugar. Add eggs, milk, and margarine. Mix until well combined. Place batter into large measuring cup. Pour batter onto hot waffle iron. Allow waffles to cook until browned on both sides. Serves 6.

Nutritional analysis per serving: 276 cal, 0 g fiber, 9.6 g fat, 98.2 mg chol, 509 mg sodium

VEGETABLES

Almond Green Rice

¾ cup milk
1 egg, beaten
2 cups cooked white rice
½ cup (2 ounces) shredded sharp
   Cheddar cheese
6 tablespoons dried parsley
½ teaspoon salt
3 tablespoons diced onion
5-ounce can mushroom pieces, drained
1 tablespoon butter, melted
½ cup roasted almonds

In large bowl, combine milk and beaten egg. Add rice, cheese, parsley, salt, onion, mushrooms, and butter. Stir until well combined. Put mixture into lightly greased 2-quart casserole dish. Cover and bake at 350°F for 40–45 minutes. Sprinkle with almonds before serving. Serves 8.

Nutritional analysis per serving: 209 cal, 0.45 g fiber, 14 g fat, 61 mg chol, 464 mg sodium

Apple-Carrot Casserole ★

6 carrots, peeled
1 20-ounce can sliced apples
½ cup sugar
2 tablespoons margarine
⅛ teaspoon paprika, if desired

Slice carrots crosswise into ½-inch thick rounds. Cook carrots in small amount of salted water for 12 minutes or until tender. Drain off water. Spoon half of carrots into lightly greased 2-quart casserole dish. Then add half the apples. Repeat with remaining carrots and apples. Sprinkle sugar over mixture. Dot with margarine and sprinkle with paprika. Bake at 350°F for 35–40 minutes, or until liquid becomes syrupy. Serves 6.

Nutritional analysis per serving: 186 cal, 2.6 g fiber, 4.4 g fat, 0 mg chol, 72.5 mg sodium

Asparagus and Pea Casserole

1 10.5-ounce can asparagus spears,
   drained
2 hard-boiled eggs, chopped
2 cups sharp Cheddar cheese, grated
1 10.5-ounce can small peas, drained
⅓ cup slivered almonds
¼ cup (4 tablespoons) margarine
¼ teaspoon black pepper
¾ cup milk
1 10.5-ounce can cream of mushroom
   soup
cracker crumbs

Preheat oven to 350°F and grease 2-quart baking dish with margarine. Place drained asparagus in baking dish. Add chopped eggs and 1 cup of cheese. Add peas and half of almonds. Dot with margarine. Season with black pepper. In separate bowl, combine milk and soup. Mix well. Pour mixture over layers in baking dish. Top with cracker crumbs and remaining almonds and cheese. Bake for 30 minutes, or until golden brown. Serves 10.

Nutritional analysis per serving: 252.5 cal, 1 g fiber, 18.2 g fat, 91 mg chol, 796 mg sodium

Baked Cheese Grits +

18 cups water
3 tablespoons salt
4½ cups uncooked regular grits
1½ cups butter or margarine
12 cups medium-sharp Cheddar cheese,
    shredded and divided
18 eggs, beaten

Combine water and salt; bring to a boil. Stir in grits; cook until done, following package directions. Remove from heat. Add butter and 11¼ cups cheese; stir until completely melted. Add a small amount of hot grits to eggs, stirring well; stir egg mixture into remaining grits. Pour grits into large, lightly greased chafing pan; sprinkle with remaining ¾ cup cheese. Bake at 350°F for 1 hour and 15 minutes. Serves 24.

Nutritional analysis per serving: 394 cal, 3 g fiber, 23 g fat, 219 mg chol, 1205 mg sodium

Baked Spicy Potatoes √ ★

4 tablespoons Dijon-style mustard
1 teaspoon cumin
½ teaspoon cayenne pepper
2 teaspoons paprika
1 teaspoon chili powder
16 small red potatoes

Preheat oven to 400°F. Spray baking pan with vegetable oil. Place mustard and spices in bowl and stir to blend. Make deep holes in potatoes with tines of fork. Add potatoes to spice mixture. Toss to coat evenly. Pour potatoes and coating mixture into baking pan, separating potatoes. Bake about 1 hour, until potatoes are tender. Serves 4.

Nutritional analysis per serving: 346 cal, 8 g fiber, 2 g fat, 0 mg chol, 200 mg sodium

Baked Tomatoes √ ★

6 tomatoes, sliced
garlic powder, parsley, and oregano to
    taste
½ cup low-fat mayonnaise
mozzarella cheese

Layer sliced tomatoes in shallow casserole dish. Do not grease dish. Sprinkle tomatoes with spices and any other seasonings you like. Drop dollops of mayonnaise over top of tomato slices and sprinkle mozzarella cheese over top. Bake in preheated 350°F oven until cheese browns (about 20 minutes). Serves 6. (May reduce calories and fat by using low-fat and/or lite cheese.)

Nutritional analysis per serving: 230 cal, 2 g fiber, 17 g fat, 25 mg chol, 321 mg sodium

Baked Vidalia Onions ★

6 Vidalia onions, washed and peeled
6 beef bouillon cubes
6 pats butter or margarine

Cut small slits in top of onions; put 1 bouillon cube and 1 pat of butter in each one. Bake at 350°F for approximately 25 minutes, or until tender. Serves 6.

Nutritional analysis per serving: 61 cal, 1 g fiber, 4 g fat, 0.1 mg chol, 913 mg sodium

Broccoli Casserole

¼ cup margarine, melted
1 cup herb-seasoned stuffing mix,
    divided
1 medium onion, chopped
1 16-ounce can cream-style corn
1 10.5-ounce can condensed cream of
    mushroom or celery soup
1 egg, beaten
1 package frozen chopped broccoli,
    cooked and drained

Combine margarine and ¾ cup stuffing mix. Stir in onion, corn, soup, egg, and broccoli until well mixed. Top with remaining stuffing mix. Bake at 350°F in lightly greased 2-quart casserole dish for 30–35 minutes. Serves 8.

Nutritional analysis per serving: 189 cal, 0.84 g fiber, 9.8 g fat, 35.3 mg chol, 685.7 mg sodium

Broccoli Casserole

2 packages frozen broccoli, cooked and
  drained
1 stick (½ cup) margarine, melted
1 envelope dry onion soup mix
1 cup chopped nuts
1 5-ounce can sliced water chestnuts,
  drained
1 teaspoon bacon bits

Combine broccoli, margarine, soup mix,
nuts, water chestnuts, and bacon bits in lightly
greased 2-quart baking dish. Bake at 350°F
for 10 minutes, or until thoroughly heated.
Serves 8.

Nutritional analysis per serving: 355 cal,
1.5 g fiber, 30.5 g fat, 0.7 mg chol, 243 mg
sodium

Broccoli Casserole √

1 3-pound package broccoli
2 large onions
2 cloves garlic, minced
1 stick margarine
4 10½-ounce cans mushroom soup
1 cup sharp cheese
1 4-ounce can mushrooms
1 cup blanched almonds
1 5-ounce can water chestnuts
1 cup bread crumbs
salt and pepper to taste

Cook broccoli according to package directions. Drain well. Sauté onions and garlic
in margarine. Add broccoli. Add soup,
cheese, mushrooms, ¾ cup almonds, water
chestnuts, and ½ cup bread crumbs. Add salt
and pepper to taste. Mix well. Pour into
3-quart casserole pan. Cover with remaining
almonds and crumbs. Cook at 300°F until
bubbly. Freezes well. May make individual
casseroles if desired. Serves 8. (May reduce
calories and fat by using low-fat and/or lite
mushroom soup.)

Nutritional analysis per serving: 241 cal,
4 g fiber, 17 g fat, 8 mg chol, 261 mg sodium

Brown Rice ★

1 medium green bell pepper, diced
1 medium onion, diced
2 tablespoons margarine
1 cup brown rice
2½ cups cold water
1 teaspoon salt
1–2 tablespoons soy sauce, to taste

Sauté bell pepper and onion in margarine
until tender. Add rice, water, salt, and soy
sauce. Simmer, covered, for about 30 minutes,
or until rice is tender. Serves 4.

Nutritional analysis per serving: 109 cal,
0.4 g fiber, 6 g fat, 0 mg chol, 1112.8 mg
sodium

Cabbage and Noodle Casserole

1 medium onion, sliced
1 tablespoon margarine
1 small head of cabbage, shredded or
  chopped
1 teaspoon caraway seeds
½ teaspoon celery seeds
⅓ cup dry white wine
2 cups chicken broth
2 tablespoons all-purpose flour
½ cup plain low-fat yogurt
2 tablespoons sour cream
1–2 tablespoons cider vinegar, to taste
4 ounces egg noodles, cooked
2 tablespoons Parmesan cheese
2 tablespoons fine bread crumbs
¼ cup slivered almonds

In large saucepan, sauté onions in margarine until translucent. Add cabbage, caraway
seeds, and celery seeds. Cook for 1 minute.
Add wine and simmer for 10 minutes. In small
bowl, combine chicken broth and flour. Mix
well. Add broth mixture to cabbage. Cook
over medium heat for 2 minutes. Remove
from heat. Add yogurt, sour cream, vinegar,
and noodles. Spoon mixture into a 1½-quart,
shallow baking dish. Bake, uncovered, for 20
minutes. Sprinkle cheese, bread crumbs, and
almonds on top. Bake at 350°F until mixture

begins to bubble and brown, about 30 minutes. Serves 4.

Nutritional analysis per serving: 295.4 cal, 2.7 g fiber, 14.4 g fat, 12.7 mg chol, 524.7 mg sodium

Cajun Cabbage

1 large head cabbage, cored and
    quartered
1 clove garlic, minced
4 medium onions, chopped
1 pound fresh mushrooms, sliced
1 cayenne pepper pod or 1 tablespoon
    ground cayenne
1 cup white wine
2 teaspoons salt
1 pound hot smoked sausage, cut in
    2-inch pieces

Layer cabbage, garlic, onions, mushrooms, and pepper in large pot. Mix together two cups of water with wine and salt, and pour over mixture in pot. Put sausage on top. Cover and simmer until cabbage is tender but still crisp. Serves 12.

Nutritional analysis per serving: 479 cal, 1.3 g fiber, 38 g fat, 89 mg chol, 143 mg sodium

Carla's Tomato Quiche

2 medium-sized Charleston tomatoes,
    fully ripe
pastry for 1 9-inch pie crust
2 eggs
1½ cups milk
2 cups shredded Swiss cheese
½ cup green pepper, chopped
½ cup onions, chopped
1¼ teaspoons salt
¼ teaspoon ground black pepper

Dice 1 tomato into small cubes; slice second tomato; set both aside separately. Roll pastry to fit 9-inch pie pan. Place in pie pan and flute edges. Prick bottom and sides of pastry. Refrigerate for 10 minutes. Bake in preheated 450°F oven until golden brown, about 8 minutes. Remove from oven. Reduce

oven temperature to 325°F. In medium bowl, lightly beat eggs. Stir in milk, cheese, green pepper, onion, salt, black pepper, and reserved diced tomato. Pour into baked pie shell. Bake at 325°F for 30 minutes. Top with reserved sliced tomatoes. Bake until knife inserted in center comes out clean, about 25 minutes longer. Let pie stand at room temperature for 10 minutes before cutting. Serves 4.

Nutritional analysis per serving: 521 cal, 2 g fiber, 30 g fat, 138 mg chol, 1312 mg sodium

Carrot Casserole

2 pounds carrots, scraped
1 large can evaporated milk
¼ cup water
2 teaspoons sugar
2 teaspoons dry mustard
1 cup Cheddar cheese, grated
½ cup mayonnaise
1 small onion, chopped
¼ cup butter
1 cup cracker crumbs

Cut carrots in 1-inch pieces and cook in milk and water. When tender, mash; do not drain. Add sugar, mustard, cheese, and mayonnaise. Sauté onions in butter and add to above mixture. Combine well. Pour into casserole dish and top with cracker crumbs. Bake at 350°F for 20–30 minutes. Serves 8.

Nutritional analysis per serving: 341 cal, 4 g fiber, 22 g fat, 41 mg chol, 328 mg sodium

Carrot-Lima-Squash Medley + ★

1 cup sugar
2 tablespoons plus 2 teaspoons
    cornstarch
4 teaspoons salt
½ teaspoon dillweed
2⅔ cups orange juice
2 pounds carrots, peeled and diagonally
    sliced (about 6 cups)
4 cups fresh lima beans
2 medium yellow squash, sliced
2 medium zucchini, sliced

Combine sugar, cornstarch, salt, and dill-weed in a small saucepan; mix well. Stir in orange juice. Cook over medium heat, stirring constantly, until thickened and bubbly. Reduce heat to low to keep sauce warm. Steam carrots ten minutes; add limas and squash. Steam 10 to 15 minutes or until tender. Serve sauce over vegetables. Serves 24.

Nutritional analysis per serving: 112 cal, 3 g fiber, 0 g fat, 0 mg chol, 382 mg sodium

Cauliflower Casserole

1 package frozen cauliflower
1 8-ounce cream cheese
1 can cream of mushroom soup
1 package Ritz crackers, crumbled
½ stick margarine, melted

Cook cauliflower according to directions. Drain. Place cream cheese in warm pot, add drained cauliflower, and mix. Add mushroom soup. Mix well and pour into casserole dish. Top with crushed crackers and top with melted margarine. Bake in preheated 350°F oven for 30 minutes. Serves 6.

Nutritional analysis per serving: 749 cal, 5 g fiber, 54 g fat, 42 mg chol, 1471 mg sodium

Cheese-Frosted Cauliflower

1 medium head of cauliflower
¼ teaspoon salt
½ cup salad dressing
2 teaspoons prepared mustard
1 cup shredded medium Cheddar cheese

Remove leaves, trim base from cauliflower, and wash. Precook whole head in boiling salt water 12 to 15 minutes. Drain. Break cauliflower into serving sections. Place in 1½-quart baking dish. Sprinkle with salt. Combine salad dressing and mustard. Spread over cauliflower. Top with cheese. Bake in 350°F oven for 15 minutes or until cheese is melted and bubbly. Serves 5.

Nutritional analysis per serving: 232 cal, 5 g fiber, 19 g fat, 24 mg chol, 516 mg sodium

Corn Pie ★

3 eggs
2 tablespoons flour
1 teaspoon sugar (heaping)
½ teaspoon salt
½ cup milk
1 quart corn, cut from cob
1 tablespoon butter

Beat eggs, flour, sugar, salt, and milk together. Stir in corn. Dot with butter. Bake at 350°F for 45 minutes. Serves 8.

Nutritional analysis per serving: 122 cal, 2 g fiber, 3 g fat, 84 mg chol, 184 mg sodium

Corn Pudding

2 cups milk
2 cups corn
¼ cup chopped green pepper
2 tablespoons butter, melted
1 tablespoon sugar
salt and pepper, to taste
3 eggs, beaten
¼ cup (1 ounce) grated cheese
¼ cup corn flakes, crushed

Combine milk, corn, green pepper, butter, sugar, and seasonings. Mix well. Add eggs. Stir to mix well. Pour mixture into lightly greased 9 × 13-inch baking dish. Bake at 350°F for 45 minutes, or until pudding becomes firm. Sprinkle cheese and corn flakes over top of pudding. Bake an additional 5 minutes, or until cheese melts. Serves 6.

Nutritional analysis per serving: 256 cal, 1.3 g fiber, 12 g fat, 167 mg chol, 387 mg sodium

Creole Okra and Tomatoes ★

1 large onion, chopped
2 tablespoons margarine
4 ripe tomatoes, chopped
⅓ cup chopped green bell pepper
2 pounds fresh okra, sliced
salt and pepper, to taste

In large skillet, sauté onions in margarine until transparent and tender. Add tomatoes, green pepper, and okra. Season with salt and pepper. Cover and simmer over low to medium heat for 40 minutes, stirring occasionally. Serves 8.

Nutritional analysis per serving: 150 cal, 0.2 g fiber, 11.6 g fat, 0 mg chol, 276.4 mg sodium

Dilly Green Beans +

    8 eggs, hard-cooked
    6 pounds fresh green beans
    4 cups onion, chopped
    1 cup butter or margarine, melted
    2 tablespoons salt
    dash pepper
    2 tablespoons dill seeds

Cut eggs in half and remove yolk. Chop egg whites and sieve egg yolks; set aside. Remove strings from beans, cut into 2-inch pieces, and wash thoroughly. Cook beans, covered, in lightly salted water until tender (about 20–25 minutes); drain well and set aside. Sauté onion in butter until tender. Add green beans and seasonings, tossing lightly. Cook over medium heat until heated thoroughly. Remove from heat; garnish with chopped egg white and sieved egg yolks. Serves 24.

Nutritional analysis per serving: 126 cal, 2 g fiber, 10 g fat, 71 mg chol, 658 mg sodium

Easy Potato Casserole +

    3 32-ounce packages frozen shredded
        hash brown potatoes, thawed
    3 10.75-ounce cans cream of potato
        soup, undiluted
    3 10.75-ounce cans cream of celery
        soup, undiluted
    3 8-ounce cartons commercial sour
        cream
    3 medium onions, chopped
    1½ cups green pepper, chopped
    1½ teaspoons salt
    ⅜ teaspoon pepper
    3 cups 4 ounces Monterey Jack cheese,
        shredded

Combine all ingredients except cheese; stir well. Spoon potato mixture into three greased, shallow 2-quart casseroles. Bake at 325°F for 1 hour and 15 minutes. Sprinkle with cheese and bake an additional 15 minutes. Serves 24.

Nutritional analysis per serving: 379 cal, 1 g fiber, 23 g fat, 23 mg chol, 801 mg sodium

Eggplant Casserole

    3 strips bacon
    3 cups eggplant
    1 cup tomatoes, cooked and mashed, or
        1 can tomatoes
    1 medium onion, chopped fine
    1 cup Cheddar cheese
    ½ cup chopped green pepper
    1 egg, beaten
    2 teaspoons baking powder
    ½ cup bread crumbs
    salt and pepper, to taste

In skillet, cook bacon until crisp; break into small pieces and reserve. Peel and slice eggplant. Leave eggplant in salt water 1 hour, then cook until tender. Drain and mash eggplant. Add tomatoes, onion, cheese, green pepper, egg, bacon, and baking powder. Mix well; put in greased baking dish. Sprinkle top of dish with bread crumbs. Bake about 35 minutes at 350°F. Serves 8.

Nutritional analysis per serving: 116 cal, 2 g fiber, 7 g fat, 44 mg chol, 218 mg sodium

Eggplant Casserole

    1 medium-size eggplant, peeled and
        cubed
    1 small onion, chopped
    1 green bell pepper, chopped
    12 saltine crackers, crushed
    2 tablespoons margarine
    salt and pepper, to taste
    1 egg
    1 cup milk
    ½ cup (2 ounces) grated Cheddar cheese

In small saucepan, cook eggplant, onion, and pepper in enough water to boil vegetables until just tender. Drain water. Add crackers, margarine, salt, and pepper. Pour mixture into 2½-quart casserole dish. In separate small bowl, beat egg and milk lightly. Pour egg and milk mixture over eggplant mixture. Sprinkle top of casserole with grated cheese. Bake at 350°F for 25 minutes, or until bubbling and light brown. Serves 4.

Nutritional analysis per serving: 214 cal, 0.8 g fiber, 14.8 g fat, 91.6 mg chol, 414.7 mg sodium

Eggplant Casserole

2 large onions, chopped
6 tablespoons margarine, divided
1 pound eggplant, peeled, cooked, and cubed
3 hard-cooked eggs, chopped
1 cup milk
½ pound (2 cups) grated Cheddar cheese
1½ cups cracker crumbs, divided
salt and pepper, to taste

In small skillet, sauté onions in 3 tablespoons margarine until transparent. In large bowl, combine eggplant, eggs, milk, cheese, and 1 cup cracker crumbs. Pour mixture into greased 2-quart casserole dish. Sprinkle with remaining ½ cup cracker crumbs and dot with remaining 3 tablespoons melted butter. Bake at 350°F for 1 hour. Serves 5.

Nutritional analysis per serving: 390 cal, 0.6 g fiber, 28.2 g fat, 196.8 mg chol, 579.4 mg sodium

Eggplant Casserole +

8 to 10 pounds fresh eggplant
Salted water to cover (1 teaspoon salt per quart of water)
2 cups sour cream
1 quart chicken or meat stock
1 cup margarine, melted
1 tablespoon paprika
1 tablespoon black pepper
1 quart bread crumbs

Peel and cut eggplant crosswise into ¼-inch thick slices. Drop into boiling water. Cook just until tender, about ten minutes. Lift out of water and place in layers in greased, shallow baking pans. Combine sour cream, chicken stock, melted margarine, and seasonings. Pour over eggplant and shake pan to distribute sauce. Sprinkle with bread crumbs and bake at 350°F for about 40 minutes, or until mixture is well blended and slightly brown. If mixture becomes too dry, add small amount of stock. Grate cheese, if desired, and sprinkle over bread crumbs. Return to oven for a few minutes to melt and/or brown. Variation: For 1-dish meal, add 4 pounds of ground, seasoned, and cooked meat to sauce before pouring over eggplant. Serves 50.

Nutritional analysis per serving: 95 cal, 2 g fiber, 7 g fat, 8 mg chol, 118 mg sodium

Eggplant Casserole

2 pounds eggplant, peeled and cubed
1 onion, chopped
1 green bell pepper, chopped
1 red bell pepper, chopped
1 tablespoon vegetable oil
1 egg, beaten
1 cup seasoned dry bread crumbs
salt and pepper, to taste
1 cup (4 ounces) shredded Cheddar cheese
1–2 tablespoons Picante sauce, to taste

Cook eggplant in small amount of water until tender. Drain liquid. Mash eggplant. In skillet, sauté onion and peppers in oil until tender. Remove from heat. In bowl, combine eggplant, egg, bread crumbs, and seasonings. Mix well. Add onion mixture. Spoon half of eggplant mixture into lightly greased 2-quart casserole dish. Sprinkle with half of cheese. Spoon remaining eggplant over cheese and sprinkle with remaining cheese. Top evenly with Picante sauce. Bake at 350°F for 30 minutes. Serves 8.

Nutritional analysis per serving: 150.4 cal, 0.8 g fiber, 7.8 mg chol, 373.7 mg sodium

Eggplant Company Casserole

1 pound eggplant (1 eggplant), peeled and cubed
1 egg, slightly beaten

⅓ cup milk

½ cup onion, chopped

1 10.75-ounce can condensed cream of
  mushroom soup

1¼ cup herb seasoned stuffing mix,
  divided

1 cup (4 ounces) grated cheese

2 tablespoons margarine, melted

Cook eggplant in boiling, salted water until tender, about 7 minutes. Drain. In large
bowl, combine egg, milk, onion, soup, and ¾
cup of stuffing mix. Mix until well blended.
Add eggplant. Stir until just combined. Spoon
mixture into lightly greased 2-quart casserole
dish. Crush remaining ½ cup stuffing mix.
Sprinkle crushed stuffing mix and cheese over
top of casserole. Dot with margarine. Bake at
375°F for 30 minutes. Serves 8.

Nutritional analysis per serving: 185 cal,
0.3 g fiber, 11.7 g fat, 51.6 mg chol, 594 mg
sodium

Eggplant Olé

1 pound eggplant

2 tablespoons water

2 cups seeded and chopped tomatoes

1 4-ounce can chopped green chili
  pepper, drained

½ teaspoon oregano

¼ teaspoon ground cumin

salt and pepper, to taste

½ cup (2 ounces) shredded Monterey
  Jack cheese

cilantro or parsley to garnish, optional

Rinse eggplant and peel, if desired. Cut
eggplant into ½-inch thick round slices. Place
eggplant in 9 × 13-inch microwave-safe baking dish. Overlap slices as needed, and add
water. Cover with plastic wrap or paper towels.
Cook on 100% power (high) for 5–7 minutes,
or until eggplant is tender. Turn dish once while
cooking. Drain liquid when done. In small mixing bowl, combine tomatoes, chili peppers,
oregano, cumin, salt, and pepper. Mix well.
Top eggplant with tomato mixture. Place dish
in microwave. Cook on high power for 1–2

minutes, or until completely heated. Sprinkle
cheese over top. Cover and allow mixture to sit
for 2–3 minutes, or until cheese melts. Sprinkle
with cilantro or parsley. Serves 6.

Nutritional analysis per serving: 88.4 cal,
0.74 g fiber, 5.8 g fat, 16.6 mg chol, 283 mg
sodium

Eggplant Parmesan

½ cup cornmeal

¼ cup Parmesan cheese

1 1-pound eggplant, peeled and sliced in
  ½-inch disks

½ cup butter or margarine

1 8-ounce can pizza sauce

1 cup (8 ounces) mozzarella cheese,
  grated

2 tablespoons dry parsley

Preheat oven to 400°F. In small dish, combine cornmeal and Parmesan cheese. Dip eggplant slice in melted butter and coat with
cornmeal and Parmesan mixture. Place coated
eggplant slice on greased jelly roll pan. Continue until each piece is coated and placed in
pan; do not layer slices. Spread pizza sauce
evenly on top of eggplant. Combine mozzarella and parsley and sprinkle over sauce. Bake
for 15 minutes. Serves 4.

Nutritional analysis per serving: 546 cal,
0.4 g fiber, 39 g fat, 43.4 mg chol, 1342 mg
sodium

Fancy Potatoes

1 cup onions, diced

1 10.5-ounce can cream of chicken soup,
  diluted

1 16-ounce container sour cream

1 stick (½ cup) margarine, melted

8 ounces sharp Cheddar cheese, grated

salt and pepper, to taste

2 pounds frozen hash browns, thawed

1 cup corn flakes, optional

Preheat oven to 375°F. In bowl, combine
onions, soup, sour cream, margarine, cheese,
and seasonings. Mix well. Put one layer of
hash browns in 9 × 13-inch baking pan.

Spread mixture on top of hash browns. Sprinkle corn flakes over top of casserole. Bake for 1 hour. Serves 8.

Nutritional analysis per serving: 680 cal, 0.5 g fiber 43.5 g fat, 43.3 mg chol, 881 mg sodium

Festive Spinach Casserole

2 pounds fresh spinach
1 tablespoon milk
8 ounces cream cheese
¼ teaspoon dry Italian seasoning
⅓ cup light spread (40% less fat and calories)
1 cup Italian-flavored bread crumbs
6 cherry tomatoes

Preheat oven to 350°F. Wash fresh spinach thoroughly and cook 5 to 8 minutes (in water clinging to spinach). Drain and chop. Mix milk with cream cheese until smooth. Combine spinach, cream cheese, and dry Italian seasoning mix. Pour into 1½ quart casserole dish. Melt spread, toss with Italian-flavored bread crumbs, and sprinkle over casserole. Bake 20–30 minutes until bubbly and hot (lightly browned). Cut cherry tomatoes in half, place cut-side down around casserole dish, and place back in turned-off oven to heat. Serves 6.

Nutritional analysis per serving: 316 cal, 14 g fiber, 25 g fat, 55 mg chol, 568 mg sodium

Five-Minute Cabbage ★

2 tablespoons margarine
1 cup chopped celery
1 cup chopped onion
1 cup shredded cabbage
1 green bell pepper, chopped
salt and pepper, to taste

Melt margarine in saucepan over medium heat. Stir in vegetables. Cover tightly and cook for 5 minutes. Season with salt and pepper and serve immediately. Serves 6.

Nutritional analysis per serving: 49 cal, 0.52 g fiber, 3.9 g fat, 0 mg chol, 420 mg sodium

French-Cooked Green Peas ★

lettuce leaves, washed
2 10-ounce packages frozen green peas, thawed
1 teaspoon salt
1 teaspoon sugar
¼ cup sauterne

Line small, shallow casserole with lettuce leaves. Pour peas over lettuce. Sprinkle peas with salt and sugar. Pour sauterne over peas. Cover with lettuce. Cover casserole and bake at 350°F for 45 minutes. Serves 5.

Nutritional analysis per serving: 59 cal, 0 g fiber, 0.44 g fat, 0 mg chol, 433 mg sodium

Fresh Corn Chowder √ ★

1 cup chopped onion
6 cups fresh corn kernels
3 cups chicken stock
½ cup bell pepper, chopped
½ teaspoon rosemary
½ teaspoon black pepper
1 teaspoon basil, chopped
½ teaspoon thyme
cayenne pepper to taste

Preheat large heavy pan over medium heat. Spray with vegetable oil. Sauté onion until clear. Add half of corn and sauté 4 to 5 minutes until it softens. Add 2 cups of chicken stock and cook about 20 minutes. Transfer mixture to blender and puree until smooth. Return puree to pan on medium heat. Add bell pepper and spices, remaining chicken stock, and corn. Cook, while stirring, about 10 minutes more until chowder is thick and creamy. Garnish with fresh basil if desired. Serves 6.

Nutritional analysis per serving: 732 cal, 19 g fiber, 11 g fat, 54 mg chol, 105 mg sodium

Fried Cucumbers

1 teaspoon salt
1 teaspoon pepper
½ cup all-purpose flour
2 cucumbers, pared and sliced
½ cup chopped onion
½ cup cooking oil

Salt, pepper, and flour cucumber slices. Fry with chopped onion in cooking oil until brown. Serves 4.

Nutritional analysis per serving: 322 cal, 1.5 g fiber, 28 g fat, 0 mg chol, 538 mg sodium

Glazed Carrots ★

1 pound carrots, peeled and sliced into
  ¼-inch thick rounds
salt and pepper, to taste
1 tablespoon butter
¼ cup orange marmalade

In saucepan, add carrots and just cover with water. Add salt and pepper. Cook until carrots are almost tender. Drain liquid. Melt butter with marmalade. Stir until well blended. Add butter and marmalade to carrots. Cook for about 3 minutes over low heat to glaze, stirring to coat evenly. Serves 5.

Nutritional analysis per serving: 162 cal, 0.7 g fiber, 9.3 g fat, 24.8 mg chol, 112 mg sodium

Grated Sweet Potato Salad √ ★

1 large can pineapple chunks
½ cup sugar
3 large raw sweet potatoes, peeled and
  grated

Bring pineapple chunks (with liquid) and sugar to boil. Pour over raw sweet potatoes and toss well. Bake in 350°F oven for 25 minutes. Serve hot as vegetable or cold as salad. Serves 4.

Nutritional analysis per serving: 205 cal, 3 g fiber, 0 g fat, 0 mg chol, 10 mg sodium

Green Beans Almandine ★

1 pound fresh green beans
1 tablespoon slivered almonds
1 tablespoon butter or margarine
1 teaspoon lemon juice

Slice green beans French-style (length-wise). Parboil or steam beans in small amount of water until tender. Drain. Sauté almonds in butter over low heat, stirring occasionally until golden brown. Remove almonds from heat. Add lemon juice. Pour lemon juice over beans and top with almonds. Serves 4.

Nutritional analysis per serving: 110 cal, 1.2 g fiber, 9.5 g fat, 0 mg chol, 71 mg sodium

Green Chili Squash Casserole ★

2 pounds zucchini squash
1 medium onion, chopped
2 strips bacon
2 ounces green chili peppers, chopped
1 cup cracker crumbs
½ cup (2 ounces) grated Cheddar cheese

Cook squash in boiling water until tender. Drain and mash. In skillet, sauté onion and bacon. Drain. In lightly greased 2-quart baking dish, combine squash, onion, bacon, and green chili peppers. Sprinkle cracker crumbs and cheese over top of mixture. Bake at 400°F for 30 minutes. Serves 8.

Nutritional analysis per serving: 148.8 cal, 0.1 g fiber, 7 g fat, 16.8 mg chol, 278.6 mg sodium

Grits Souffle √

1 cup raw grits
3 eggs, separated
1 stick butter
Worcestershire sauce to taste
1 cup sharp Cheddar cheese
1 teaspoon salt
garlic to taste

Cook grits as directed on package. To hot, cooked grits, add butter, cheese, beaten egg yolks, and all seasonings. Mix until all cheese is melted. Fold in stiffly beaten egg whites and pour into greased casserole pan (about ⅔ full). Bake 30 minutes at 300°F. Serve while hot. May store in refrigerator to heat and serve later. Serves 6.

Nutritional analysis per serving: 350 cal, 3 g fiber, 25 g fat, 146 mg chol, 644 mg sodium

Lima Bean Casserole

2 cups lima beans, cooked
1 cup Cheddar cheese, grated
½ cup pimentos, chopped
1 small onion, chopped fine
1½ cups thick white sauce
1 tablespoon margarine
1 cup bread crumbs

Preheat oven to 350°F. In mixing bowl, combine beans, cheese, pimentos, onion, and white sauce. Put mixture in 9 × 13-inch casserole dish. Sprinkle bread crumbs over top of mixture. Dot with margarine. Bake for 30 minutes, or until top is brown and bubbling on sides. Serves 6.

Nutritional analysis per serving: 386 cal, 2.2 g fiber. 19.6 g fat, 53.3 mg chol, 769.6 mg sodium

Lima Beans Creole +

14 cups fresh lima beans
24 slices bacon
1 cup onion, finely chopped
8 tablespoons green pepper, chopped
4 16-ounce cans whole tomatoes, undrained
2 teaspoons salt
½ teaspoon pepper

Cook beans in boiling, salted water in Dutch oven until tender (20 to 30 minutes); drain. Return beans to Dutch oven and set aside. Cook bacon until crisp. Remove from skillet, reserving 8 tablespoons drippings; crumble bacon and set aside. Sauté onion and green pepper in reserved drippings until tender. Stir onion mixture, bacon, and remaining ingredients into beans, cover, and simmer 15 minutes. Serves 24.

Nutritional analysis per serving: 177 cal, 8 g fiber, 4 g fat, 5 mg chol, 419 mg sodium

Marinated Onions

½ cup sugar
½ cup water
1 cup white vinegar
1 teaspoon salt

½ teaspoon dry dill weed or 2 teaspoons fresh chopped dill
6 cups large onions, sliced and cut into bite-size pieces

Heat sugar, water, vinegar, salt, and dill until sugar is dissolved. Pack onions into 3 pint jars. Pour warm vinegar mixture over onions. Let stand at room temperature overnight. Will keep indefinitely in refrigerator. Serves 24.

This is not a preserved product. It must be kept refrigerated.

Nutritional analysis per serving: 17.3 cal, 0 g fiber, 0 g fat, 0 mg chol, 178 mg sodium

Marinated Vegetables

½ small head cauliflower
2 carrots
1 yellow squash
1 zucchini
1 red pepper
3 mushrooms
½ cup salad oil
½ cup olive oil
½ cup white wine vinegar
1 tablespoon sugar
1 tablespoon fresh dill or 1 teaspoon dill weed
½ teaspoon salt, optional
¾ teaspoon grated lemon peel
½ teaspoon black pepper
½ cup water
1 bay leaf

Keeping all vegetables separate, cut cauliflower into 1-inch by 2-inch pieces; thinly slice carrots; cut squash lengthwise in half, then crosswise into ½-inch slices; cut zucchini into bite-size chunks; cut red pepper lengthwise into ½-inch slices; slice mushrooms ¼-inch thick. In large bowl, mix oils, vinegar, sugar, dill, salt, lemon peel, pepper, and water until well blended. In tall, 2-quart sealable container, place zucchini; top with cauliflower, red pepper, squash, carrots, and mushrooms. Pour marinade over vegetables. Place bay leaf on top. Cover and refrigerate to blend flavors.

Serve as cold vegetable dish or spoon vegetables with some marinade over mixed greens for a refreshing new salad. Serves 8.

Nutritional analysis per serving: 243 cal, 4 g fiber, 22 g fat, 0 mg chol, 162 mg sodium

Mexican Rice

1½ cups uncooked brown rice
3 tablespoons oil
1 large onion, chopped
2 pounds ground beef
1 15-ounce can tomato sauce
1 quart tomato juice
1 6-ounce can sliced ripe olives, drained
salt and pepper
1 tablespoon ground oregano, optional
1 envelope spaghetti seasoning

In skillet, fry rice in oil until brown and toasted. Remove rice from pan. Brown onions and meat. Drain fat. Transfer rice and meat to lightly greased 9 × 12-inch baking pan. Add tomato sauce, juice, olives, and seasonings. Stir until well mixed. Bake, covered, at 400°F for 1½ hours, or until rice is cooked. Serves 8.

Nutritional analysis per serving: 382.4 cal, 0.1 g fiber, 25.5 g fat, 69 mg chol, 1466 mg sodium

Microwave Okra ★

2 tablespoons olive oil
1 pound okra, sliced ½-inch thick
1 medium onion
2 jalapeño peppers
1 teaspoon curry powder
salt and pepper, to taste

Heat oil in dish at 100% power for 3 minutes. Remove from microwave oven and add okra and onion. Sprinkle peppers and curry powder over top, stirring rapidly to coat the vegetables with oil. Cook uncovered 12 minutes or until okra is brown and glazed. Stir several times during cooking. Serves 3.

Nutritional analysis per serving: 84 cal, 1 g fiber, 6 g fat, 0 mg chol, 194 mg sodium

Mushroom Rice ★

3 cups cooked rice
½ cup canned sliced mushrooms, drained
1 cup cooked green peas
2 tablespoons butter
¼ teaspoon minced onion
2 tablespoons sliced pimento
salt and pepper, to taste

In saucepan, combine rice, mushrooms, peas, butter, onion, and pimento. Cook over low heat until vegetables are thoroughly heated. Stir occasionally. Cook for 3 to 4 minutes. Serves 8.

Nutritional analysis per serving: 124 cal, 0.8 g fiber, 2.5 g fat, 6.3 mg chol, 66 mg sodium

Orange Sweet Potatoes +

1 tablespoon cornstarch
½ cup sugar
¼ teaspoon salt
¾ cup brown sugar
¼ cup butter
1 cup orange juice
6 baked sweet potatoes

Blend cornstarch, sugar, salt, and brown sugar thoroughly. Combine butter and orange juice and heat. Stir starch mixture into hot juice. Cook and stir about 5 minutes, or until mixture thickens. Peel and slice baked potatoes in ¾-inch slices. Pour syrup over potatoes. Bake 40 minutes in 350°F oven. Garnish with orange slices if desired. Serves 12.

Nutritional analysis per serving: 175 cal, 2 g fiber, 4 g fat, 10 mg chol, 93 mg sodium

Oven-Fried Okra ★

1¼ cups cornmeal
pepper to taste
½ teaspoon salt
4 cups fresh okra, cut in 1-inch slices
vegetable cooking spray

Combine first three ingredients. Dredge okra in cornmeal mixture (okra must be moist for cornmeal mixture to coat well). Lightly coat jelly roll pan with cooking spray. Spread okra in single layer and bake at 350°F for 30 to 40 minutes. Serves 6.

Nutritional analysis per serving: 141 cal, 3 g fiber, 1 g fat, 0 mg chol, 184 mg sodium

Oven-Roasted Potatoes ★

1 envelope onion-mushroom soup mix
2 tablespoons cooking oil
1 teaspoon oregano
salt and pepper, to taste
6 medium potatoes, washed and sliced
   (skin on)

Preheat oven to 400°F. Combine soup mix, oil, and spices. Mix well. Place potatoes in large baking pan. Pour soup mixture over potatoes. Toss to thoroughly combine. Bake for 1 hour, or until potatoes are golden brown and tender. Serves 6.

Nutritional analysis per serving: 457.5 cal, 0 g fiber, 18.5 g fat, 0 mg chol, 127.4 mg sodium

Parmesan Potatoes ★

¼ cup sifted flour
¼ cup grated Parmesan cheese
½ teaspoon salt
⅛ teaspoon pepper
6 large potatoes (about 3 pounds),
   peeled and quartered
¼ cup butter or margarine

Combine flour, cheese, salt, and pepper. Coat potatoes well with cheese mixture. Melt butter in 9 × 12-inch baking dish. Place potatoes in layer in dish. Bake at 375°F for about 1 hour, turning once during baking. Serves 12.

Nutritional analysis per serving: 80 cal, 0 g fiber, 4.4 g fat, 1.3 mg chol, 167 mg sodium

Pineapple-Carrot Sauce with Brown Rice ★

1 20-ounce can unsweetened pineapple
   tidbits
2 large carrots, sliced into rounds
1 large onion, sliced
1 green bell pepper, sliced into strips
1 tablespoon cornstarch
3 cups hot, cooked brown rice
2 tablespoons almonds, sliced and
   toasted

Drain pineapple and reserve liquid. Simmer carrots, onion, and bell pepper in pineapple juice until tender. To thicken sauce, mix cornstarch with 1 tablespoon water. Add to liquid in pot and cook, stirring constantly, until thickened. Add pineapple tidbits and warm through. Serve over cooked brown rice and top with almonds. Serves 6.

Nutritional analysis per serving: 108 cal, 1.4 g fiber, 2.7 g fat, 0 chol, 10.6 mg sodium

Potato Casserole

4 large potatoes, peeled
½ pound American cheese
2 cups milk
1 stick (½ cup) margarine
1 teaspoon salt
1 cup sour cream
6 slices bacon, fried and crumbled

Preheat oven to 350°F. Boil potatoes in unsalted water until done. Cool and grate. Place potatoes in 9 × 13-inch baking pan. In saucepan, melt cheese, milk, margarine, and salt. Cook over low heat, stirring constantly. Pour cheese mixture over potatoes. Mix until combined. Bake for 30 minutes, or until golden brown. Remove from oven and top with sour cream and bacon bits. Return to oven for additional 10 minutes. Serves 8.

Nutritional analysis per serving: 343.2 cal, 0 g fiber, 26.6 g fat, 40 mg chol, 612.3 mg sodium

Potato Morsel Casserole

2 tablespoons margarine
3 tablespoons all-purpose flour
2½ cups milk
1½ cups (6 ounces) grated Cheddar
   cheese
1 pound potato morsels (tater tots),
   thawed
1 tablespoon minced onion

2 tablespoons parsley
salt and pepper, to taste
⅛ teaspoon paprika, optional

Preheat oven to 450°F. In saucepan, melt margarine. Add flour and mix until smooth. Gradually add milk, stirring constantly. Cook over medium heat for 3 minutes, stirring frequently. Stir in 1 cup of cheese until melted. Add morsels, onion, parsley, and seasonings. Cook additional 3 minutes, stirring constantly. Pour mixture into lightly greased 9 × 13-inch baking pan. Sprinkle with remaining ½ cup cheese and paprika. Bake for 5–10 minutes, or until browned. Serves 8.

Nutritional analysis per serving: 333 cal, 0.01 g fiber, 22.5 g fat, 32.6 mg chol, 551 mg sodium

Potatoes Gourmet +

18 medium potatoes
⅓ cup butter or margarine, melted
6 cups Cheddar cheese, shredded
3 8-ounce cartons commercial sour
    cream
9 green onions, chopped
1 tablespoon salt
¾ teaspoon pepper
6 tablespoons butter or margarine

Cover potatoes with salted water and bring to boil; reduce heat and cook about 30 minutes or until tender. Cool slightly. Peel and coarsely shred potatoes, set aside. Combine ⅓ cup melted butter and cheese in a heavy saucepan; cook over low heat, stirring constantly, until cheese is partially melted. Combine potatoes, cheese mixture, sour cream, onion, salt and pepper; stir well. Spoon potato mixture into large, greased chafing pan; dot with 6 tablespoons butter. Cover and bake at 300°F for 25 minutes. Serves 24.

Nutritional analysis per serving: 319 cal, 2 g fiber, 21 g fat, 42 mg chol, 532 mg sodium

Red Beans and Rice √ ★

1 pound red beans
4 cups water

1 tablespoon bacon drippings
1 ham hock or 6 ounces boiled ham
2 large onions, chopped
2 cloves garlic, minced
½ teaspoon black pepper
1 teaspoon salt
¼ teaspoon red pepper

Wash beans. Cover in water and soak overnight. Drain. Heat drippings in 4-quart saucepan over medium heat. Add ham and sauté 10 minutes. Remove ham, stir in onions and garlic, and sauté 5 minutes. Add beans, seasonings, water, and ham. Bring to boil. Place cover on saucepan. Cook over low heat about 6 hours. Stir and mash frequently during last 2 hours of cooking. Serve with cooked, hot rice. May cook in pressure cooker at 15 pounds pressure for 1½ to 2 hours. When pressure goes down, remove cover and stir before serving. Serves 8.

Nutritional analysis per serving: 149 cal, 4 g fiber, 4 g fat, 14 mg chol, 566 mg sodium

Rice Pilaf ★

1 cup rice
2½ cups water
2 chicken or beef bouillon cubes
1 tablespoon margarine
3 teaspoons chopped onion
1½ cups frozen peas
3 teaspoons finely chopped celery

In large saucepan, combine rice, water, bouillon cubes, margarine, and onion. Cook for 5 minutes over high heat, or until water begins to boil. Add peas and celery. Boil for 2 minutes. Remove from heat and cover. Allow rice to stand for 10 minutes. Do not stir during cooking or standing time. Serves 5.

Nutritional analysis per serving: 97 cal, 2 g fiber, 2.6 g fat, 0 mg chol, 389 mg sodium

Savory Vegetable Platter ★

3 cups beef broth
½ teaspoon tarragon
1 head cauliflower, trimmed

5 carrots, peeled and sliced into 2-inch pieces
½ pound fresh whole green beans
5 stalks celery, sliced into 2-inch pieces
2 tablespoons butter
2 tablespoons sesame seed
2 tablespoons lemon juice

In saucepan, heat broth and tarragon to boil. Add cauliflower. Cover and simmer for 10 minutes. Add remaining vegetables. Cover and simmer for 20 minutes. In separate small saucepan or microwave oven, combine butter, seeds, and juice. Put cauliflower in center of platter and arrange carrots, green beans, and celery around it. Drizzle sesame butter sauce over vegetables. Serves 10.

Nutritional analysis per serving: 64.5 cal, 1.34 g fiber, 3.5 g fat, 6.2 mg chol, 241 mg sodium

Scalloped Asparagus

2 packages frozen asparagus
1 cup (4 ounces) grated Cheddar cheese
2 cups medium white sauce (below)
4 hard-cooked eggs, chopped
1 tablespoon bread crumbs
1 teaspoon butter

Cook asparagus according to package directions until tender. Drain off liquid. Place layer of asparagus in 2-quart casserole dish. Alternate layers of asparagus, cheese, white sauce, and eggs. Top with bread crumbs and dot with butter. Bake at 350°F until bubbly, about 20 minutes.

White Sauce:

2 tablespoons butter
2 tablespoons finely chopped onion
2 tablespoons finely chopped green bell pepper
2 tablespoons flour
2 cups milk

Sauté onion and bell pepper in butter. Mix in flour until well blended. Gradually add milk while stirring. Bring to boil over medium heat, stirring constantly. Reduce heat and cook for an additional 5 minutes. Serves 8.

Nutritional analysis per serving: 231 cal, 0.04 g fiber, 14.6 g fat, 174.6 mg chol, 243 mg sodium

Skillet Tomato-Okra-Onion Stir-Fry ★

1 cup okra, cut into pieces
3–4 fresh tomatoes, chopped
½ cup chopped onion
½ cup chopped green pepper
2 tablespoons cooking oil
salt and pepper, to taste
1 teaspoon sugar

In large pan, put ¼ cup water and cook okra for 5 minutes over medium heat. Add tomatoes. Cook until tender. Add onions and green pepper. Continue to cook over low heat. Add oil, salt, pepper, and sugar. Stir ingredients until well combined. Simmer for about 5 minutes, or until thoroughly heated. Serve over rice, if desired. Serves 8.

Nutritional analysis per serving: 53.4 cal, 0.64 g fiber, 3.6 g fat, 0 mg chol, 273 mg sodium

Southern Fried Cabbage ★

2 tablespoons cooking oil
4 cups chopped or shredded cabbage
1 small onion, chopped
salt and pepper, to taste
⅛ teaspoon ground nutmeg
1 teaspoon sugar
1–2 tablespoons white vinegar, to taste

Heat oil over medium heat in large skillet. Add cabbage, onion, and seasonings. Stir until combined. Simmer, covered, for 10 minutes. Combine sugar and vinegar together; stir until sugar is dissolved. Pour vinegar over cabbage and simmer an additional 5 minutes. Stir just before serving to mix. Serves 8.

Nutritional analysis per serving: 44.2 cal, 0.5 g fiber, 3.5 g fat, 0 mg chol, 140 mg sodium

Spanish Rice ★

6 slices bacon
1 small onion, diced
1 cup long grain white rice, uncooked

1½ cups cooked or canned tomatoes,
   with juice
1½ cups water
salt and pepper, to taste

In large frying pan, fry bacon until crisp. Remove bacon from pan, crumble, and save for garnish. Pour off bacon fat. Add onion and rice to skillet. Cook over medium heat, stirring constantly until onions are soft. Add tomatoes and water. Cover and simmer over low heat for 30 minutes, or until liquid is absorbed. Season with salt and pepper, to taste. Serves 5.

Nutritional analysis per serving: 94 cal, 0.63 g fiber, 4 g fat, 6.4 mg chol, 239 mg sodium

Speedy Veggies ★

4 large ears yellow corn, halved
1 large onion, cut into 8 wedges
2 green bell peppers, sliced into strips
1 tablespoon margarine
salt and pepper, to taste

Set steamer basket into large pan that has been filled with ½ inch of water. Place corn in basket. Add onion wedges and peppers around corn. Bring to boil over high heat. Reduce heat, cover pan, and simmer vegetables for 10 to 15 minutes, until desired tenderness. Transfer vegetables to large serving dish. Top with margarine and seasonings. Serves 4.

Nutritional analysis per serving: 119 cal, 2 g fiber, 4 g fat, 0 mg chol, 48.3 mg sodium

Spinach Casserole

2 10-ounce packages frozen chopped
   spinach, cooked and drained
½ cup mayonnaise
1 10.75-ounce can cream of mushroom
   soup
2 eggs, well beaten
1 tablespoon dry sherry, optional
½ cup (2 ounces) grated Cheddar
   cheese, divided

Combine spinach, mayonnaise, soup, eggs, sherry, and ¼ cup cheese in lightly greased

2-quart casserole dish. Mix well. Top with remaining ¼ cup cheese. Bake at 350°F for 30 minutes, or until lightly browned. Serves 10.

Nutritional analysis per serving: 247 cal, 0.5 g fiber, 23.6 g fat, 77.2 mg chol, 461.4 mg sodium

Squash and Cheese Casserole

4 cups sliced summer squash (about
   3 pounds raw)
5 tablespoons butter or margarine
1 cup grated cheese (Velveeta or
   Cheddar)
1 teaspoon baking powder
1 teaspoon salt
2 beaten eggs
½ cup flour
½ teaspoon pepper

Wash and slice squash. In small amount of water, cook until tender; drain. Add butter while squash is still hot. Combine other ingredients except for ⅓ cup cheese. Pour into greased, 1-quart casserole dish. Top with remaining cheese. Bake at 350°F for 20 minutes. Serves 8.

Nutritional analysis per serving: 196 cal, 2 g fiber, 14 g fat, 88 mg chol, 477 mg sodium

Squash Casserole

2 cups cooked squash
2 eggs
1 cup grated sharp cheese
2 cups cracker crumbs
¾ stick margarine
½ teaspoon salt
1 cup chopped onion
1 cup evaporated milk

Mash cooked squash. Add all other ingredients and mix thoroughly. Pour into greased 8-inch square baking dish and bake in preheated 350°F oven for 40 minutes. Serve with crunchy chilled salad and hot sourdough bread. Serves 6.

Nutritional analysis per serving: 451 cal, 2 g fiber, 20 g fat, 124 mg chol, 499 mg sodium

Squash Casserole ★

    3 cups cooked yellow squash
    1 large onion, diced
    1 green bell pepper, chopped
    1 8-ounce package cornbread stuffing
      mix
    2 tablespoons margarine, melted
    1 large carrot, grated
    1 10.75-ounce can condensed cream
      soup (chicken, mushroom, or celery)

Cook squash in small amount of water. Steam onion and bell pepper in microwave oven in 2 tablespoons of water for 1 minute, or until soft. Put stuffing mix in food processor or blender and crush into small pieces, adding margarine while blending. Put half of stuffing mix in bottom of lightly greased 9 × 13-inch baking pan. In large bowl, combine squash, carrot, soup, onion, and green peppers. Stir until well combined. Add squash mixture to baking pan. Cover with remaining stuffing. Bake at 350°F for 30 minutes. Serves 12.

Nutritional analysis per serving: 75 cal, 0.6 g fiber, 3.8 g fat, 2.2 mg chol, 303 mg sodium

Squash Stir-Fry ★

    2 large zucchini squash
    2 large yellow summer squash
    1 large onion, chopped
    2 tablespoons cooking oil
    3 drops sesame oil
    3 drops soy sauce

Slice squash into ¼-inch thick rounds. Sauté squash and onion in oil over medium-high heat, stirring constantly, until tender-crisp. Remove skillet from heat. Add sesame oil and soy sauce to taste, and mix lightly. Serves 8.

Nutritional analysis per serving: 52.4 cal, 0.44 g fiber, 4 g fat, 0 mg chol, 44.5 mg sodium

Stir-Fry Green Beans ★

    1 pound fresh green beans
    3 tablespoons olive oil
    3 cloves garlic, pressed

    ½ teaspoon sugar
    1 tablespoon fresh lemon juice
    2 tablespoons dry sherry
    ½ teaspoon black pepper

In large saucepan, parboil beans for 2½ minutes. In skillet, heat oil and sauté garlic. Add green beans. Sauté for 2 minutes. Add remaining ingredients and cook for 1½ minutes. Serves 4.

Nutritional analysis per serving: 122 cal, 1.2 g fiber, 10.2 g fat, 0 mg chol, 4.4 mg sodium

Summer Squash Casserole

    6 medium summer squash, cooked
    2 large onions, chopped
    ½ stick (¼ cup) margarine
    3 carrots, peeled and grated
    8 ounces sour cream
    1 10.5-ounce can cream of chicken soup
    ¾ cup sharp cheese
    ½ cup Ritz crackers or herb stuffing mix
    ⅛ teaspoon black pepper

Preheat oven to 350°F. In saucepan, boil squash and onion in small amount of water. Cook until tender. Drain liquid. Add margarine, carrots, sour cream, soup, and cheese. Mix well. Pour mixture into a 9 × 13-inch casserole dish. Sprinkle with crushed crackers or stuffing mix and pepper. Bake for 30 minutes. Serves 8.

Nutritional analysis per serving: 296 cal, 1.64 g fiber, 23.7 g fat, 27 mg chol, 584.3 mg sodium

Summer Squash Casserole

    4 summer squash, about 6 inches long,
      sliced into ¼-inch rounds
    2–3 tablespoons margarine or butter
    ¾ cup crushed cheese crackers
    3 tablespoons sour cream
    ¼ teaspoon basil
    ⅛ teaspoon thyme
    salt and pepper, to taste
    1 teaspoon Parmesan cheese
    ⅛ teaspoon paprika

Steam or parboil squash until tender-crisp. Drain and save liquid. Transfer squash to lightly greased 1-quart baking dish. Gently add margarine, crushed crackers, sour cream, herbs, and seasonings. If mixture seems dry, add some of reserved cooking liquid. Sprinkle with cheese and paprika. Bake at 350°F, uncovered, for 20 minutes, or until lightly browned. Serves 5.

Nutritional analysis per serving: 230.4 cal, 1.2 g fiber, 13 g fat, 13.5 mg chol, 392 mg sodium

Summer Squash in a Jacket ★

6 medium-size summer squash
1 teaspoon salt
2 tablespoons margarine
¾ cup crushed saltines
1 teaspoon sage
2 drops hot sauce, or to taste
1 medium onion, finely chopped
2 tablespoons finely chopped banana pepper
2 tablespoons mayonnaise
½ teaspoon seasoning salt
salt and pepper, to taste

In saucepan, boil whole squash in salted water until slightly tender. Remove from pan and cool. Slice squash in half lengthwise. Spoon out inside of squash with small spoon, and place in large mixing bowl. Reserve shells. Add remaining ingredients to mashed squash. Mix until well combined. Spoon mixture back into squash shells. Place shells on baking dish. Bake at 350°F for 20 minutes or until light brown. Serves 12.

Nutritional analysis per serving: 69.3 cal, 0.05 g fiber, 4.3 g fat, 1.4 mg chol, 274.3 mg sodium

Sweet Potato Bake

4 large sweet potatoes, peeled and baked
½ stick (¼ cup) margarine at room temperature
1 cup sugar
1 teaspoon vanilla extract

1 6.5-ounce can crushed pineapple, drained
1 large apple, peeled, cored, and diced
½ cup shredded coconut
½ cup chopped pecans
½ cup brown sugar
1 teaspoon cinnamon
pecan halves to garnish
1 tablespoon maple syrup to garnish

Beat potatoes with electric mixer while still warm. Add margarine, sugar, and vanilla while mixing. Stir in pineapple. Line bottom of lightly greased 9 × 13-inch baking dish. Spoon sweet potato mixture over apples. Combine coconut, pecans, brown sugar, and cinnamon. Sprinkle nut mixture over sweet potatoes. Garnish with pecan halves and drizzle with maple syrup. Bake at 350°F for 20 minutes. Serves 12.

Nutritional analysis per serving: 287 cal, 1.4 g fiber, 11.4 g fat, 0 mg chol, 198 mg sodium

Sweet Potato Crunch

3 cups boiled, mashed sweet potatoes
1 cup sugar
1½ sticks butter or margarine, at room temperature, divided
½ cup milk
1 teaspoon cinnamon
2 egg yolks, beaten
2 egg whites, beaten
1 cup brown sugar
2 cups oatmeal
1 cup chopped pecans

In large bowl, combine sweet potatoes, sugar, ½ stick (4 tablespoons) butter or margarine, milk, and cinnamon. Mix well. Thoroughly mix in egg yolks. Fold in egg whites. Pour into 9 × 12-inch baking dish. Combine 1 stick butter or margarine, brown sugar, oatmeal, and pecans. Sprinkle evenly over top of potato batter. Bake at 350°F for about 45 minutes, or until toothpick inserted near center comes out clean. This dish may be served hot or cold. Serves 6.

Nutritional analysis per serving: 302 cal, 0 g fiber, 10.2 g fat, 94 mg chol, 310.5 mg sodium

Sweet Potato Pone ★

2 eggs, beaten
1 cup milk
½ teaspoon nutmeg
2 cups grated raw sweet potato
1 cup sugar
1 teaspoon cinnamon
2 tablespoons melted margarine

Cream eggs, sugar, and milk. Add other ingredients and mix well. Place in 2-quart casserole dish and bake in preheated 350°F oven about 1 hour. Serves 8.

Nutritional analysis per serving: 216 cal, 0 g fiber, 4 g fat, 22 mg chol, 57 mg sodium

Sweet Potatoes and Apples ★

4 tablespoons margarine
¼ cup brown sugar
½ teaspoon salt
¼ teaspoon nutmeg
4 medium sweet potatoes, cooked and peeled
3 apples, peeled and cored
¼ cup hot water

Preheat oven to 350°F. Melt margarine; add sugar, salt, and nutmeg. Thinly slice potatoes and apples. In 2-quart casserole or 9-inch square baking pan, make layer of potatoes, then apples, then sugar mixture, using about ⅓ of each. Repeat, making two or more layers. Add hot water. Cover and bake for 1 hour. Serves 8.

Nutritional analysis per serving: 158 cal, 3 g fiber, 6 g fat, 16 mg chol, 200 mg sodium

Sweet Potatoes with Coconut +

16 pounds sweet potatoes
1¼ cups sugar
2 tablespoons cinnamon
½ pound butter or margarine
1¼ teaspoons salt
2 pounds grated coconut

Clean potatoes thoroughly. Place on sheet pans and bake at 375°F approximately 45 minutes, or until tender. Cut potatoes and scoop out pulp, discarding skin. Put through food mill and thoroughly blend in all remaining ingredients, except coconut. Place in clean pans and refrigerate until firm. With No. 8 ice cream scoop and portion scale, weigh out 50 4-ounce portions. Form into round, flat patties. Roll in coconut. Place on brown paper on sheet pan and refrigerate until ready to cook. Sauté lightly in butter or margarine, turning when brown. Remove to sheet pans and finish heating in 350°F oven for 10 to 15 minutes. Serves 50.

Nutritional analysis per serving: 359 cal, 1 g fiber, 13 g fat, 0 mg chol, 197 mg sodium

Swiss Corn Bake ★

16 ounces frozen whole kernel corn
2 eggs, beaten
1½ cups Swiss cheese, shredded
2 5-ounce cans evaporated milk
¼ cup onion, chopped
salt and pepper, to taste
¾ cup bread crumbs
2 tablespoons margarine, melted

Cook corn according to package directions; drain. In medium bowl, combine eggs, 1 cup of cheese, milk, onion, salt, and pepper. Stir in drained corn. Turn mixture into 8-inch, round casserole dish. Place dish on baking sheet. Bake in preheated 350°F oven for 20 minutes. Toss bread crumbs with remaining cheese and melted margarine. Sprinkle bread mixture over top of corn mixture and bake 5 to 10 minutes more or until golden and bubbly. Let stand 5 minutes before serving. Serves 6.

Nutritional analysis per serving: 301 cal, 0 g fiber, 15 g fat, 101 mg chol, 231 mg sodium

Three-Corn Casserole

1 16-ounce can whole kernel corn
1 16-ounce can cream-style corn
1 stick (½ cup) margarine, melted

2 eggs, beaten
1 cup sour cream
1 small box corn muffin mix

Combine all ingredients. Pour mixture into lightly greased 2-quart casserole dish. Bake at 350°F for 45 minutes. Serves 16.

Nutritional analysis per serving: 164.6 cal, 0 g fiber, 9.8 g fat, 40.6 mg chol, 361 mg sodium

Tomato Casserole ★

4 slices of white bread, toasted and cubed
2 tablespoons margarine or butter
½ teaspoon garlic salt
1 teaspoon basil leaves
1 28-ounce can whole tomatoes
½ cup (1½ ounces) Parmesan cheese

In skillet, brown toast in margarine. Mix toast with garlic, salt and basil and set aside. Empty tomatoes (with juice) into shallow, 2-quart baking dish. Top tomatoes with bread crumbs. Sprinkle cheese on top. Bake at 350°F for 30 minutes. Serves 10.

Nutritional analysis per serving: 156 cal, 0.6 g fiber, 10.7 g fat, 9 mg chol, 476.4 mg sodium

Tomato Pie

1 9-inch unbaked deep-dish pie shell
5 large tomatoes, peeled and sliced thick
½ teaspoon salt
½ teaspoon pepper
3 teaspoons dried basil
½ teaspoon dried oregano
½ teaspoon garlic powder
¾ cup reduced-calorie mayonnaise
1¼ cups sharp Cheddar cheese, grated
1 small can fried onion rings

Preheat oven to 375°F. Bake pie shell for 10 minutes. Remove from oven. Layer tomatoes in shell. Sprinkle each layer with salt, pepper, basil, oregano, and garlic powder. Combine mayonnaise and cheese. Spread mayonnaise mixture over tomatoes. Bake at 350°F for 20 to 25 minutes or until brown. Remove pie from oven and allow to stand for 5 minutes before serving. Put onion rings over top just before serving. Serves 8.

Nutritional analysis per serving: 403.3 cal, 0.6 g fiber, 29 g fat, 48.4 mg chol, 615.7 mg sodium

Veg-All Casserole

2 16-ounce cans Veg-all, mixed vegetables
¼ cup onion, chopped
¼ cup green bell pepper, chopped
1 5-ounce jar pimento
½ cup reduced-calorie mayonnaise
12–14 saltine crackers, crushed
6 tablespoons margarine, melted

Preheat oven to 375°F. Grease 2-quart casserole dish with margarine. In large mixing bowl, combine Veg-all, onion, green pepper, pimento, and mayonnaise. Stir until well mixed. Spoon mixture into prepared casserole dish. Sprinkle cracker crumbs on top and dot with margarine. Bake for 25 minutes. Serves 8.

Nutritional analysis per serving: 245 cal, 0.1 g fiber, 20.5 g fat, 8 mg chol, 512 mg sodium

Vegetable Casserole

1 16-ounce can Veg-all, drained
1 8.5-ounce can water chestnuts, sliced
1 medium onion, chopped
1 cup reduced-calorie mayonnaise
1 cup Cheddar cheese, grated
1 cup cracker crumbs
margarine

Preheat oven to 350°F. In 2-quart casserole dish, combine Veg-all, water chestnuts, onion, and mayonnaise. Mix well. Bake for 20 minutes, stirring once. Remove casserole from oven and sprinkle with cheese and cracker crumbs. Dot dish with a few pats of butter or margarine. Return casserole to oven. Bake, uncovered an additional 25 minutes, or until golden brown. Serves 8.

Nutritional analysis per serving: 180 cal, 0.1 g fiber, 10 g fat, 30.5 mg chol, 360 mg sodium

Vegetable Casserole

1 can white shoepeg corn, drained
1 can French-style green beans, drained
½ cup onion, chopped
½ cup celery, chopped
1 can cream of celery soup
½ cup sour cream
½ cup grated cheese
¼ teaspoon salt
dash pepper
Topping:
1 roll Ritz crackers crushed
½ cup butter, melted

Mix all ingredients, except topping, and place in greased, 2-quart casserole dish. Top with cracker crumbs and drizzle with melted butter. Bake 45 minutes in 300°F oven or 30 minutes in 350°F oven. Serves 10.

Nutritional analysis per serving: 221 cal, 1 g fiber, 17 g fat, 25 mg chol, 470 mg sodium

Vegetable Herb Cheesecake

1 tablespoon butter or margarine
½ cup fine, dry bread crumbs
3 cups zucchini, grated
1 tablespoon salt
3 tablespoons butter or margarine
1 cup onion, finely chopped
2 cloves garlic, crushed
1 cup (about ½ lb) carrots, grated
3 tablespoons flour
½ teaspoon basil
½ teaspoon oregano
¼ cup finely chopped parsley
1 tablespoon lemon juice, fresh or frozen
3 cups ricotta cheese
1 cup (4 oz) mozzarella cheese, grated
½ cup Parmesan cheese
4 large eggs
3 medium-sized tomatoes

Butter 10-inch springform pan. Lightly coat bottom and sides of pan with dry bread crumbs. Preheat oven to 375°F. Put grated zucchini in a colander over bowl. Sprinkle with salt. Allow to sit for 10 to 15 minutes. Squeeze moisture out of zucchini with clean towel or with strong paper towels. Sauté onions in butter or margarine. When onions are limp, add zucchini, garlic, carrots, flour, basil, and oregano. Stirring constantly, cook over medium heat for 10 minutes. Remove from heat. Stir in parsley and lemon juice. In large bowl, beat cheeses and eggs together until smooth. Add vegetable mixture and stir until thoroughly blended. Pour mixture into prepared springform pan. Bake at 375°F for 30 minutes. While cheesecake is baking, slice tomatoes into uniform ¼ inch slices. Cut slices in half. When cheesecake has baked for 30 minutes, remove from oven. Decorate cheesecake by placing tomato slices in circles around top. Reduce oven temperature to 350°F. Return cheesecake to oven. Bake for 30 minutes. Turn off oven. Open oven door and allow cheesecake to sit undisturbed for 15 minutes before cutting and serving. Serves 12.

Nutritional analysis per serving: 247 cal, 1 g fiber, 14 g fat, 111 mg chol, 513 mg sodium

Vegetable Sandwich

1 8-ounce cream cheese, softened at
    room temperature
¼ cup celery, grated
¾ cup carrots, grated
¼ cup cucumber, grated and drained
¼ cup bell pepper, grated
¼ cup onion, grated
mayonnaise as needed
mixed-grain bread

Combine ingredients; add enough mayonnaise to mix. Let chill overnight. When ready to serve, add more mayonnaise if needed. Spread on two slices mixed-grain bread. Serves 6.

Nutritional analysis per serving: 396 cal, 11 g fiber, 14 g fat, 42 mg chol, 143 mg sodium

Vidalia Onion Pie

2 pounds Vidalia onions, peeled and
 sliced thin
½ cup real butter
3 eggs, beaten
1 cup sour cream
½ teaspoon pepper
¼ teaspoon salt
dash of Tabasco sauce
1 9-inch pie shell, unbaked
½ cup grated Parmesan cheese

Sauté onions in butter. Combine eggs and
sour cream. Add onions and stir in seasonings.
Pour into pie shell and top with cheese. Bake
in preheated 450°F oven for 20 minutes, reduce heat to 325°F, and cook 20 minutes more
or until brown and bubbly. (May reduce calories and fat by using light sour cream, Egg
Beaters, and Heart Healthy cheese.) Serves 6
to 8.

Nutritional analysis per serving: 329 cal,
2 g fiber, 25 g fat, 96 mg chol, 379 mg sodium

Wadmalaw Sweet Onions ★

2 teaspoons olive oil
4 Wadmalaw sweet onions
½ teaspoon salt and pepper
garlic powder
parsley flakes

Lightly coat microwave-safe baking dish
with olive oil. Peel onions and place in dish.
Add small amount of olive oil to onions, then
salt and pepper. Sprinkle with garlic powder
and parsley flakes. Cover with plastic wrap
and vent one corner. Bake in microwave, on
high, about 10 minutes for four onions. Do
not overcook. Serves 4.

Nutritional analysis per serving: 233 cal,
2 g fiber, 2 g fat, 0 mg chol, 310 mg sodium

Yellow Fluff Rice ★

1¾ cups chicken broth
1 cup regular rice, uncooked
⅓ cup finely chopped celery
½ cup diced onion
½ cup small garden peas

½ cup chopped pimento
1 teaspoon salt
2 drops yellow food coloring
⅓ cup sliced fresh mushrooms
parsley to garnish

Combine all ingredients except parsley in
lightly greased, 1-quart baking dish. Bake at
350°F uncovered for 1 hour. Garnish with
parsley. Serves 6.

Nutritional analysis per serving: 123 cal,
0.6 g fiber, 8.2 g fat, 0 mg chol, 413 mg sodium

Zucchini Dressing

2 cups zucchini squash, cooked and
 drained
1 large onion, chopped
2 cups cornbread crumbs
1 10.75-ounce can condensed cream of
 chicken soup
½ stick (¼ cup) margarine
1 green bell pepper, chopped
2 eggs, beaten
1 teaspoon sage

Combine all ingredients in large bowl,
tossing to mix evenly. Transfer mixture to
lightly greased 9 × 13-inch baking dish. Bake
at 350°F for 30 minutes. Serves 12.

Nutritional analysis per serving: 111 cal,
0.12 g fiber, 3.3 g fat, 48.5 mg chol, 335 mg
sodium

Zucchini Pie

4 cups sliced zucchini
1 cup chopped onion
¼ cup margarine
2 tablespoons parsley
salt and pepper, to taste
⅛ teaspoon garlic
⅛ teaspoon basil
⅛ teaspoon oregano
2 eggs, beaten
2 cups (8 ounces) grated Muenster, Jack,
 or mozzarella cheese
1 can refrigerated crescent rolls
2 teaspoons spicy mustard

Sauté zucchini and onion in margarine until tender. Mix in parsley and all seasonings. Mix eggs and cheese together, stirring until well combined. Separate crescent rolls into 8 triangles. Place triangles in 8 × 12-inch casserole dish. Press dough over sides and bottom of dish to form crust. Spread mustard evenly over bottom. Pour vegetable mixture over mustard. Bake at 350°F for 20 minutes. Remove from oven and allow to sit for 10 minutes before cutting. Serves 8.

Nutritional analysis per serving: 390 cal, 0.2 g fiber, 23.8 g fat, 103 mg chol, 592.5 mg sodium

ENTRÉES

BEEF

Barbecue Meatballs ★

1 pound lean ground beef
1 cup bread crumbs
½ cup milk
Barbecue Sauce:
1½ tablespoons Worcestershire sauce
½ cup water
½ cup catsup
½ cup chopped onions
pepper to taste
½ cup chopped bell pepper
¼ cup brown sugar
1 teaspoon salt

Combine meat, bread crumbs, and milk in mixing bowl. Shape into 1-inch balls. Place meatballs in baking dish in single layer. In separate bowl, combine remaining ingredients to make barbecue sauce. Pour sauce over meatballs. Bake, uncovered, at 350°F for 1 hour. Serves 4.

Nutritional analysis per serving: 418 cal, 0.3 g fiber, 15 g fat, 73.3 mg chol, 880.4 mg sodium

Barbecued Hamburgers ★

3 tablespoons cooking oil
1 pound ground beef, shaped into
    4 patties
½ cup chopped onion
1 cup chopped celery
2 tablespoons vinegar
¾ cup catsup

½ teaspoon dry mustard
½ cup water

In 12-inch skillet, add oil. Brown patties in oil over medium heat. Drain excess fat from skillet. Add onion, celery, vinegar, catsup, mustard, and water. Stir well. Return hamburgers to skillet. Simmer over low heat for 30 minutes. Serve on buns. Serves 4.

Nutritional analysis per serving: 384 cal, 0.43 g fiber, 26 g fat, 65.5 mg chol, 607.3 mg sodium

Barbecued Round Steak ★

1½ pounds round steak
2 tablespoons cooking oil
1 large onion, diced
¾ cup vinegar
1 tablespoon sugar
1 teaspoon paprika
2 tablespoons Worcestershire sauce
½ cup catsup
1 teaspoon salt
1 teaspoon powdered mustard
½ teaspoon pepper

Slice steak into 1-inch wide strips. In 12-inch skillet, add oil and brown steak strips on all sides. Put meat into 2-quart casserole dish or 9 × 13-inch baking dish. Drain excess oil from skillet. Add onion, vinegar, sugar, paprika, Worcestershire sauce, catsup, salt, mustard, and pepper. Simmer for five minutes. Pour mixture over steak and cover. Bake at 350°F for 1 hour, uncover and bake an additional 30 minutes. Serves 6.

Nutritional analysis per serving: 228 cal, 0.11 g fiber, 11 g fat, 61 mg chol, 961 mg sodium

Beef-Brisket Barbecue ★

4 pounds fresh beef brisket
1½ cups barbecue sauce, divided
1 cup water, divided
½ teaspoon salt
½ teaspoon pepper

Put brisket in 9 × 13-inch baking dish, fat-side up. Cover brisket with 1 cup barbecue sauce and ½ cup water. Cover pan with foil. Roast at 350°F for 3 hours. Remove brisket from oven, cool completely, and refrigerate for 12 hours. Remove meat from refrigerator and skim off fat. Slice meat against grain. Return meat to pan. Add remaining ½ cup barbecue sauce, ½ cup water, salt, and pepper to meat. Reheat thoroughly in oven at 350°F for about 20 minutes. Spoon sauce over slices. Serves 8.

Nutritional analysis per serving: 311 cal, 0 g fiber, 13.8 g fat, 99 mg chol, 895 mg sodium

Beef-Pork Barbecue

1 18-ounce bottle barbecue sauce
½ cup catsup
2 tablespoons Worcestershire sauce
½ cup brown sugar
6 cups cooked pork, cubed
6 cups cooked beef, cubed

In large pot, combine barbecue sauce, catsup, Worcestershire sauce, and brown sugar. Mix well. Cook over medium heat, stirring constantly, for 10 minutes. Stir in meat. Cook, covered, on low heat for 60 minutes, or until meat is tender when pierced with a fork. Serves 16.

Nutritional analysis per serving: 471.5 cal, 0 g fiber, 25.2 g fat, 132 mg chol, 836 mg sodium

Beef Stroganoff +

2-pound round steak
1 stick butter
salt and pepper, to taste

4 medium onions, chopped
1 8-ounce can tomato paste
½ cup water
1 8-ounce can mushrooms
2 cups sour cream
cooked noodles

Cut beef in long, thin strips. Melt butter in skillet and brown meat. Season with salt and pepper. Add chopped onions, tomato paste, and water. Simmer for 1½ hours, or until meat is tender. About 30 minutes before serving, add mushrooms and sour cream. Heat slowly; high temperature will curdle cream. Serve on top of cooked noodles. Serves 10.

Nutritional analysis per serving: 509 cal, 1 g fiber, 43 g fat, 152 mg chol, 622 mg sodium

Beefy Baked Beans + ★

5 pounds ground beef
2½ cups onion, chopped
1 No. 10 can pork and beans
5–10 tablespoons vinegar
2½ teaspoons salt
1¼ teaspoons hot sauce
2¼ cups catsup
5 tablespoons Worcestershire sauce
1¼ teaspoons pepper

Cook ground beef and onion until meat is browned, stirring to crumble meat. Drain well. Combine beef mixture and remaining ingredients; stir well. Spoon bean mixture into five 1½-quart casserole dishes. Bake, uncovered, at 350°F for 30 minutes. Serves 25.

Nutritional analysis per serving: 445 cal, 8 g fiber, 26 g fat, 86 mg chol, 1174 mg sodium

Chinese Beef and Noodles ★

½ pound boneless top sirloin, thinly sliced
¼ cup oil
½ teaspoon minced garlic
4 medium carrots, sliced
4 stalks celery, sliced
1 small head cabbage
1 cup water

1 8-pounce package egg noodles
4 ounces fresh mushrooms, sliced
1 8-ounce package snow peas
½ cup soy sauce

In wok, stir-fry beef in hot oil. Remove beef; add garlic, carrots, celery, and cabbage to wok and stir-fry until carrots are crisp and tender. Add ½ cup water and reduce heat. Simmer, covered, for 15 minutes. Cook noodles in boiling water until tender. Drain. Add noodles, beef, mushrooms, and snow peas to vegetable mixture in wok. Stir in soy sauce and ½ cup water. Heat to serving temperature, stirring constantly. Serves 8.

Nutritional analysis per serving: 281 cal, 3 g fiber, 13 g fat, 19 mg chol, 613 mg sodium

Chuck

1 pound lean ground beef
2 small onions, chopped
1 green bell pepper, chopped
3 tablespoons vegetable oil
5 ounces egg noodles, cooked
1 cup milk

Preheat oven to 325°F. In skillet, brown ground beef, onions, and peppers in vegetable oil. In baking dish, combine noodles and ground beef. Add milk to mixture. Bake, covered, for 30 minutes. Serves 4.

Nutritional analysis per serving: 497 cal, 0.36 g fiber, 29 g fat, 112 mg chol, 94.6 mg sodium

Easy Rice and Beef Casserole

1 cup rice
1 16-ounce can roast beef, chopped
1 10.75-ounce can condensed beef
    consommé
¾ cup water
salt and pepper, to taste
1 tablespoon butter

Mix rice, roast beef, soup, water, and seasonings together in 2-quart casserole dish. Stir until well combined. Dot with butter. Bake covered at 350°F for 35 minutes. Serves 4.

Nutritional analysis per serving: 214.3 cal, 0 g fiber, 11.2 g fat, 67.4 mg chol, 1126.3 mg sodium

Ground Beef Stroganoff

1 pound lean ground beef
1 medium onion, chopped
¼ teaspoon paprika
¾ teaspoon salt
⅛ teaspoon pepper
1 10.75-ounce can condensed cream of
    mushroom soup
1 cup sour cream

In large skillet, cook ground beef and onion together over medium heat until beef is brown and onions are translucent. Drain excess fat. Add seasonings and soup. Cook over low heat, uncovered and stirring frequently, for 20 minutes. Add sour cream and heat through; do not boil. Serve with noodles or rice. Serves 4.

Nutritional analysis per serving: 428 cal, 0.16 g fiber, 32.5 g fat, 97 mg chol, 1120 mg sodium

Hamburger Casserole

1 pound lean ground beef
½ cup chopped onion
3 ounces cream cheese
1 10.75-ounce can condensed cream of
    mushroom soup
1 12- to 16-ounce can corn or peas,
    drained
salt and pepper, to taste
1 small can refrigerated biscuits (5
    biscuits)

In large skillet, cook ground beef and onion together over medium heat until beef is brown and onion is transparent. Drain excess fat. Add cream cheese and soup. Mix well. Stir in corn (or peas) and seasoning. Pour mixture into lightly greased, 2-quart casserole dish. Separate biscuits, cut each in half, and place half-circles around edge of casserole. Bake at 375°F for 20 to 25 minutes, or until biscuits are brown. Serves 5.

Nutritional analysis per serving: 594 cal, 0.9 g fiber, 36.7 g fat, 106.8 mg chol, 1312.4 mg sodium

Hamburger Casserole ★

1½ pounds lean ground beef
1 large onion, sliced thin
6 medium potatoes, sliced thin
salt and pepper, to taste

Shape beef into six patties. Layer hamburgers, onions, and potatoes in lightly greased 9 × 13-inch pan, ending with potatoes. Season with salt and pepper. Cover pan with foil. Bake at 350°F for 45–60 minutes, or until potatoes are done. Serves 8.

Nutritional analysis per serving: 311 cal, 0.08 g fiber, 15 g fat, 70 mg chol, 66.3 mg sodium

Hamburger-Bean Casserole ★

1 pound hamburger
1⅓ cup onions, chopped
1 teaspoons chili powder
1 teaspoon Worcestershire sauce
1 pint tomatoes
1 can kidney beans
Topping:
1 cup self-rising cornmeal
2 tablespoons shortening
1 cup milk

In an oven-proof skillet or casserole brown hamburger and onions. Add remainder of ingredients and simmer. Blend topping mixture and spread on top of meat mixture. Bake in 425°F preheated oven for 20 minutes or until brown. Serves 8.

Nutritional analysis per serving: 369 cal, 6 g fiber, 20 g fat, 48 mg chol, 435 mg sodium

Hamburger-Corn Casserole

1½ pounds ground beef
1 cup chopped onions
1 12-ounce can whole kernel corn, drained
1 10.75-ounce can condensed cream of mushroom soup
1 10.75-ounce can condensed cream of chicken soup
1 cup sour cream
½ cup chopped pimentos
¾ teaspoon salt, optional
½ teaspoon monosodium glutamate, optional
¼ teaspoon black pepper
3 cups cooked egg noodles (al dente)
bread crumbs

In 12-inch skillet, cook beef until brown. Drain fat. Add onions and cook until they are transparent and tender. Add corn, soups, sour cream, pimentos, salt, monosodium glutamate, and pepper. Mix well. Gently stir in cooked noodles. Pour mixture into 2-quart casserole dish. Sprinkle with bread crumbs. Bake at 350°F for 30 minutes. Serves 6.

Nutritional analysis per serving: 546 cal, 0.2 g fiber, 28 g fat, 116 mg chol, 1351 mg sodium

Layer Dinner ★

1 pound lean ground beef
2 potatoes, sliced
1 medium onion, sliced
2 carrots, peeled and sliced into rounds
½ cup rice
salt and pepper, to taste
2 cups canned whole tomatoes

Layer ground beef, potatoes, onion, carrots, and rice in 2-quart, lightly greased casserole dish. Season with salt and pepper, then pour tomatoes over top. Bake at 350°F, covered, for 1 hour. Serves 4.

Nutritional analysis per serving: 344 cal, 1.6 g fiber, 15.4 g fat, 70 mg chol, 338.2 mg sodium

Meal-in-One

1 pound lean ground beef or ground turkey
1 small onion, chopped
1 15-ounce can green peas
1 15-ounce can stewed tomatoes
1½ cups cubed potatoes

In skillet, brown meat. Drain fat. Add onions. Cook until transparent. Add peas, tomatoes, and potatoes. Cook over medium heat until potatoes are tender. Serve alone or over rice. Serves 4.

Nutritional analysis per serving: 379 cal, 4.5 g fiber, 16.5 g fat, 70 mg chol, 482 mg sodium

Meat Loaf ★

1½ pounds lean ground beef
1 egg
½ cup bread crumbs
¼ onion, chopped
¼ cup milk
¼ cup steak sauce
½ teaspoon salt
¼ teaspoon pepper

In mixing bowl, combine all ingredients. Mix well. Shape into 4 × 8-inch loaf pan. Bake for 1 hour at 350°F. Allow meat loaf to remain in pan for five minutes before removing. Remove meat loaf to a platter to slice. Serves 6.

Nutritional analysis per serving: 282 cal, 0.02 g fiber, 6.3 g fat, 117.5 mg chol, 866.3 mg sodium

Meat Pie

1 pound ground beef
1 medium onion, chopped
salt and pepper, to taste
½ cup condensed cream of mushroom soup
1 egg
1 slice of bread, toasted and crumbled
2 cups mashed potatoes
¼ cup (1 ounce) grated cheese

In large skillet, brown ground beef. Add onion, salt, and pepper and cook until tender. Remove from heat and drain. Add half of soup, egg, and bread crumbs. Mix well. Transfer mixture to 2-quart casserole dish. Cover meat mixture with mashed potatoes. Mix remaining soup with cheese and spread it over potatoes. Bake at 325°F for 25 minutes, or

until light brown and thoroughly heated. Serves 8.

Nutritional analysis per serving: 313.3 cal, 0.1 g fiber, 20.3 g fat, 81 mg chol, 631.4 mg sodium

Mexican Casserole ★

2 pounds ground beef
2 bell peppers, chopped
1 onion, chopped
1 16-ounce can tomato sauce
1 15-ounce can whole tomatoes
1 teaspoon sugar
1 cup cooked white rice
1 15-ounce can corn, drained
1 tablespoon chili powder
½ teaspoon seasoning salt
1 tablespoon garlic powder
½ cup (2 ounces) grated Cheddar cheese, divided

In skillet, brown beef. Add peppers and onions. Cook until tender. Drain liquid. Add tomato sauce, tomatoes, and sugar. Stir until combined, and cook over medium heat for 5 minutes. In 2-quart casserole dish, combine rice, corn, spices, and ¼ cup grated cheese. Add beef and tomato mixture to casserole dish. Mix well. Sprinkle remaining cheese on top. Bake at 350°F for 25 minutes, or until cheese is completely melted. Serves 8.

Nutritional analysis per serving: 390 cal, 1.24 g fiber, 20.4 g fat, 76.5 mg chol, 1089 mg sodium

Porcupine Meatballs ★

1 pound lean ground beef
¾ cup long grain rice, uncooked
garlic salt, onion salt, and pepper, to taste
2 10.75-ounce cans condensed tomato soup
2 cups water
½ small cabbage, cut into 8 wedges

In bowl, combine meat, rice, and spices. Form meat mixture into meatballs that are slightly smaller than a walnut. Do not press meatballs together too tightly because the rice will need to expand. Pour soup and water into large pot (or Crock-Pot). Mix thoroughly. Add meatballs. Bring mixture just to boil. Cover and simmer for an hour or longer. Add cabbage about 30 minutes before serving. Cook until cabbage is at tenderness desired. Serves 4.

Nutritional analysis per serving: 379 cal, 1.3 g fiber, 17.5 g fat, 70 mg chol, 1141 mg sodium

Quick Sloppy Joes ★

1 pound ground beef
1 medium onion, chopped
1 10-ounce can tomato soup
1 teaspoon sugar
1 teaspoon mustard
1 tablespoon catsup
4 hamburger buns

Brown ground beef with onion in skillet, stirring until crumbly; drain. Add soup, sugar, mustard, and catsup; mix well. Simmer for 5 to 10 minutes. Serve on buns. Serves 4.

Nutritional analysis per serving: 434.7 cal, 1.7 g fiber, 32.2 g fat, 84.7 mg chol, 745.3 mg sodium

Quick Sloppy Joes ★

1 pound ground beef
1 large onion, chopped
½ green pepper, chopped
2 tablespoons prepared mustard
¾ cup catsup
1 teaspoon salt
6 hamburger buns

In skillet, brown beef, onion, and pepper. Drain off fat. Add remaining ingredients. Mix well. Cook over medium heat for 30 minutes, stirring occasionally. Serve warm on hamburger buns. Serves 6.

Nutritional analysis per serving: 194.4 cal, 0.2 g fiber, 11.3 g fat, 46 mg chol, 388 mg sodium

Round Steak de Parmesan + ★

7 pounds boneless round steak, ¾-inch thick
5 eggs, beaten
1⅔ cups milk
2⅓ cups fine dry bread crumbs
2 tablespoons salt
¾ teaspoon pepper
5 tablespoons seasoned salt
1 cup butter
2⅓ cups water
1¼ teaspoons dried whole oregano
1¼ teaspoons Parmesan cheese, grated
1 No. 10 can small onions
1¼ teaspoons salt
1¼ teaspoons paprika

Trim excess fat from steak; pound to ½-inch thickness. Cut steak into serving-size pieces. Combine eggs and milk; beat well. Combine bread crumbs, 2 tablespoons salt, pepper, and seasoned salt. Dip steak in egg mixture, dredge in bread crumb mixture, and brown in butter. Place steak in large, lightly greased chafing pan. Add water and sprinkle with oregano and cheese. Add onions to steak; sprinkle with 1¼ teaspoons salt and paprika. Cover tightly and bake at 325°F for 1 hour and 15 minutes or until tender. Serves 30.

Nutritional analysis per serving: 294 cal, 1 g fiber, 14 g fat, 119 mg chol, 1058 mg sodium

Simple Ground Beef Casserole

1 pound lean ground beef
2 tablespoons vegetable oil
2 medium size onions, sliced
5 white potatoes, peeled and sliced
1 10.5-ounce can cream of mushroom soup
1 10.5-ounce soup can of water
1 5-ounce jar pimentos (optional)

Preheat oven to 325°F. In small skillet, brown ground beef in vegetable oil. Alternate layers of ground beef, onions, and potatoes in 2-quart casserole dish. Pour mushroom soup and water over layers. Add pimentos. Bake, covered for 45 minutes, or until potatoes are done. Serves 5.

Nutritional analysis per serving: 415.3 cal, 0.3 g fiber, 22 g fat, 57.2 mg chol, 557.4 mg sodium

Slumgullion √

1½ pounds lean ground beef
1½ cups bell pepper, chopped
1 cup catsup
2 teaspoons Italian seasoning
1 teaspoon chili powder
1 teaspoon marjoram
1 16-ounce can whole tomatoes
1½ cups onion, chopped
3 teaspoons oregano
1 teaspoon garlic powder
1 teaspoon paprika
salt and pepper, to taste
2 cups cooked white rice

In large pot, brown ground beef. Drain excess fat. Add remaining ingredients (except rice) to pot and cook over low heat for 45 minutes. Spread cooked rice evenly in 9 × 13-inch lightly greased baking pan. Cover with sauce. Allow mixture to sit for 15 minutes before serving. Serves 8.

Nutritional analysis per serving: 408 cal, 3 g fiber, 12 g fat, 52 mg chol, 579 mg sodium

Steak in a Bag

1 large slice London Broil (thin)
½ stick softened margarine
salt, pepper, garlic powder, to taste
1 cup Cheddar cheese, grated

Preheat oven to 350°F. Coat meat with butter and spices. Place meat inside brown grocery bag and pat on cheese (it will stick to margarine). Fold end of bag closed and staple. Place on cookie sheet and bake about 1 hour. Bag will smell like it is burning. Serves 4.

Nutritional analysis per serving: 367 cal, 0 g fiber, 26 g fat, 80 mg chol, 370 mg sodium

Super Burgers

1 tablespoon shortening
1 medium onion, chopped
½ green bell pepper, chopped
1 pound ground beef
salt and pepper, to taste
2 tablespoons catsup
1 can cream of mushroom soup

Heat shortening in skillet. Cook onion and pepper until soft. Add ground beef and cook until brown. Add salt, pepper, catsup, and mushroom soup; stir thoroughly. Turn heat down to low and cook slowly for about 45 minutes. Stir occasionally. Serve on warm hamburger buns. Serves 4.

Nutritional analysis per serving: 434.7 cal, 1.7 g fiber, 32.2 g fat, 84.7 mg chol, 745.3 mg sodium

Supper Casserole

1½ pounds lean ground beef
½ onion, chopped
1½ cups frozen corn
½ cup pimento, chopped
3 cups egg noodles, cooked
½ teaspoon salt
½ teaspoon pepper
1 cup sour cream
1 cup saltine cracker crumbs
3 tablespoons butter
½ cup shredded cheese

Preheat oven to 350°F. Lightly grease shallow, 2-quart casserole dish. In large skillet, sauté beef until it just turns color. Add onion and cook until transparent. Stir in corn, pimento, and precooked noodles. Season with salt and pepper. Add sour cream. Stir until well mixed. Spoon mixture into casserole dish. Sprinkle with saltine cracker crumbs. Dot with butter and cheese. Bake for 30 minutes. Serves 6.

Nutritional analysis per serving: 910 cal, 0.5 g fiber, 38.4 g fat, 220.3 mg chol, 541.6 mg sodium

Swiss Steak ★

2 pounds round steak
2 teaspoons salt and pepper
4 tablespoons flour (about ¼ cup)
¼ cup oil
2 cans tomato sauce
2 cups warm water
1 large onion, chopped
1 bell pepper, diced
2 teaspoons Worcestershire sauce
1 tablespoon prepared mustard

Divide steak into serving pieces. Mix salt, pepper, and flour. Pound into steak. Brown steak in oil in 2-quart pot. Mix other ingredients and bring to boil. Return browned steak to sauce mixture and simmer, covered, on top of stove about 30 minutes. Serve over cooked rice. Serves 6.

Nutritional analysis per serving: 340 cal, 2 g fiber, 16 g fat, 67 mg chol, 1443 mg sodium

Weiner Schnitzel

4 boneless veal chops or steaks
salt and pepper, to taste
½ cup all-purpose flour
1 egg, slightly beaten
1 cup bread crumbs
3 tablespoons butter
juice of one lemon
lemon slices, garnish
anchovies, garnish
capers, garnish
parsley, garnish

Pound chops or steaks until flat. Sprinkle with salt and pepper. Coat chops with flour, then egg, then bread crumbs. In large skillet, heat butter. Brown chops in skillet, about 3 minutes on each side. Sprinkle with lemon juice and arrange on hot serving platter. Garnish with lemon slices, anchovies, capers, and parsley. Serves 4.

Nutritional analysis per serving: 889 cal, 0 g fiber, 48 g fat, 366 mg chol, 467 mg sodium

Yum-a-Setta (Amish Recipe)

2 pounds hamburger
salt and pepper, to taste
1 teaspoon brown sugar
¼ onion, chopped
1 can tomato soup
1 package egg noodles
1 can cream of chicken soup
1 8-ounce package cheese, grated

Brown hamburger with salt and pepper, brown sugar, and onion. Add tomato soup. Cook egg noodles in boiling water and drain. Add cream of chicken soup. Layer hamburger mixture and noodle mixture in casserole dish with grated cheese between layers. Bake in preheated 350°F oven about 30 minutes. Serves 8.

Nutritional analysis per serving: 729 cal, 0 g fiber, 45 g fat, 129 mg chol, 687 mg sodium

CHEESE AND EGGS

Cheese Souffle

1½ cups milk
1 cup coarse bread crumbs
1 tablespoon butter or margarine
½ pound (2 cups) grated Cheddar cheese
4 eggs, separated
salt and pepper, to taste

Preheat oven to 350°F. Grease 2½-quart souffle dish or casserole dish with margarine. Heat milk, bread crumbs, and butter in top of double boiler. Add cheese to hot mixture and stir until melted. Beat egg yolks until light and creamy. Gradually add cheese mixture to egg yolks, stirring constantly. Season with salt and pepper. Beat egg whites until stiff peaks form. Fold cheese mixture into egg whites. Pour mixture into prepared dish. Bake for 30 to 35 minutes, or until just set. Serves 4.

Nutritional analysis per serving: 356 cal, 0 g fiber, 22 g fat, 315.7 mg chol, 845.4 mg sodium

Corn-Rice-Cheese Bake ★

1 5-ounce package saffron-flavored
   yellow rice
1 10.75-ounce can condensed cream of
   chicken soup
1 12-ounce can Mexican-style corn
nonstick vegetable coating spray
1 cup (4 ounces) grated sharp Cheddar
   cheese

Cook rice in saucepan, according to directions on package. Gently mix soup and corn with rice. Transfer mixture to 2-quart casserole dish that has been lightly treated with nonstick vegetable spray. Sprinkle grated cheese on top. Bake at 350°F, uncovered, for 20 to 30 minutes. Serves 4.

Nutritional analysis per serving: 364 cal, 0 g fiber, 14.4 g fat, 36 mg chol, 1389 mg sodium

Egg Cups ★

½ teaspoon butter or margarine
1 slice bread, crust removed
1 egg
1 tablespoon grated cheese

Preheat oven to 350°F. Butter one custard cup. Butter bread on both sides and place inside cup. Break egg into cup and sprinkle with cheese. Bake for 15 minutes, or until yolk has jelled. Serves 1.

Nutritional analysis per serving: 181.8 cal, 0.44 g fiber, 10.2 g fat, 225.6 mg chol, 244.4 mg sodium

Egg Rolls +

2 pounds browned hamburger, cooked
   chicken, or shrimp
1 8-ounce can mushrooms
2 8.5-ounce can bamboo shoots
2 tablespoons ground ginger
1 teaspoon salt
1 teaspoon monosodium glutamate
   (MSG), if desired
3 cups celery, diced
1 medium onion, chopped
2 16-ounce cans bean sprouts
2 8.5-ounce cans water chestnuts

5 tablespoons soy sauce, or to taste
1 teaspoon sugar
1 egg beaten
3 packages egg roll skins

In large bowl, combine all ingredients, except egg and egg roll skins. Mix until well combined. Beat egg and set aside. Fill egg roll skins with 2 tablespoons of filling and roll as directed on package. Seal roll with beaten egg. Deep fry rolls at 350°F until brown. Serve with sweet and sour sauce or soy sauce. Egg rolls will freeze well. Reheat in a 350°F oven for 15 to 20 minutes, turning once. Serves 50.

Nutritional analysis per serving: 60 cal, 0.1 g fiber, 2.5 g fat, 16.5 mg chol, 178 mg sodium

Macaroni and Cheese Casserole

1 cup elbow macaroni
2 tablespoons butter or margarine
½ pound (2 cups) grated sharp Cheddar
   cheese, divided
2 cups milk, scalded
2 eggs, beaten
½ teaspoon salt
¼ teaspoon red pepper

Cook macaroni according to package directions. Drain well and return to pot. Add butter to macaroni and stir until butter melts. Add 1½ cups of cheese. In separate bowl, slowly add scalded milk to eggs, stirring constantly. Pour milk mixture into macaroni and cheese. Season to taste. Stir gently to mix well. Pour mixture into greased, 2-quart casserole dish. Sprinkle with remaining ½ cup of cheese. Bake at 350°F for 30 minutes, or until golden brown. Serves 8.

Nutritional analysis per serving: 540 cal, 0 g fiber, 28.3 g fat, 183 mg chol, 671 mg sodium

Macaroni and Cheese Casserole

8 ounces small elbow macaroni
1½ cups (6 ounces) grated sharp
   Cheddar cheese
6 eggs

3 cups milk
2 tablespoons margarine
⅛ teaspoon black pepper

Cook macaroni according to package directions. In 9 × 13-inch greased baking dish, alternate layers of cooked macaroni and cheese to make 2 or 3 layers. In small bowl, beat eggs and milk. Pour egg mixture over macaroni and cheese layers. Dot with margarine and sprinkle with pepper. Bake at 300°F for 60 to 90 minutes, or until golden brown and set. Serves 8.

Nutritional analysis per serving: 331 cal, 0 g fiber, 17.4 g fat, 240 mg chol, 262 mg sodium

Microwave Macaroni and Cheese

1 can Cheddar cheese soup
¾ cup milk
1½ cups Cheddar cheese, shredded
3 cups macaroni, cooked

In 2-quart, microwave-safe casserole dish, stir soup and milk until blended. Stir in cheese and macaroni. Cover and microwave on high for 10 minutes (stir at 5 to 6 minutes). Remove and let stand for 5 minutes before serving. Serves 6.

Nutritional analysis per serving: 282 cal, 1 g fiber, 14 g fat, 42 mg chol, 544 g sodium

PORK/LAMB

Apple Butter Pork Roast ★

2 pounds boneless pork loin roast
2 cloves garlic
1½ tablespoons dry mustard
1½ cups apple butter
1 tablespoon caraway seeds
½ teaspoon thyme

Rub roast with garlic and mustard. Spread roast with ½ cup of apple butter. Sprinkle top with caraway seeds and thyme. Let stand in refrigerator 1 hour before cooking. Roast uncovered at 300°F for 1 hour per pound of meat. Baste frequently with pan juices and remaining apple butter. Serves 8.

Nutritional analysis per serving: 388 cal, 0 fiber, 26 g fat, 77 mg chol, 53 mg sodium

Bacon Quiche Cups

8 ounces cream cheese, softened
2 tablespoons milk
2 eggs
½ cup grated Swiss cheese
1 medium onion, chopped
1 10-count can flaky biscuits
5 slices bacon, cooked until crisp

Grease regular size muffin tin. In small bowl, beat cream cheese, milk, and eggs. Stir in cheese and onions. Separate biscuits into 10 or more (depending on desired thickness of crust). Place individual dough in each greased muffin cup and press down on bottom and sides. Divide bacon and place half in bottom of cups. Spoon over about 1 tablespoon of egg mixture and top with remaining bacon. Bake in preheated 375°F oven about 15 minutes. Serves 10.

Nutritional analysis per serving: 186 cal, 0 g fiber, 13 g fat, 76 mg chol, 328 mg sodium

Baked Pork Chops with Apple Raisin Stuffing ★

6 rib pork chops, 1½ inches thick
5 tablespoons chopped onion
1½ cups dry bread crumbs
3 tablespoons butter or margarine
1 large green apple, peeled, cored, sliced thin
5 tablespoons seedless raisins
½ teaspoon salt
½ teaspoon nutmeg
¼ teaspoon cinnamon
1 tablespoons water
salt and pepper, to taste

Split chops through the middle, starting from outer or fatty edge and leaving meat attached to bone. Spread open like a book. Pound both sides as thin as you would for scallopini. To make stuffing, sauté onion and bread crumbs in butter or margarine. Remove from heat. Add apple, raisins, salt, nutmeg, cinnamon, and water. Mix well. Divide stuffing into 6 equal portions and spread on open chops. Fold chops together and fasten with toothpicks. Season with salt and pepper, to taste. Bake at 350°F for 1½ hours, until tender. Turn chops once and drain off excess fat once or twice during baking. Season with salt and pepper. Serves 6.

Nutritional analysis per serving: 480 cal, 0.6 g fiber, 28.5 g fat, 73 mg chol, 429 mg sodium

Dirty Rice √

2 pounds pork sausage, ground
1 pound hamburger meat
1 large onion
4 green onions, chopped
4 cups cooked rice
chopped parsley

Sauté meat in heavy pan until brown. Add small amount of water if needed. Add chopped onion and cook until onion is tender. Add green onions and cook about 2 minutes more. Add rice and mix well. Top with parsley. Serves 8.

Nutritional analysis per serving: 704 cal, 0 g fiber, 47 g fat, 134 mg chol, 1506 mg sodium

Easy Skillet Supper

3 strips bacon, cut into 1-inch pieces
1½ pounds lean ground beef, shaped into 6 patties
1 small onion, sliced
3 potatoes, peeled and sliced
2 carrots, cut into strips and quartered
1 green bell pepper, sliced in rings
salt and pepper, to taste

Cover bottom of large frying pan with bacon pieces. Layer beef patties, onions, potatoes, carrots, and bell pepper rings. Salt and pepper to taste. Cook over medium heat for 5 minutes, until bacon sizzles. Add ½ cup water and turn heat to low. Cook 50 to 60 minutes or until carrots and potatoes are tender. Add more water as needed. Serves 6.

Nutritional analysis per serving: 307.5 cal, 6 g fiber, 15.2 g fat, 74 mg chol, 172.5 mg sodium

Electric Skillet Pork Chops ★

4 ½-inch thick pork chops
vegetable spray or 1 tablespoon vegetable oil
paprika (optional)
⅓ cup Parmesan cheese, grated
½ teaspoon salt
¼ teaspoon black pepper
4 cups white potatoes, sliced thin
2 medium onions, sliced
4 medium carrots, peeled and diced
¾ cup hot water
1 tablespoon lemon juice

Trim excess fat from pork chops. Lightly grease skillet with vegetable spray. Sprinkle chops with paprika. Place chops in skillet and brown on both sides. Drain excess grease. In small bowl, combine cheese, salt, and pepper. Pour half of cheese mixture over meat. Add potatoes, onions, and carrots. Sprinkle remaining cheese mixture over potatoes. Add hot water and lemon juice. Cover skillet and simmer over low heat. Cook for 40 minutes or until vegetables are done. Serves 4.

Nutritional analysis per serving: 615 cal, 1.4 g fiber, 35.5 g fat, 86 mg chol, 681.7 mg sodium

Fantastic Breakfast Casserole

1 cup hot cooked grits
1 box Jiffy Cornbread Mix
4 eggs, beaten
1¾ cups hot milk
½ stick butter
salt and pepper to taste
1 pound hot bulk sausage, cooked and drained
1 cup cheese, grated

Mix grits, cornbread mix, eggs, hot milk, and butter. Add salt and pepper to taste. Layer sausage alternately with grits mixture in 9 × 13-inch casserole dish. Top with cheese. Bake in preheated 325°F oven for 45 minutes. Serves 8.

Nutritional analysis per serving: 482 cal, 0 g fiber, 32 g fat, 185 mg chol, 1164 mg sodium

Farm Casserole

2 cups cooked, cubed chicken
1½ cups green peas, fresh, frozen, or canned
1 15-ounce can cream-style corn
4 ounces Cheddar cheese, diced
¼ cup chopped onion
1 cup evaporated milk
1 tablespoon Worcestershire sauce
1 teaspoon pepper
1 can refrigerator biscuits

Lightly grease 2-quart casserole dish. Layer chicken, peas, corn, cheese, and onion in dish. In small bowl, combine milk, Worcestershire sauce, and pepper. Pour over layered mixture. Bake at 375°F for 30 minutes, or until bubbly around edges. Top with biscuits and continue baking until biscuits are golden brown (10 to 15 minutes). Serves 8.

Nutritional analysis per serving: 345.3 cal, 2.5 g fiber, 9.2 g fat, 48.8 mg chol, 1156.7 mg sodium

Farmer's Breakfast ★

6 slices bacon, cut into 2-inch pieces
1 small green bell pepper, chopped
2 tablespoons onion, finely chopped
3 large potatoes, cooked, peeled, and diced
½ cup sharp Cheddar cheese, shredded
6 eggs
salt and pepper, to taste

In medium size skillet, fry bacon over low heat until crisp. Remove bacon pieces from skillet and reserve 3 tablespoons of grease and drain rest. Add pepper, onions, and potatoes to skillet. Cook over medium heat until potatoes are brown. Sprinkle cheese over potatoes and stir until cheese begins to melt. Break eggs into skillet on top of mixture. Reduce

heat to low. Cook, stirring gently, until eggs are done. Season with salt and pepper and top with bacon. Serves 6.

Nutritional analysis per serving: 215 cal, 0.14 g fiber, 12 g fat, 289 mg chol, 232.5 mg sodium

Ham and Cheese Chowder

4 white potatoes, peeled and diced
1 cup diced celery
1 cup diced carrots
½ cup chopped onions
2 teaspoons salt
½ teaspoon pepper
1 stick (½ cup) butter
½ cup all-purpose flour
4 cups milk
½ pound (2 cups) grated sharp Cheddar cheese
2 cups cubed ham

In saucepan, bring 3 cups of water to boil. Add potatoes, celery, carrots, and onions. Reduce heat, add salt and pepper, and simmer until potatoes are fork-tender. In separate saucepan, melt butter. Add flour, stirring constantly to blend. Gradually add milk, stirring constantly to prevent lumping. Heat until thick and smooth. Add cheese while stirring. Add ham, vegetables, and cooking liquid to milk mixture. Stir well to combine. Simmer chowder for 30 minutes. Serves 8.

Nutritional analysis per serving: 637 cal, 0.4 g fiber, 45 g fat, 134.2 mg chol, 1852.4 mg sodium

Ham Loaf

1 envelope plain gelatin
1 cup crushed cracker crumbs
3 hard-boiled eggs, finely chopped
1 teaspoon salt
3 cups ground ham
1 cup mayonnaise
2 tablespoons lemon juice

In top of double boiler, dissolve gelatin in cold water, according to package directions. In large bowl, combine all remaining ingredients.

Add dissolved gelatin to ham mixture. Pour mixture into loaf pan or individual serving dishes. Chill 12 to 24 hours. Serves 6.

Nutritional analysis per serving: 491 cal, 0 g fiber, 37 g fat, 185 mg chol, 1287.6 mg sodium

Lamb Chops with Tarragon Tomato Sauce ★

    6 1-inch thick lean lamb loin chops
    ⅛ teaspoon pepper
    1 8-ounce can tomato sauce, no salt
       added
    2 tablespoons dry vermouth
    ¾ teaspoon dried whole tarragon
    ⅛ teaspoon garlic powder
    3 cups hot cooked rice

Remove excess fat from chops. Lightly grease large skillet. Heat over medium heat until hot, then add chops. Cook chops for 4 minutes per side, or until brown. Remove chops from skillet and place them on a paper towel. Sprinkle chops with pepper. Wipe skillet clean with paper towel. Add tomato sauce, vermouth, tarragon, and garlic powder to skillet. Stir over medium heat until well combined. Add chops to skillet. Bring to boil. Reduce heat, cover, and simmer for 20 minutes, or until chops are tender. Serve over rice. Serves 6.

Nutritional analysis per serving: 232 cal, 0 g fiber, 6.2 g fat, 57 mg chol, 599 mg sodium

Low Country Sausage √

    1 pound hot sausage, sliced
    1 medium onion, chopped
    1½ cups long grain rice
    1¼ cups V-8 juice
    ½ teaspoon chili powder
    ⅔ cup picante sauce
    1 teaspoon salt
    1¾ cups water
    ½ teaspoon thyme
    1 medium bell pepper, chopped

Cook sausage over medium heat about 2 minutes. Add onion, stirring occasionally until onion is translucent. Add rice and mix well. Stir in remaining ingredients except bell pepper. Bring to boil, reduce heat, cover, and simmer 20 minutes or until liquid is absorbed. Stir in bell pepper. Remove from heat. Let stand covered for 5 minutes before serving. Serves 8.

Nutritional analysis per serving: 265 cal, 1 g fiber, 9 g fat, 32 mg chol, 904 mg sodium

Marinated Pork Roast + ★

    4 tablespoons dry mustard
    1 cup soy sauce
    2 teaspoons ground ginger
    4 teaspoons whole thyme leaves
    4 cloves garlic, minced
    1 8–10 pound pork loin roast, boned,
       rolled, and tied
    2 10-ounce jars apricot preserves or jelly
    2 tablespoons soy sauce

Combine first five ingredients in shallow dish, stirring well. Place roast in dish; cover and marinate 3 to 4 hours in refrigerator, turning occasionally. Remove roast from marinade and place on rack in shallow roasting pan. Insert meat thermometer at angle into thickest part of roast. Bake, uncovered, in 325°F oven until thermometer registers 170°F (2½ to 3 hours total cooking time). Combine preserves and 2 tablespoons soy sauce in small saucepan; cook over low heat, stirring occasionally, until preserves melt. Serve with sliced roast. Garnish as desired. Serves 28.

Nutritional analysis per serving: 261 cal, 0 g fiber, 7 g fat, 135 mg chol, 760 mg sodium

Mexican Pork and Beans ★

    2 tablespoons flour
    4 pork chops, cubed
    1 cup thick and chunky salsa
    2 tablespoons lime juice
    ¾ teaspoon chili powder
    ½ teaspoon garlic powder
    1 16-ounce can kidney beans, drained
    2 medium bell peppers, cubed

Shake flour into Reynolds baking bag. Place on baking sheet. Add pork, salsa, lime juice, chili powder, and garlic powder. Shake to blend. Spoon beans and peppers around meat. Close bag. Punch slits in top of bag. Bake at 350°F until pork is tender, about 35 to 40 minutes. Let stand in bag for 5 minutes before serving. Serves 4.

Nutritional analysis per serving: 427 cal, 8 g fiber, 23 g fat, 77 mg chol, 568 mg sodium

Pork Chops Italiano + ★

24 pork chops, cut 1-inch thick
salt and pepper, to taste
¼ cup vegetable oil
3 pounds fresh mushrooms, sliced
6 medium onions, chopped
5 small cloves garlic, crushed
12 medium green peppers, cut into
    thin strips
¼ cup lemon juice
1 5-ounce can tomato sauce
1½ teaspoons whole oregano or basil

Sprinkle pork chops with salt and pepper; brown on both sides in hot oil. Place chops in large chafing pan; cover with mushrooms and set aside. Add onion, garlic, and green pepper to skillet; cook until tender. Add remaining ingredients and simmer 5 minutes; pour over chops. Bake at 350°F for 1 hour or until chops are done. Serves 24.

Nutritional analysis per serving: 339 cal, 1 g fiber, 26 g fat, 77 mg chol, 94 mg sodium

Pork Savory +

3 pounds lean pork, cut in 1-inch pieces
1½ teaspoons salt
½ teaspoon pepper
1 tablespoon fat or oil
3 cups water
2½ cups carrots, sliced
1 cup sifted flour
3 cups dairy sour cream
3½ cups potatoes, diced
1½ cups green lima beans
1 tablespoons onions, finely chopped

Sprinkle pork with 1½ teaspoons salt and pepper. Brown in fat or oil. Add water, cover, and simmer until meat is tender. Cook carrots in small amount of water until almost tender. Combine flour and sour cream; beat until smooth. Add vegetables and salt; blend well. Combine with meat and broth. Bake uncovered in moderate oven (375°F) for 1 hour. Remove cover and continue baking 30 minutes to brown top. Serves 25.

Nutritional analysis per serving: 273 cal, 2 g fiber, 15 g fat, 64 mg chol, 190 mg sodium

Potato Flakes Oven Fried Pork Chops ★

vegetable spray or vegetable oil
⅓ cup dry potato flakes
4 pork chops or chicken breasts
salt and pepper, to taste

Preheat oven to 350°F. Line baking pan with aluminum foil. Lightly grease foil with vegetable spray. Sprinkle half of instant potato flakes evenly on baking pan. Rinse meat and season with salt and pepper. Place meat into baking pan and sprinkle with remaining potato flakes. Put pan on bottom rack of oven. Bake uncovered for 45 minutes. Turn meat once while baking. Serves 4.

Nutritional analysis per serving: 383 cal, 0 g fiber, 33 g fat, 71.7 mg chol, 42.6 mg sodium

Quiche

4 medium eggs
8 bacon slices or ½ cup ham
8 ounces Swiss or Monterey Jack cheese
¼ cup minced onion
1 cup milk
pepper, to taste
1 9-inch pastry shell

Preheat oven to 350°F. In large bowl, beat eggs. Add bacon slices, cheese, onion, milk, and pepper. Pour mixture into unbaked pie shell. Bake for 40 to 45 minutes, or until golden brown and firm. Serves 8.

Nutritional analysis per serving: 317 cal, 0 g fiber, 22.5 g fat, 173 mg chol, 373.5 mg sodium

Sausage and Broccoli Casserole +

4 pounds sausage links, cut into small
  pieces
4 10.5-packages frozen chopped broccoli
1 cup mild Cheddar cheese, shredded
12 tablespoons green pepper, chopped
12 tablespoons onion, chopped
8 tablespoons all-purpose flour
12 eggs, hard-cooked and sliced
4 10.75-ounce cans cream of mushroom
  soup
1 1/3 cups milk
2 cups dry bread crumbs
12 tablespoons butter or margarine,
  melted
12 tablespoons fresh parsley, minced
hot, cooked rice

Cook sausage until browned; drain. Cook broccoli according to package directions; drain well. Place broccoli in large, lightly greased chafing pan. Combine sausage, cheese, green pepper, onion, parsley, and flour in medium bowl; spoon half of sausage mixture over broccoli in casserole. Top sausage mixture with egg slices; spoon remaining sausage mixture over eggs. Combine soup and milk; pour over casserole. Combine bread crumbs and butter; sprinkle over casserole. Bake at 375°F for 30 minutes. Serve over cooked rice. Serves 24.

Nutritional analysis per serving: 632 cal, 3 g fiber, 37 g fat, 180 mg chol, 1373 mg sodium

Sausage-Cheese Casserole √

8 slices bread, crusts removed
1 pound pork sausage (hot)
1/2 pound sharp cheese, grated
3 or 4 eggs
1 cup milk
salt and pepper, to taste
1 teaspoon dry mustard

In casserole, layer bread, sausage, and cheese. Repeat layers. Beat together eggs, milk, salt, pepper, and mustard. Pour mixture over bread and cheese. Chill 1 hour (or overnight). Bake at 350°F for 35 minutes. Serves 8.

Nutritional analysis per serving: 446 cal, 0 g fiber, 31 g fat, 184 mg chol, 1089 mg sodium

Sausage Quiche

1 9-inch deep dish pastry pie shell,
  unbaked
1/2 pound hot bulk sausage, browned
  and drained
1/2 cup sliced fresh mushrooms
1/2 cup chopped onions
1/4 teaspoon oregano
1/4 teaspoon basil
1/4 teaspoon ground red pepper
1/2 teaspoon salt
1/2 cup (2 ounces) shredded sharp
  Cheddar cheese
1/2 cup (2 ounces) shredded Swiss cheese
1/4 cup chopped green pepper
1 1/2 cups evaporated skim milk
3 eggs, beaten

Preheat oven to 400°F. Bake pie shell for 3 minutes. Reduce oven temperature to 350°F. Mix together browned sausage, mushrooms, onions, oregano, basil, red pepper, salt, cheeses, green pepper, milk, and eggs. Pour mixture into pie shell and bake for 50 minutes, or until set. Serves 6.

Nutritional analysis per serving: 439.3 chol, 0.05 g fiber, 28.3 g fat, 187.8 mg chol, 831.5 mg sodium

Special Pork Chops ★

1/4 teaspoon salt
1/2 teaspoon pepper
1/2 cup all-purpose flour
4 1/2-inch-thick pork chops
2 tablespoons vegetable oil
1 onion, sliced
1 lemon, sliced
4 tablespoons brown sugar

Preheat oven to 375°F. In small bowl, add salt, pepper, and flour. Dip each chop in flour, covering both sides. In frying pan, heat oil and add chops. Brown chops on both sides. Remove chops from pan and place them in baking pan. Place slice of onion and lemon on each chop. Sprinkle 1 tablespoon of brown sugar on each chop. Cover pan with foil or lid. Bake for 30 minutes. Serves 4.

Nutritional analysis per serving: 502 cal, 0.2 g fiber, 33.3 g fat, 71.7 mg chol, 180.8 mg sodium

Stuffed Pork Chops ★

    6 1½-inch-thick pork chops, with
        pockets
    ¼ teaspoon salt
    ¼ teaspoon pepper
    ½ cup grated sharp cheese
    2 tablespoons margarine
    2 tablespoons orange juice
    1½ cups toasted bread crumbs or cubes
    ½ cup peeled and chopped apple
    ⅓ cup raisins
    1 teaspoon celery seed or ⅓ cup
        chopped celery

Preheat oven to 350°F. Sprinkle inside and outside of chop with salt and pepper. In small mixing bowl, combine remaining ingredients. Stuff chops with stuffing mixture. Place chops in baking dish. Bake for 1 hour. Remove from oven and cover with foil. Bake an additional 15 minutes. Serves 6.

Nutritional analysis per serving: 526.4 cal, 0.33 g fiber, 34.4 g fat, 82.8 mg chol, 428.7 mg sodium

Western Omelet + ★

    ¾ pound bacon, diced
    1½ pound onions, diced
    1½ pound green peppers, diced
    ¾ pound ham trimmings, diced
    90 eggs, medium to large size
    1 pint milk
    ½ ounce salt
    ¼ teaspoon white pepper
    butter as needed

Dice bacon, onions, and green peppers into ¼-inch pieces. Fry diced bacon; add onions and green peppers and sauté until onions are transparent but not brown. Add diced ham trimmings and heat thoroughly. Remove from heat. Break eggs into bowl; add milk, salt, and white pepper and beat well. Heat butter in frying pan and pour off excess fat. Add western mixture, allowing 1 ounce per serving, and egg mixture, equivalent to 2 eggs per serving. Cook over hot fire, continuously moving frying pan back and forth until eggs become firm but are still soft in middle. Use spatula and fold eggs in from bottom of frying pan toward opposite rim from handle to form pointed oval. Allow to brown lightly, and then turn onto plate or pan. Serves 50.

Nutritional analysis per serving: 199 cal, 0 g fiber, 13 g fat, 393 mg chol, 428 mg sodium

Winter Pork Surprise ★

    4 potatoes
    4 tablespoons Cheddar cheese, shredded
    6 pork chops
    1 can cream of mushroom soup, diluted

Slice potatoes into bottom of Crock-Pot. Sprinkle cheese on potatoes, layer pork chops, and pour diluted soup over top. Set Crock-Pot on high and cook 6 to 8 hours. Serves 4.

Nutritional analysis per serving: 688 cal, 5 g fiber, 21 g fat, 132 mg chol, 510 mg sodium

POULTRY

Baked Chicken Special

    6 boneless, skinless chicken breast halves
    1 tablespoon lemon juice
    ½ teaspoon black pepper
    2 tablespoons cooking oil
    3 tablespoons butter or margarine
    1 2-ounce jar sliced mushrooms
    ½ cup cooking sherry
    8 ounces sour cream
    1 10.75-ounce can condensed cream of
        chicken soup
    4 tablespoons bread crumbs
    1 teaspoon sesame seeds

Season chicken breasts with lemon juice and pepper. Sauté chicken in oil until lightly browned and tender. Melt butter or margarine in 2-quart casserole dish. Layer sautéed chicken and sliced mushrooms in casserole dish. Mix together sherry, sour cream, and soup. Pour over chicken. Top with bread crumbs and sesame seeds. Bake at 350°F for 1 hour. Serves 6.

Nutritional analysis per serving: 515.5 cal, 0 g fiber, 37.3 g fat, 90 mg chol, 745 mg sodium

Baked Chicken Supreme ★

2½–3 pounds chicken fryer pieces, skinned
1 teaspoon salt
1 teaspoon pepper
¼ teaspoon paprika
½ teaspoon tarragon
3 tablespoons lemon juice
2 teaspoons soy sauce
¼ cup sherry
1 cup chicken broth, divided
1 medium onion, diced
2 tablespoons cornstarch
1 cup plain yogurt
2 tablespoons fresh parsley, chopped

Arrange chicken pieces in 9 × 13-inch baking dish. Sprinkle salt, pepper, paprika, and tarragon on chicken. Mix together lemon juice, soy sauce, sherry, ½ cup chicken broth, and onion. Pour mixture over chicken. Bake, uncovered, at 425°F for 20 minutes. Remove from oven. Baste with pan drippings. Cover and bake an additional 20 minutes at 375°F. When chicken is done, transfer pieces to warm platter. To make sauce, add remaining ½ cup chicken broth to baking pan and simmer on stove for 2 minutes, stirring constantly. In separate bowl, combine cornstarch, yogurt, and parsley. Mix well. Add gradually to chicken broth, stirring constantly. Cook until heated through; do not boil. Serves 5.

Nutritional analysis per serving: 132.4 cal, 0.13 g fiber, 2.1 g fat, 33.5 mg chol, 924.3 mg sodium

Cheese and Chicken

6 boneless, skinless chicken breast halves
1 10.75-ounce can condensed cream of chicken soup
8 ounces (1 cup) sour cream
1 cup bread crumbs
1 cup (4 ounces) grated Cheddar cheese

Put chicken in 2-quart casserole dish. Combine soup and sour cream. Pour this mixture over chicken. Bake for 45 minutes at 350°F. Combine bread crumbs and cheese. Sprinkle mixture over chicken. Bake an additional 30 minutes. Serves 6.

Nutritional analysis per serving: 405.5 cal, 0 g fiber, 20 g fat, 107 mg chol, 755 mg sodium

Cheezy Chicken

4 chicken breast halves, skinned
3 cups cheese crackers, crushed
¼ cup butter or margarine, melted

Brush chicken pieces with butter. Roll in cracker crumbs. Arrange pieces in flat microwave baking dish. Cover with waxed paper. Microwave on high for 12 to 15 minutes. Rotate dish ½ turn halfway through microwaving time. Let stand, covered, 2 to 3 minutes. Serves 4.

Nutritional analysis per serving: 523 cal, 0.1 g fiber, 23 g fat, 150 mg chol, 623 mg sodium

Chicken and Dressing Casserole ★

3 cups cooked, cubed chicken
2½ cups chicken broth
1 10.75-ounce can condensed cream of celery soup
2 tablespoons margarine, melted
3 cups baked corn bread, crumbled
1 cup white bread, crumbled
3 eggs

Put chicken in 2-quart casserole dish. Combine broth, soup, margarine, breads, and eggs. Stir until well mixed. Pour over chicken.

Bake at 350°F for 30 to 40 minutes, or until set and lightly browned. Serves 7.

Nutritional analysis per serving: 667 cal, 0 g fiber, 32 g fat, 293.4 mg chol, 1258 mg sodium

Chicken and Herb Rice ★

1 10.75-ounce can condensed cream of chicken soup
1 10.75-ounce can condensed onion soup
1 10.75-ounce can condensed beef bouillon
1 10.75-ounce can water
5- or 6-serving package herb rice
3 pounds chicken parts

Mix soups and water together until blended. Mix rice into soup. Put chicken parts in lightly greased 9 × 13-inch baking pan, skin side up. Pour soup mixture over chicken. Bake at 350°F for 45 minutes, or until chicken is tender. Serves 6.

Nutritional analysis per serving: 468 cal, 0 g fiber, 19.2 g fat, 116.3 mg chol, 1061.5 mg sodium

Chicken Breast Casserole ★

6 small boneless, skinless chicken breast halves
¼ cup all-purpose flour
salt and pepper, to taste
2 tablespoons margarine
1 10.75-ounce can condensed cream of chicken soup
½ cup water
½ cup diced celery
¼ cup diced onion

Dredge chicken in flour and lightly salt and pepper. In 12-inch skillet, heat margarine and lightly brown chicken on both sides over medium heat. In small bowl, combine soup, water, celery, and onion. Place chicken in 9 × 13-inch baking pan. Spoon soup mixture over chicken pieces. Bake for 45 minutes at 325°F, or until chicken is tender when pierced with fork. Serves 6.

Nutritional analysis per serving: 234 cal, 0.14 g fiber, 8.3 g fat, 72.4 mg chol, 529.6 mg sodium

Chicken, Broccoli, and Rice Casserole ★

1 whole chicken or 4–5 chicken breasts
1 10-ounce package frozen, chopped broccoli
½ cup onion, diced
½ cup celery, diced
1 teaspoon margarine
1 10-ounce can cream of mushroom soup or cream of chicken soup
1 cup grated American cheese
1½ cups cooked rice
2 tablespoons bread crumbs

Boil chicken until completely cooked. De-bone and skin chicken and cut into bite-size pieces. Cook broccoli according to package directions and drain. In skillet, sauté onion and celery in margarine. Add broccoli, soup, and cheese to skillet mixture. Stir in cooked rice and chicken. Place mixture in 2-quart casserole dish. Top with bread crumbs. Bake at 350°F for 45 minutes. Serves 5.

Nutritional analysis per serving: 575.3 cal, 1.3 g fiber, 34.8 g fat, 102.3 mg chol, 1350.8 mg sodium

Chicken Casserole

9 slices white bread, crust removed
1 8-ounce can sliced mushrooms
1 8-ounce can water chestnuts, drained and sliced
4 eggs
1 8-ounce can cream of mushroom soup
1 5-ounce jar pimento, drained
4 cups chicken, diced
½ cup butter
½ cup mayonnaise
9 slices Cheddar cheese, grated
1 teaspoon salt
1 8-ounce can cream of celery soup
¼ cup buttered bread crumbs

Cut bread into bite-size pieces. Line 2-quart baking dish or 9 × 13-inch baking pan with bread. In large bowl, combine remaining ingredients. Stir until combined. Pour over bread in baking dish. Allow ingredients to marinate 6 hours in refrigerator before cooking. Bake at 350°F for 1 to 1½ hours. Serves 8.

Nutritional analysis per serving: 661.6 cal, 0 g fiber, 36.5 g fat, 261.8 mg chol, 1270.2 mg sodium

Chicken Casserole ★

1 cup long grain white rice
2 cups boiling water
1 frying chicken, cut up
1 stick (½ cup) margarine or butter
1 envelope dry onion soup mix
salt and pepper, to taste

In 2-quart casserole dish, combine rice with boiling water. Place chicken over rice. Dot margarine over chicken. Sprinkle onion soup over top. Salt and pepper to taste. Cover dish. Cook for 1 hour at 350°F or until chicken is done (juices run clear). Serves 6.

Nutritional analysis per serving: 227.2 cal, 0 g fiber, 18.7 g fat, 23.2 mg chol, 307 mg sodium

Chicken Casserole ★

1 cup uncooked rice
1 tablespoon seasoning salt
1 10.75-ounce can condensed cream of
    mushroom soup
¾ cup water
3 pounds chicken fryer parts
¼ cup mayonnaise

Lightly grease 9 × 13-inch baking pan or 2-quart casserole dish. Combine rice, salt, soup, and water. Pour into prepared pan. Place chicken on rice with skin side up. Do not overlap pieces. Lightly spread mayonnaise on exposed chicken skin. Cover pan and bake at 300°F for 2 hours. Uncover for last 30 minutes of cooking to brown chicken. Serves 8.

Nutritional analysis per serving: 100 cal, 0 g fiber, 3.8 g fat, 21.2 mg chol, 1131.4 mg sodium

Chicken Casserole + ★

2½ cups Uncle Ben's uncooked rice
½ large can water
1 tablespoon sugar
½ large can mushroom soup
⅓ cup onion soup mix
¾ cup soy sauce
salt and pepper, to taste
20 chicken breasts, split

Allow 1¼ cups uncooked rice for each chafing pan. Mix all other ingredients except chicken. Pour this over rice and stir to mix. Place chicken on top of rice. Pat down gently to get some of sauce on top of chicken. Make sure rice stays on bottom. Cover with foil and cook about 2 hours at 350°F. Serves 20.

Nutritional analysis per serving: 334 cal, 0 g fiber, 7 g fat, 147 mg chol, 914 mg sodium

Chicken Casserole with Curry ★

2 cups boned chicken
1 cup chopped celery
⅛ teaspoon dry mustard
1 teaspoon chopped onion
½ cup almonds
1½ cups cooked rice
1 can cream of chicken soup
½ teaspoon salt and pepper
¾ cup plain low-fat yogurt
⅛ teaspoon curry powder
¼ cup water
1 tablespoon lemon juice

Mix all ingredients together. Place in casserole dish and bake in preheated 350°F oven for 20 to 25 minutes. (Good topped with 1 cup herbed seasoning mix before baking.) Serves 8.

Nutritional analysis per serving: 240 cal, 1 g fiber, 10 g fat, 42 mg chol, 435 mg sodium

Chicken Chowder ★

2 cups chicken broth
1 cup frozen cut broccoli
1 medium carrot, grated
¼ cup quick brown rice
1 tablespoon dried minced onion

dash of pepper
1 cup milk
1 tablespoon all-purpose flour
1½ cups chicken, cooked and cubed

Stir broth, broccoli, carrots, rice, onion, and pepper together in 3-quart pot. Bring to boil. Reduce heat, cover, and simmer for 12 to 15 minutes or until vegetables are tender. Stir together milk and flour. Stir into broth mixture. Cook and stir over medium heat until mixture thickens. Cook, while stirring, for 1 minute one more. Stir in chicken. Cook about 3 minutes longer. Good with slaw and cornbread on a cold, rainy day. Serves 4.

Nutritional analysis per serving: 779 cal, 3 g fiber, 29 g fat, 221 mg chol, 587 mg sodium

Chicken Ciapinna ★

1 frying chicken, skinned and cut into
   pieces
salt and pepper, to taste
¼ cup margarine
2 8-ounce cans tomato sauce
½ cup red wine
¾ cup onions, chopped
1 clove garlic, minced
3 teaspoons parsley
1 bay leaf, crushed
1 tablespoon basil, crushed
1 pound raw shrimp, cleaned
cooked rice

Season skinned chicken pieces with salt and pepper and brown slowly in butter. Debone. Mix tomato sauce, wine, onions, garlic, parsley, bay leaf, basil, and pepper. Place in 2-quart heavy pot. Cover and simmer until chicken is tender. Add shrimp, being sure they are covered in sauce. Cover and cook 5 to 10 minutes until shrimp are tender. Serve in hot soup plates over cooked rice. Serves 6.

Nutritional analysis per serving: 209 cal, 1 g fiber, 10 g fat, 152 mg chol, 697 mg sodium

Chicken Hot Dish ★

2 cups cooked, diced chicken
½ cup diced onions
1 cup diced celery
1 10.75-ounce can condensed cream of
   mushroom soup
2 cups chow mein noodles, divided
1 cup chicken broth
¼ cup chopped cashews

Combine chicken, onions, celery, soup, 1½ cups noodles, and chicken broth in 2-quart casserole dish. Top with remaining ½ cup noodles and cashews. Bake at 350°F for 45 minutes. Serves 4.

Nutritional analysis per serving: 506.3 cal, 0.43 g fiber, 25.9 g fat, 70.9 mg chol, 1952.7 mg sodium

Chicken-Noodle Casserole ★

1 chicken, cut into pieces
1 8-ounce package of noodles
1 cup onions, chopped
1 can cream of celery soup
1 cup Cheddar cheese, grated
1 cup bell pepper, chopped
1 can mushroom soup
salt and pepper, to taste

Boil chicken until done. Remove chicken, debone, skin, and cut into bite-size pieces. Cook noodles in chicken water. Drain. Mix all ingredients together and place in greased 9 × 13-inch baking dish. Bake in preheated 350°F oven until bubbly. Serves 8.

Nutritional analysis per serving: 246 cal, 1 g fiber, 11 g fat, 47 mg chol, 554 mg sodium

Chicken Parmigiana +

12 whole chicken breasts, split, boned,
   and skinned
8 eggs, slightly beaten
4 teaspoons salt
4 teaspoons pepper
3 cups fine, dry bread crumbs
2 cups vegetable oil
4 15-ounce cans tomato sauce
1 teaspoon dried whole basil

½ teaspoon garlic powder
4 tablespoons butter or margarine
2 cups Parmesan cheese, grated
2 pounds mozzarella cheese, thinly sliced
 and cut into triangles

Place each chicken breast on sheet of waxed paper. Flatten to ¼-inch thickness, using meat mallet or rolling pin. Combine eggs, salt, and pepper. Dip chicken breasts into egg mixture and roll each in bread crumbs. Brown chicken in hot oil in large skillet; drain on paper towels. Place chicken in a lightly greased chafing pan. Drain oil from skillet. Combine tomato sauce, basil, and garlic powder in skillet. Bring to boil, and simmer 10 minutes or until thickened. Stir in butter. Pour mixture over chicken, and sprinkle with Parmesan cheese. Cover and bake at 350°F for 30 minutes. Uncover and arrange mozzarella cheese slices on top. Bake 10 additional minutes. Serves 24.

Nutritional analysis per serving: 616 cal, 2 g fiber, 39 g fat, 182 mg chol, 913 mg sodium

Chicken-Pepper-Onion Skillet ★

1 pound skinless, boneless chicken
 breasts, cut into strips
3 tablespoons soy sauce
2 teaspoons cornstarch
⅛ teaspoon garlic powder
⅛ teaspoon sugar
1 large bell pepper, sliced
1 large onion, sliced
½ pound fresh mushrooms, sliced
¼ cup vegetable oil, divided
½ cup water
5-ounce can water chestnuts, drained
 and sliced
cooked rice

Combine chicken, soy sauce, cornstarch, garlic powder, and sugar; set aside. In 12-inch skillet, over medium to medium-high heat, sauté peppers, onions, and mushrooms in 2 tablespoons oil. Remove vegetables from skillet. Add remaining 2 tablespoons of oil.

Cook chicken mixture, stirring constantly for about 5 minutes, or until chicken is tender. Return vegetables to skillet. Add water and water chestnuts. Heat to boiling, stirring constantly. Remove from heat. Serve over hot rice. Serves 4.

Nutritional analysis per serving: 434.6 cal, 0.36 g fiber, 20 g fat, 65.3 mg chol, 842 mg sodium

Chicken Pie

1 3–4 pound chicken, cooked, skinned,
 and boned
1 cup chicken broth
1 6-ounce can mushrooms, drained and
 sliced
1 10-ounce can cream of celery soup
1 10-ounce can cream of onion soup
2 16.5-ounce cans mixed vegetables,
 drained
Topping:
1 cup self-rising flour
1 teaspoon baking powder
1 stick (½ cup) margarine, melted
1 cup milk

Preheat oven to 350°F. Grease 2-quart casserole dish with margarine. Cut chicken into bite-size pieces. In bowl, combine chicken, broth, mushrooms, celery and onion soups, and mixed vegetables. Stir until well combined. Pour chicken mixture into casserole dish. In separate bowl, combine flour, baking powder, margarine, and milk. Mix well. Pour the batter evenly over chicken mixture. Bake for 60 minutes or until crust is golden brown. Serves 8.

Nutritional analysis per serving: 291 cal, 0 g fiber, 17.8 g fat, 40.3 mg chol, 1366 mg sodium

Chicken-Rice Casserole ★

1¼ cups onion, chopped
1 tablespoon margarine
1 5-ounce can of chicken
1 14.5-ounce can chicken broth
1 cup sharp cheese, grated
½ cup rice, uncooked

Cook onion in margarine until tender. Mix in chicken, broth, cheese, and rice. Pour into casserole dish. Bake covered in preheated 375°F oven about 1 hour. Serves 4.

Nutritional analysis per serving: 278 cal, 1 g fiber, 16 g fat, 50 mg chol, 721 mg sodium

Chicken Risotto ★

6 tablespoons margarine or butter, divided
1 pound boneless, skinless chicken breasts, cut in bite-size pieces
1 clove garlic, pressed
1½ cups long grain rice, uncooked
½ cup fresh mushrooms, sliced
3 green onions, chopped
3 cups chicken broth
1 tablespoon fresh dill, minced
1 teaspoon basil
½ cup (2 ounces) grated mozzarella cheese

Melt 2 tablespoons butter in large skillet. Sauté chicken in butter over medium heat, stirring constantly, until chicken is golden brown. Remove chicken from skillet. Put remaining butter into skillet. Add garlic and rice, stirring constantly. Cook for about 5 minutes, until rice browns. Add mushrooms and green onions. Cook until mushrooms become tender, stirring constantly. Stir in chicken broth, dill, and basil. Bring to boil. Reduce heat. Cover and simmer for 15 minutes. Gradually add chicken. Continue simmering (covered) until chicken is thoroughly heated and rice is done, about 5 minutes. Top with cheese. Serve immediately. Serves 4.

Nutritional analysis per serving: 326 cal, 0 g fiber, 22.8 g fat, 26.5 mg chol, 1457.8 mg sodium

Chicken Souffle Supreme

6 slices white bread, cubed
2 cups cooked, diced chicken
¼ cup chopped green pepper
¼ cup pimento, chopped
¼ cup chopped celery
½ cup mayonnaise
¾ teaspoon seasoned salt
dash of pepper
2 beaten eggs
1½ cups milk
1 10.75-ounce can condensed cream of mushroom soup
½ cup (2 ounces) grated sharp Cheddar cheese

Put 1 cup of bread cubes in 9-inch square baking dish. Combine chicken, vegetables, and mayonnaise with seasonings and spoon over bread. Cover with remaining bread cubes. Combine eggs and milk and pour over mixture in baking dish. Cover and chill at least 1 hour or overnight. Just before baking, spoon soup over top of casserole mixture. Bake at 325°F for 1 hour, or until set. Immediately after removing from oven, sprinkle grated cheese on top. Serves 8.

Nutritional analysis per serving: 296 cal, 0.2 g fiber, 14 g fat, 121.4 mg chol, 635.4 mg sodium

Chicken Stew ★

2 large potatoes, peeled and diced
1 large onion, chopped
1 5-ounce can chunky chicken
1 8-ounce can cream-style corn
salt and pepper, to taste
¼ teaspoon herb seasoning
1 cup milk

In saucepan, combine potatoes and onion. Cover with 1 inch of water. Cook over medium heat until potatoes are tender when pierced with fork. Add chicken. Cook for 5 minutes. Add corn and seasonings. Reduce heat to low, and simmer for a few minutes until hot. Add milk, stirring gently. Cook until stew is thoroughly heated, but do not boil. Serves 4.

Nutritional analysis per serving: 188 cal, 0.16 g fiber, 2.9 g fat, 28.6 mg chol, 238.2 mg sodium

Chicken with Mushrooms ★

8 small boneless, skinless chicken breast
  halves
¼ cup all-purpose flour
3 tablespoons margarine or butter
2 tablespoons diced celery
2 tablespoons chopped green bell pepper
2 tablespoons chopped onion
1 10.75-ounce can condensed cream of
  mushroom soup
1 10.5-ounce can milk
1 3-ounce can sliced mushrooms

Coat chicken lightly with flour. In skillet,
lightly brown chicken in margarine or butter.
Remove from heat. Place chicken breasts in 9
× 13-inch baking dish or casserole. Combine
remaining ingredients. Pour mixture over
chicken. Cover. Bake for 45 minutes at 350°F.
Serve over rice, if desired. Serves 8.

Nutritional analysis per serving: 142.5
cal, 0.05 g fiber, 8.6 g fat, 18.8 mg chol, 428.7
mg sodium

Creamy Baked Chicken
with Mushrooms ★

8 small skinless, boneless chicken breast
  halves
1 tablespoon cooking oil
1 large onion, sliced thinly
8 ounces fresh mushrooms, cut in half
¼ teaspoon garlic powder
¼ teaspoon seasoned salt
1 10.75-ounce can condensed cream
  soup (onion, mushroom, or chicken)
4 ounces hard cheese, grated
½ cup bacon bits

Brown chicken in cooking oil. Transfer
chicken to deep casserole dish. Brown onions
in same skillet. Cover chicken with onions.
Brown mushrooms in skillet, sprinkling them
with garlic as they cook. Cover onions with
mushrooms. Sprinkle with salt. Heat soup in
skillet. Stir in 2 tablespoons of water, and pour
soup over casserole. Bake at 325°F for 20 minutes. Sprinkle 2 tablespoons cheese and 1 tablespoon bacon bits on each chicken breast.

Bake an additional 10 to 15 minutes, or until
cheese is melted. Serves 8.

Nutritional analysis per serving: 260 cal,
0.1 g fiber, 11.3 g fat, 94 mg chol, 564 mg
sodium

Crowd-Pleaser Chicken +

4 cans mushroom soup
4 cans water
4 cups rice
1 stick margarine, in pats
4 pounds chicken, cleaned and dried,
  salted and peppered
4 envelopes onion soup (dried)

In bottom of large baking dish or dishes,
mix together 2 cans mushroom soup, water,
and rice. Over this mixture, layer margarine,
chicken, 2 cans mushroom soup, and dried
onion soup. Pour 4 additional cans of water
over, cover, and bake at 350°F for 2 hours.
Serves 20.

Nutritional analysis per serving: 279 cal, 1
g fiber, 16 g fat, 45 mg chol, 1442 mg sodium

Diabolic Chicken ★

1 tablespoon margarine
½ cup honey
1 teaspoon salt
¼ cup prepared mustard
1 teaspoon curry powder
1 chicken, cut up

Melt margarine in shallow pan, stir in remaining ingredients except chicken. Roll chicken in mixture to coat well. Arrange chicken
meaty side up in single layer in 9 × 13-inch
baking dish. Bake 1 hour in 350°F oven or until
chicken is tender and glazed. Baste occasionally.
Serves 4.

Nutritional analysis per serving: 184 cal,
1 g fiber, 5 g fat, 53 mg chol, 782 mg sodium

Dijon Tarragon Chicken ★

4 boneless, skinless chicken breast halves
2 tablespoons lemon juice
2 teaspoons spicy mustard

¼–½ teaspoon tarragon
¼ teaspoon poultry seasoning

Place chicken in 1-quart covered casserole dish. Add lemon juice. Spread mustard on top of each chicken piece. Sprinkle chicken lightly with tarragon and poultry seasoning. Refrigerate for 1 to 2 hours. Cover and bake for 45 minutes in 350°F oven. Serves 4.

Nutritional analysis per serving: 138.5 cal, 0 g fiber, 1.7 g fat, 68.5 mg chol, 79.8 mg sodium

Easy Chicken Casserole

2 cups chicken, cooked and chopped
1 cup chicken broth
1 can cream of chicken soup
1 cup self-rising flour
1 cup milk
1 stick margarine

Mix together chicken, broth, and cream of chicken soup. Pour in 9 × 13-inch casserole dish. Mix together flour, milk, and melted margarine; pour over chicken mixture. Bake in preheated 350°F oven for 45 minutes. (May add green peas or other vegetable if desired.) Serves 8.

Nutritional analysis per serving: 435 cal, 2 g fiber, 27 g fat, 112 mg chol, 688 mg sodium

Easy Chicken Wellington

1 small box brown rice
2 egg whites, beaten
6 frozen pattie shells, thawed
6 boneless chicken breasts
salt to taste
2 egg yolks, beaten
1 can cream of chicken soup
½ soup can of milk

Cook rice according to directions. Cool. Add beaten egg whites. Roll out pattie shells to 7-inch round. Place ½ cup rice on each shell. Place chicken breast over rice. Salt to taste. Pull edges of shell over chicken and seal with water. Place on greased cookie sheet and brush tops with egg yolks. Bake uncovered in preheated 350°F oven about 30 to 45 minutes. Dilute soup with milk and heat. Serve as sauce over chicken. Serves 6.

Nutritional analysis per serving: 870 cal, 5 g fiber, 29 g fat, 270 mg chol, 386 mg sodium

Glazed Chicken ★

2 tablespoons vegetable oil
4 small skinless, boneless chicken breast halves
⅓ cup apple jelly
2 teaspoons dry sherry
2 teaspoons lemon juice
¼ teaspoon salt
¾ cup seedless red grapes, sliced in half

In 12-inch skillet, heat oil and add chicken. Cook over medium heat until done. Remove chicken from pan and keep warm. Add jelly, sherry, lemon juice, and salt to chicken. Stir in grapes after jelly has melted. Spoon glaze over chicken and serve hot. Serves 4.

Nutritional analysis per serving: 280 cal, 0 g fiber, 8.4 g fat, 68.5 mg chol, 215.2 mg sodium

Gourmet Chicken ★

1 large onion, chopped
1 tablespoon butter
4 chicken breasts
1 tablespoon oil
1 cup beef bouillon
½ pound mushrooms, sliced
salt and pepper, to taste
2 tablespoons heavy cream
fresh parsley, chopped

Sauté onions in butter and set aside. Brown chicken in oil in same pan as onions; add bouillon, mushrooms, salt and pepper, and onions. When mixture comes to boil, cover and reduce heat to low. Simmer approximately 30 minutes per pound of chicken. When done, remove chicken from pot, add cream to liquid in pot, and stir thoroughly. Serve gravy over chicken or on the side. Garnish with chopped parsley. Serves 4.

Nutritional analysis per serving: 503 cal, 0 g fiber, 27 g fat, 184 mg chol, 387 mg sodium

Grilled Marinated Turkey Breast ★

2 cups unsweetened pineapple juice
½ cup olive oil
½ cup low-sodium soy sauce
3 tablespoons cajun seasoning
4 pounds raw turkey breast, boned and sliced

Combine pineapple juice, olive oil, soy sauce, and cajun seasoning. Place turkey breast slices in a large glass container. Pour marinade over meat and turn to coat all meat. Cover and marinate in refrigerator for 12 to 24 hours, turning twice. Cook for 3 to 5 minutes per side on grill or under broiler. Serve on bun or as entrée. Serves 13.

Nutritional analysis per serving: 251 cal, 0 g fiber, 10.5 g fat, 56.5 mg chol, 2268 mg sodium

Ground Turkey Casserole ★

1 egg
1 can cream soup (celery, mushroom, or chicken)
1 pound ground turkey
1 cup celery, chopped
1 bell pepper, chopped
1 medium onion, chopped
salt and pepper, to taste

Beat egg and add ½ can of soup. Mix remaining ingredients and turkey. Place in casserole dish and top with remaining soup. Bake in preheated 350°F oven for 30 minutes. Serves 4.

Nutritional analysis per serving: 246 cal, 2 g fiber, 13 g fat, 110 mg chol, 462 mg sodium

Honey Lemon Chicken ★

¼ cup canola oil
6 tablespoons lemon juice
dash salt and pepper
1 teaspoon lemon peel, grated

2 tablespoons honey
6 chicken breast halves, skinned and boneless

Combine first 5 ingredients in shallow baking dish. Stir until well blended. Place chicken in marinade. Turn to coat. Refrigerate 30 minutes, turning once. Heat broiler or prepare grill. Remove chicken from marinade. Broil or grill 3 to 5 minutes per side. Serves 6.

Nutritional analysis per serving: 160 cal, 0 g fiber, 4 g fat, 65 mg chol, 95 mg sodium

Hot Chicken Casserole √

3 pounds cooked chicken
1 can mushroom soup
2 cups diced celery
½ cup mayonnaise
4 hard-boiled eggs, chopped
2 cans cream of chicken soup
3 teaspoons lemon juice
1 small onion, grated
1 cup slivered almonds
1 teaspoon salt
potato chips

Place all ingredients (except chips) in bowl and blend well. Pour into 2-quart casserole dish, top with crushed chips, and bake in 350°F preheated oven for 30 minutes or until bubbly. Casserole may be prepared day ahead and refrigerated. Add potato chips just before baking. Serves 10.

Nutritional analysis per serving: 411 cal, 2 g fiber, 20 g fat, 165 mg chol, 860 mg sodium

Jalapeño Chicken ★

1 whole chicken, cut-up, skin removed
1 onion, diced
4 jalapeño peppers, chopped
¼ cup soy sauce
garlic salt and black pepper, to taste
4 green onions, chopped
2 tablespoon cornstarch

Place chicken, onion, jalapeño peppers, and seasonings in flameproof casserole dish. Cover chicken with water by only ½ inch.

Bring to boil, while skimming off foam. Cover and reduce heat to simmer. Cook until chicken is done, approximately 45 minutes. Place green onions on top of chicken and simmer another 5 minutes. To thicken broth, mix cornstarch with 2 tablespoons cold water to blend. Add cornstarch to broth, stirring constantly. Simmer until thickened. Serve over hot rice, if desired. Serves 6.

Nutritional analysis per serving: 96.2 cal, 0.11 g fiber, 2 g fat, 35 mg chol, 730.2 mg sodium

Mexican Fried Chicken Breasts ★

2 tablespoons cornmeal
1 teaspoon paprika
½ teaspoon salt
⅓ teaspoon garlic powder
½ teaspoon black pepper
¼ teaspoon ground cumin
4 boneless, skinless chicken breast halves
¼ cup cooking oil

Combine cornmeal, paprika, salt, garlic powder, pepper, and cumin in plastic bag. Rinse chicken and do not pat dry. Put chicken in bag with spices. Hold tightly closed and shake vigorously to coat chicken. Heat oil in skillet for about 4 minutes on medium to medium-high. Fry chicken in oil for 8 to 10 minutes, or until juices run clear. Serves 4.

Nutritional analysis per serving: 398 cal, 0 g fiber, 16.7 g fat, 137 mg chol, 481 mg sodium

Pineapple Chicken and Rice + ★

100 pieces fresh chicken
flour, salt, and pepper, as needed
1¾ gallon pineapple juice
3 cups soy sauce
3 cups lemon juice
2½ No. 10 cans sliced pineapple
steamed white rice for 100

Toss chicken lightly in flour; season with salt and pepper. Brown each piece in deep fat. Place chicken in roasting or serving pans. Mix together remaining ingredients except for

pineapple slices. Pour liquid mixture over chicken and cover. Bake at 350°F for 40 to 45 minutes. Gently sauté pineapple slices, 1 slice per serving. Place sautéed pineapple over chicken. Return to oven for 15 minutes. Serve with steamed white rice. Serves 100.

Nutritional analysis per serving: 481 cal, 1 g fiber, 16 g fat, 166 mg chol, 634 mg sodium

Quail with Sour Cream

8 thin slices of Canadian bacon
8 quail
salt and pepper, to taste
4 slices bacon (about ¼ pound)
½ cup sour cream
½ cup condensed cream of mushroom
    soup

Line greased shallow 1-quart baking dish with Canadian bacon. Season quail with salt and pepper. Wrap each quail with half slice of bacon. Put each quail on slice of Canadian bacon. Combine sour cream and soup. Pour over quail. Bake uncovered in 275°F oven for 3 hours. Serves 16.

Nutritional analysis per serving: 304 cal, 0 g fiber, 19 g fat, 103 mg chol, 676 mg sodium

Quick and Easy Chicken Pie ★

3 cups cooked, cubed chicken
2½ cups chicken broth
1 10.75-ounce can condensed cream
    soup (mushroom or celery)
1 cup all-purpose flour
1 stick (½ cup) margarine or butter,
    room temperature
1 cup milk
2 tablespoons parsley, chopped
1 tablespoon onion powder
1 teaspoon black pepper
1 teaspoon salt

Put chicken in 9 × 13-inch baking dish. Mix together chicken broth and soup. Pour over chicken. Combine flour, margarine, milk, parsley, and seasonings. Sprinkle evenly over chicken. Bake for 30 minutes at 375°F, or until crust becomes golden brown. Serves 8.

Nutritional analysis per serving: 270 cal, 0 g fiber, 16.7 g fat, 25.4 mg chol, 1211.8 mg sodium

Scalloped Chicken ★

½ loaf white bread, cubed
1½ cups cracker crumbs
2 cups chicken broth
3 eggs, beaten
salt and pepper, to taste
¾ cup diced celery
2 tablespoons chopped onion
2 cups chicken, cooked, deboned,
　　skinned, and cubed
1 8-ounce can mushrooms, sliced
1 tablespoon margarine

Combine bread cubes and 1 cup cracker crumbs. Stir in broth, eggs, salt, pepper, celery, onion, chicken, and mushrooms. Spoon into greased, 2-quart casserole dish. Melt butter. Place remaining cracker crumbs over top and dot with butter. Bake in preheated 350°F oven for 1 hour. Serves 8.

Nutritional analysis per serving: 211 cal, 1 g fiber, 6 g fat, 83 mg chol, 504 mg sodium

Scalloped Chicken + ★

4 cups cooked chicken, cut in large
　　pieces
1 cup celery, diced
1 cup soft bread crumbs
2 tablespoons parsley, minced
2 cups chicken broth
2 teaspoons salt
4 eggs, slightly beaten
½ cup milk

Grease two 9-inch baking dishes. Alternate layers of chicken with celery, bread crumbs, and parsley. Measure chicken broth into bowl; add eggs, salt, and milk and pour over chicken. Set dishes in pan of hot water. Bake in moderate oven (350°F) 1 hour or until knife inserted in center comes out clean. Serves 12.

Nutritional analysis per serving: 190 cal, 0 g fiber, 5 g fat, 144 mg chol, 598 mg sodium

Skillet Turkey with Lentils ★

1½ cups lentils, rinsed
2 medium onions, chopped
2 cloves garlic, minced
2 tablespoons cooking oil
1 pound ground turkey
2 teaspoons low-sodium chicken
　　bouillon
2 tablespoons long-grain rice
1 teaspoon sugar
1 teaspoon salt
1 teaspoon ground cumin
½ teaspoon black pepper
1 tablespoon cider vinegar

Cook lentils in 1 quart simmering water for 20 minutes. Drain and reserve liquid. In deep skillet, sauté onions and garlic in oil. Add ground turkey and brown, stirring frequently. Dissolve bouillon in 2⅓ cups of reserved liquid. Add hot water, if necessary. Add liquid and lentils to meat mixture. Cover and simmer for 10 minutes. Stir in rice, sugar, salt, cumin, and pepper. Bring mixture to boil, then reduce heat and cover. Simmer for 30 minutes, until rice is tender and liquid is absorbed. Stir in cider vinegar just before serving. Serves 7.

Nutritional analysis per serving: 183 cal, 2.5 g fiber, 5.2 g fat, 26.2 mg chol, 1231 mg sodium

Sweet and Sour Chicken

4 small boneless, skinless chicken breast
　　halves
½ teaspoon salt
1 egg, beaten
¾ cup bread crumbs
¾ cup cooking oil
⅔ cup sugar
2 tablespoons cornstarch
1 tablespoon paprika
1 20-ounce can pineapple chunks, juice
　　reserved
¼ cup soy sauce

¼ cup white vinegar
1 green bell pepper, sliced into strips
1 large onion, sliced
2 tomatoes, sliced into wedges
cooked rice

Cut chicken breasts into 1-inch pieces. Salt chicken and dip into beaten egg and then into bread crumbs to coat. Heat oil in large skillet over medium heat. Fry chicken pieces until they are golden brown. Remove chicken pieces from skillet and drain them on a paper towel. Combine sugar, cornstarch, and paprika in skillet. Add enough water to pineapple juice to make 2 cups liquid. Mix in soy sauce and vinegar. Add liquid to skillet, stirring constantly. Continue to cook and stir until mixture begins to boil. Boil for 1 minute. Add green pepper and onion. Cover and cook for 5 minutes. Add pineapple and tomato. Cover and cook for 1 additional minute. Gently stir in chicken pieces, coating them completely with sauce. Serve over hot rice. Serves 4.

Nutritional analysis per serving: 814 cal, 2.4 g fiber, 45.5 g fat, 137.8 mg chol, 1316.3 mg sodium

Turkey Balls ★

1 pound ground turkey
½ cup bread crumbs
1 egg white
½ teaspoon salt
1 tablespoon cooking oil
2 tablespoons flour
⅛ teaspoon ground cinnamon
2 cups apple juice
1 apple, coarsely grated

Combine turkey, bread crumbs, egg white, and salt in bowl and mix well. Form into 1-inch balls. In skillet, brown balls in oil. Transfer browned turkey balls to baking dish. Add flour and cinnamon to skillet. Stir constantly until light brown. Add apple juice and grated apple. Cook until thickened. Pour over turkey balls. Bake at 350°F for 30 minutes. Serves 5.

Nutritional analysis per serving: 247 cal, 0.6 g fiber, 5 g fat, 37.4 mg chol, 1375 mg sodium

Turkey Steak with Gravy ★

2 slices of toast
1 pound ground turkey meat
3 tablespoons catsup, divided
1 tablespoon Worcestershire sauce
¾ teaspoon salt, divided
1½ teaspoons black pepper, divided
1 tablespoon vegetable oil
1 small onion, sliced
3 tablespoons all-purpose flour
2 cups water

Soften toast with 2 tablespoons water. In large mixing bowl, combine toast, turkey, 1 tablespoon catsup, Worcestershire sauce, ½ teaspoon salt, and 1 teaspoon pepper. Mix ingredients and form into 4 patties. In frying pan, brown patties in vegetable oil. Remove patties from pan and place in baking pan. Add slice of onion for top of each pattie. Add flour to meat drippings in frying pan. Stir until brown. While stirring, gradually add water. Then add remaining 2 tablespoons catsup, ¼ teaspoon salt, and ½ teaspoon pepper. Cook, stirring constantly, until thickened. Pour gravy over meat patties. Cover baking pan and bake at 375°F for 30 minutes. Serves 4.

Nutritional analysis per serving: 153 cal, 0.2 g fiber, 5 g fat, 20.6 mg chol, 765.6 mg sodium

Turkey-Zucchini Casserole ★

1 pound ground turkey
1 cup chopped celery
1 medium onion, chopped
2 tablespoons cooking oil
2 medium zucchini, sliced
1 1-pound can whole tomatoes
3 tablespoons Worcestershire sauce
1 teaspoon dried basil
1 teaspoon sugar
3 tablespoons grated Parmesan cheese
salt and pepper, to taste

In large skillet, sauté turkey, celery, and onions until turkey browns. Remove from skillet. Put oil in skillet and sauté zucchini. Alternate layers of turkey and zucchini in shallow, 2-quart baking dish. Combine tomatoes, Worcestershire sauce, basil, and sugar. Pour over casserole. Sprinkle with cheese. Bake at 350°F for 40 to 45 minutes. Serves 5.

Nutritional analysis per serving: 176 cal, 1.4 g fiber, 9 g fat, 22.8 mg chol, 765 mg sodium

Unfried Chicken √ ★

12 chicken breasts (skinless)
3 cups ice water
1 cup plain nonfat yogurt
1 cup all-purpose flour
½ teaspoon Creole seasoning
cayenne pepper to taste
½ teaspoon basil
1 cup Italian bread crumbs
½ teaspoon garlic powder
½ teaspoon black pepper
½ teaspoon thyme
½ teaspoon oregano

Preheat oven to 400°F. Spray baking sheet with vegetable oil. Place chicken in ice water. Toss bread crumbs and seasonings in large plastic bag until well mixed. Remove chicken one piece at a time, dip in yogurt, and shake in bread mixture to coat well. Place chicken on baking sheet. Repeat until all chicken is coated. Spray chicken pieces lightly with vegetable oil. Bake for 1 hour, turning pieces of chicken several times during baking for even browning. Serves 12.

Nutritional analysis per serving: 486 cal, 1 g fiber, 17 g fat, 166 mg chol, 214 mg sodium

SEAFOOD

Bar-B-Q Shrimp ★

1 pound shrimp, peeled and deveined
¾ cup barbecue sauce

Place cleaned shrimp and barbecue sauce in seal-top bag. Place in refrigerator one hour

(or overnight). Turn several times to cover shrimp well with sauce. Place shrimp on foil-lined broiler pan and broil four to five minutes on each side. Serves 2.

Nutritional analysis per serving: 314 cal, 1 g fiber, 6 g fat, 350 mg chol, 1102 mg sodium

Catfish Stew ★

½ pound bacon
4 pounds catfish
3 pounds white potatoes, diced
2 pounds onions, diced
1 cup hot water
1 10.75-ounce can condensed tomato soup
4 tablespoons butter, melted
hot sauce, to taste
salt and pepper, to taste

Fry bacon in large, heavy pot until brown. Remove bacon, leaving fat in pot. Add in layers catfish, potatoes, and onion, using about two layers of each. Add hot water, cover, and cook for 1½ hours without stirring. Mix together tomato soup, butter, hot sauce, salt, and pepper. Add to stew. Thin with additional water, if desired. Serve hot. Serves 12.

Nutritional analysis per serving: 367 cal, 0.6 g fiber, 12.3 g fat, 100 mg chol, 394 mg sodium

Crab au Gratin √ ★

2 cups white sauce
2 cups crab meat
1 chopped pimento
1 chopped bell pepper
salt and pepper to taste
½ teaspoon Worcestershire sauce
2 lemons, sliced thin
1 teaspoon parsley, chopped
1 cup grated cheese

Combine all ingredients, except cheese. Place in baking dish, sprinkle cheese on top of mixture, and bake in 350°F oven for 30 minutes. Serves 6.

Nutritional analysis per serving: 268 cal, 1 g fiber, 18 g fat, 75 mg chol, 669 mg sodium

Crab Cakes

1 pound fresh lump crab meat, picked over for shell and flaked
2 tablespoons fresh flat leaf parsley, chopped
1 teaspoon Dijon mustard
⅛ teaspoon cayenne pepper
1 large egg
⅓ cup dry bread crumbs
2 tablespoons heavy cream
1 tablespoon fresh lemon juice
2 teaspoons snipped fresh chives
½ teaspoon lemon zest, grated
freshly ground pepper, to taste
1 large egg yolk
½ cup light packed fresh bread crumbs
4 tablespoons (½ stick) unsalted butter
prepared tartar sauce

Preheat oven to 250°F. Place all ingredients except dry bread crumbs, butter, and tartar sauce in mixing bowl and stir to combine. Shape into 8 (2½-inch) patties, gently squeezing out excess liquid. Spread dry bread crumbs in shallow bowl and coat both sides of each patty with bread crumbs, gently shaking off excess. Heat half the butter in large skillet over medium heat. Add half the crab cakes and cook, until golden brown for four to six minutes, turning once. Keep warm in oven. Repeat with remaining butter and cakes. Serve hot with tartar sauce. Serves 8.

Nutritional analysis per serving: 177 cal, 0 g fiber, 11 g fat, 131 mg chol, 712 mg sodium

Curried Shrimp ★

¾ pounds cooked shrimp
¼ cup onion, chopped
3 tablespoons butter, melted
3 tablespoons flour
1 teaspoon salt
dash pepper
1 teaspoon curry powder
¼ teaspoon powdered ginger

2 cups milk
rice

Cut large shrimp in half. Cook onion in butter until tender. Blend flour and seasonings. Add milk gradually and cook until thick, stirring constantly. Add shrimp; heat. Serve in a rice ring or over rice. Serves 6.

Nutritional analysis per serving: 251 cal, 1 g fiber, 6 g fat, 102 mg chol, 855 mg sodium

Easy Fish Fillets ★

1 clove garlic, minced
1 tablespoon minced onion
½ teaspoon thyme
2 tablespoons olive oil
1 tablespoon white wine vinegar
⅛ teaspoon oregano
salt and pepper, to taste
4 5-ounce fresh fish fillets, any type

Preheat oven to 450°F. Combine garlic, onion, thyme, olive oil, vinegar, oregano, salt, and pepper. Spread one tablespoon of mix on each fish fillet. Allow fish to marinate with mixture for 30 minutes in refrigerator. Bake for 10 minutes per inch of thickness of fillets (measured at thickest part). Serves 4.

Nutritional analysis per serving: 156 cal, 0.02 g fiber, 7.5 g fat, 43 mg chol, 82.5 mg sodium

Golden Shrimp Casserole ★

8 slices bread, cubed
2 cups cooked shrimp
1 3-ounce can mushrooms, drained and sliced
½ pound sharp cheese, grated
3 eggs
2 cups milk
½ teaspoon salt
½ teaspoon dry mustard
dash paprika

Place half of bread crumbs in greased 7 × 11-inch baking dish. Add shrimp, mushroom, and half of cheese. Top with remaining bread and cheese. Beat together eggs, milk, and seasonings. Pour over mixture. Let stand in refrigerator one hour. Bake in preheated 325°F oven 40 to 45 minutes or until set. Serves 6.

Nutritional analysis per serving: 330 cal, 1 g fiber, 16 g fat, 150 mg chol, 1015 mg sodium

Grilled Honey Grouper

2 cups honey
1 cup soy sauce
1½ teaspoons fresh ground pepper
2 large grouper fillets
4 cups olive oil
2 tablespoons Dijon mustard
¼ cup lemon juice

Mix all ingredients together. Stir well. Marinate grouper fillets in covered bowl in refrigerator for two hours. Spray grill basket with vegetable oil. Place fish in basket (or on outside grill). Cook, basting with extra sauce, until golden brown on outside. (May substitute chicken for fish). Serves 4.

Nutritional analysis per serving: 2597 cal, 1 g fiber, 220 g fat, 31 mg chol, 3711 mg sodium

Grilled Shark Steak ★

8 shark steaks
Marinade:
4 cloves of garlic, crushed
1 teaspoon dry mustard
4 tablespoons parsley
½ cup olive oil
2 teaspoons salt
¼ teaspoon pepper
6 tablespoons lemon juice

Place shark steaks in baking dish, leaving some room between each one. Pour marinade over them and marinate in refrigerator for at least four hours. Cook on grill until done. Serves 8.

Nutritional analysis per serving: 253 cal, 0 g fiber, 19 g fat, 43 mg chol, 601 mg sodium

Hot Seafood Pie +

10 cups crushed potato chips, divided
2 cups margarine, melted

8 6.50-ounce cans crab meat, drained and flaked
8 4.50-ounce cans medium shrimp, drained
4 cups celery, chopped
2 cups green pepper, chopped
4 tablespoons grated onion
4 tablespoons lemon juice
1 teaspoon salt
1 cup pimento, chopped
4 cups mayonnaise
2 cups shredded Cheddar cheese

Combine 6 cups crushed potato chips and margarine; press into 9-inch pie plate. Bake at 375°F for 5 minutes. Cool. Combine crab meat, shrimp, celery, green pepper, onion, lemon juice, salt, pimento, and mayonnaise in large bowl; stir well. Spoon mixture into potato chip crust. Combine remaining crushed potato chips and cheese; sprinkle on top. Bake at 375°F for 10 minutes or until cheese melts. Serves 28.

Nutritional analysis per serving: 402 cal, 1 g fiber, 31 g fat, 124 mg chol, 858 mg sodium

Hot Shrimp Sandwiches ★

1 small onion, chopped
1 medium green bell pepper, chopped
1 stalk of celery, chopped
1 tablespoon olive oil
garlic powder, to taste
black pepper, to taste
½ pound shrimp, cooked, peeled, and deveined
½ cup mayonnaise
1 5-ounce jar chopped pimento
6 hamburger buns
½ cup (2 ounces) grated Cheddar cheese

Sauté onion, green pepper, and celery in olive oil. Cook until onion becomes transparent. Remove vegetables from heat. Sprinkle with garlic powder and pepper. Add shrimp to skillet. In separate small bowl, combine mayonnaise and pimentos. Mix well. Add mayonnaise mixture to shrimp mixture. Place three tablespoons of mixture on each hamburger bun half. Sprinkle each with two teaspoons of cheese. Broil until cheese melts. Serves 6.

Nutritional analysis per serving: 424 cal, 0.3 g fiber, 21 g fat, 96 mg chol, 891.6 mg sodium

Marinated Fish ★

¼ cup soy sauce
¼ cup dry Sherry or Madeira
¼ cup olive oil
juice of 1 orange (¼ cup)
2 cloves garlic, chopped
1 tablespoon minced fresh ginger or powdered ginger
2 tablespoons orange rind, grated
2 pounds fresh tuna, fish steaks, or fillets, ¾ inch thick

Combine soy sauce, sherry, olive oil, orange juice, garlic, ginger, and orange rind in shallow dish or pan. Add fish and marinate for 30 minutes in refrigerator. Place over hot coals and cook 2 to 3 minutes on each side or until just done. Serves 6.

Nutritional analysis per serving: 320 cal, 0 g fiber, 16 g fat, 57 mg chol, 729 mg sodium

Maryland Crab Cakes

1 pound crab meat
3 eggs
2 tablespoons mayonnaise
3 tablespoons prepared mustard
1 cup crushed saltine crackers
3 tablespoons cooking oil

Combine crab meat, eggs, mayonnaise, and mustard. Shape mixture into 8 patties. Roll each pattie in crushed crackers. Fry in oil over medium heat until cakes are golden brown on both sides. Serves 8.

Nutritional analysis per serving: 168 cal, 0 g fiber, 98 g fat, 136.8 mg chol, 296 mg sodium

Orange Roughy with Peppercorn Sauce ★

2 orange roughy fillets
1 teaspoon green peppercorns
3 tablespoon light sour cream

½ teaspoon dill weed
1 tablespoon fat-free mayonnaise
2 teaspoons Parmesan cheese

Spray baking dish with cooking spray. Place fillets in 10-inch baking dish. Cover and place in preheated 350°F oven for 10 minutes. Soak peppercorns in small bowl of water for two minutes. Drain and crush with spoon. Add sour cream, dill, mayonnaise, and Parmesan cheese. Mix. Remove fish from oven after 10 minutes, uncover, and spoon cream sauce over fish. Bake, uncovered, an additional five minutes. Serve hot. Serves 2.

Nutritional analysis per serving: 190 cal, 0 g fiber, 14 g fat, 19 mg chol, 155 mg sodium

Quick and Easy Gourmet Seafood ★

1 medium onion, chopped
1 teaspoon cooking oil
1 cup sliced mushrooms
1 small can (6 ounces) crab meat, rinsed and drained
1 small can (6 ounces) shrimp, rinsed and drained
1 10.75-ounce can condensed cream of mushroom soup
1 soup can milk

Sauté onion in oil. Add mushrooms, crab meat, and shrimp. Stir-fry for two minutes. Mix together soup and milk. Gradually add soup mixture to seafood mixture, stirring constantly. Heat thoroughly. Serve hot over rice or pastry shells, if desired. Serves 4.

Nutritional analysis per serving: 242 cal, 0.2 g fiber, 11 g fat, 124 mg chol, 881 mg sodium

Salmon Casserole ★

2 tablespoons butter
2 tablespoons all-purpose flour
1¾ cups milk
1 15-ounce can salmon
¼ cup bread crumbs

In small saucepan, combine butter, flour, and milk. Cook over low heat, stirring constantly, until mixture is smooth and thick. Put salmon in casserole dish. Pour sauce over salmon. Sprinkle bread crumbs evenly over casserole. Bake at 350°F for 30 minutes, or until casserole bubbles and crumbs brown. Serves 4.

Nutritional analysis per serving: 305.5 cal, 0 g fiber, 15.5 g fat, 71.8 mg chol, 674.4 mg sodium

Salmon Loaf ★

1 16-ounce can salmon
½ cup corn bread, crumbled
1 egg
½ cup chopped onion
½ cup mayonnaise

Combine all ingredients in large bowl. Mix well. Put mixture into loaf pan and bake at 400°F for 30 minutes. Serves 4.

Nutritional analysis per serving: 356 cal, 0.2 g fiber, 20 g fat, 160 mg chol, 1028 mg sodium

Salmon Patties

1 15-ounce can pink salmon
1 egg
⅓ cup minced onion
½ cup all-purpose flour
1½ teaspoons baking powder
¼ cup cooking oil

Drain salmon and save 2 tablespoons of liquid. Combine salmon, egg, and onion until sticky. Stir in flour. Dissolve baking powder in salmon liquid. Add liquid to salmon mixture. Form mixture into 12 patties. Fry patties in oil over medium heat until they are golden brown. Drain on paper towels when cooked. Serves 4.

Nutritional analysis per serving: 732 cal, 0 g fiber, 63 g fat, 131 mg chol, 778 mg sodium

Scallops Fettuccini ★

½ pound scallops
1 clove garlic, minced
2 tablespoons salted butter or margarine
¼ pound fettuccini noodles, cooked
1 tablespoon Parmesan cheese

Sauté scallops and garlic in butter until scallops become opaque, about 5 minutes. Serve over hot fettuccini, sprinkled with cheese. Serves 2.

Nutritional analysis per serving: 262 cal, 0 g fiber, 6.5 g fat, 15.5 mg chol, 60 mg sodium

Scampi ★

2 teaspoons Worcestershire sauce
¼ cup sherry
1 clove garlic
2 tablespoons lemon juice
1 teaspoon sugar
1 pound raw shrimp, peeled
¼ cup parsley, minced

Mix ingredients well. Arrange shrimp in single layer. Spoon sauce over shrimp. Broil at low heat for five minutes. Remove from broiler and let stand five minutes. Sprinkle parsley over shrimp. Broil for three minutes. Spoon over hot rice and sprinkle with Parmesan cheese if desired. Serves 4.

Nutritional analysis per serving: 135 cal, 0.2 g fiber, 2 g fat, 172 mg chol, 196 mg sodium

Seafood Casserole

⅓ cup chopped onions
¼ cup melted butter
¼ cup all-purpose flour
1 teaspoon salt
½ teaspoon white pepper
1 cup half and half
1 cup milk
2 tablespoons lemon juice
1 6-ounce package frozen crab meat, thawed and flaked
1 cup cooked shrimp, peeled and deveined
1 5-ounce can sliced water chestnuts, drained
2 cups cooked rice
2 tablespoons pimento, chopped
1 cup (4 ounces) grated Cheddar cheese, divided

In deep skillet, sauté onions in butter until tender. Add flour, salt, and pepper. Continue to cook until bubbling. Gradually add half and half and milk. Cook over low heat, stirring constantly until smooth and thick. Remove from heat. Add lemon juice, crab, shrimp, water chestnuts, rice, pimento, and ½ cup of the cheese. Stir all ingredients until well mixed. Spoon mixture into two-quart, lightly greased casserole dish. Sprinkle remaining cheese on top of casserole. Bake at 325°F for 30 minutes. Serves 7.

Nutritional analysis per serving: 382.7 cal, 0.1 g fiber, 18.4 g fat, 129.2 mg chol, 857.6 mg sodium

Shellfish Sorrento ★

2 10.75-ounce cans condensed cream of mushroom soup
1 10.75-ounce can condensed cream of shrimp soup
1 cup milk
8 ounces elbow macaroni, cooked
1 6.5-ounce can crab meat
1 5-ounce can shrimp
¼ cup pimento
1 3-ounce can sliced mushrooms
½ teaspoon garlic salt or powder
⅛ teaspoon cayenne pepper
1 cup grated Parmesan cheese
2 tablespoons butter

In large saucepan, heat soup and milk until it begins to bubble. Add macaroni, shellfish, pimento, mushrooms, and seasonings. Stir in half of cheese. Spoon mixture into lightly greased, 3-quart casserole dish. Sprinkle with remaining cheese and dot with butter. Brown mixture under broiler, about five minutes. Serves 8.

Nutritional analysis per serving: 431.4 cal, 0 g fiber, 20.4 g fat, 96.3 mg chol, 1637.7 mg sodium

Shrimp Creole √

2½ pounds whole shrimp
1 tablespoon butter
½ cup onions, chopped
2 tablespoons bell pepper, chopped
1 clove garlic, minced
1 tablespoon flour
1 can tomato paste (8 oz)
½ can water (4 oz)
2 tablespoons parsley, chopped
⅛ teaspoon pepper sauce
¼ teaspoon black pepper
⅛ teaspoon thyme
1 teaspoon salt

Peel, devein, and wash shrimp. Melt butter in large skillet over medium heat. Add onion and green pepper. Sauté until soft (about 6 minutes). Stir in garlic. Remove from stove and blend in flour until smooth. Add tomato sauce and simmer 5 minutes. Add water, stirring to blend. Add shrimp and remaining ingredients. Cover and simmer 40 minutes. Serve over cooked, hot rice. Serves 4.

Nutritional analysis per serving: 418 cal, 3 g fiber, 11 g fat, 438 mg chol, 1042 mg sodium

Shrimp Creole ★

2 pounds raw shrimp, shelled and deveined
1 cup chopped onion
1 cup chopped green bell pepper
6 tablespoons margarine
1 bay leaf
4 cups canned whole tomatoes, chopped in juice
1 10.75-ounce can condensed tomato soup
5 ounces water
2 tablespoons all-purpose flour
¼ teaspoon black pepper
1 teaspoon salt
2 teaspoons chili powder
½ teaspoon minced garlic
¼ teaspoon pepper sauce
1 tablespoon soy sauce

Cook shrimp in lightly salted, boiling water for five minutes. Do not overcook. In large, deep skillet, sauté onions and bell pepper in margarine until tender. Add bay leaf, tomatoes, soup, water, flour, pepper, salt, chili powder, garlic, pepper sauce, and soy sauce. Simmer, stirring frequently, for one hour, or until liquid thickens. Add shrimp. Cook an additional ten minutes, or just long enough to warm shrimp. Remove bay leaf. Serve over hot rice, if desired. Serves 8.

Nutritional analysis per serving: 250 cal, 1 g fiber, 10.4 g fat, 170 mg chol, 1109 mg sodium

Shrimp-Okra Gumbo √ ★

2 tablespoons oil
2 medium onions, chopped
2 pounds okra, sliced
1 gallon hot water
¾ cup tomatoes, canned
salt and pepper to taste
½ clove garlic
½ teaspoon cayenne pepper
4 pounds shrimp

Heat oil in heavy saucepan. Add onions and okra and fry until brown around edges. Cook on low heat, stirring occasionally, until okra does not stick to pan (about 1 hour). Add water gradually, about 1 cup every few minutes. Add tomatoes. Add salt and pepper to taste. Add garlic and cayenne pepper. Add peeled shrimp and cook 15 minutes longer. Serve in soup bowls over heaping servings of rice. Serves 8.

Nutritional analysis per serving: 311 cal, 1 g fiber, 8 g fat, 344 mg chol, 420 mg sodium

Shrimp on Wild Rice Pilaf √ ★

Rice:
¼ millet
½ cup onion, chopped
¼ cup carrot, chopped
¼ cup celery, chopped
¼ cup bell pepper, chopped
¼ cup wild rice
½ cup brown rice
2 cups chicken stock
1 tablespoon soy sauce
1 tablespoon milk
1 teaspoon chili paste

2 cloves garlic, minced
1 teaspoon coriander
1 teaspoon lime zest
Shrimp:
16 medium shrimp
1 onion cut into chunks
16 cherry tomatoes
16 mushrooms
1 bell pepper, cubed

Toast millet in medium pan about 2 minutes. Preheat heavy pan over medium heat. Spray with vegetable oil. Add onion, carrot, celery, and bell pepper. Sauté until vegetables are limp. Add toasted millet, wild rice, and brown rice. Stir in chicken stock and soy sauce, stir, and bring to boil. Cover and reduce heat to low. Simmer 45 minutes. While rice is cooking, in large zip-lock bag, combine milk, chili paste, garlic, coriander, and lime zest. Stir well. Add shrimp, onion, tomatoes, mushrooms, and peppers. Toss to coat. Place in refrigerator to marinate about 30 minutes. Preheat grill. On skewers, thread 2 shrimp and chunks of marinated vegetables, alternating on skewers. Place bell pepper cube on end. Grill 4 minutes on each side until shrimp are pink and vegetables charred slightly. Fluff rice and divide it among 4 plates. Top with 2 skewers. Serves 4.

Nutritional analysis per serving: 272 cal, 8 g fiber, 3 g fat, 44 mg chol, 715 mg sodium

Shrimp Pasta ★

1 cup chopped onion
½ clove garlic
⅓ cup olive oil
2 16-ounce cans stewed tomatoes
½ teaspoon basil
½ teaspoon salt
¼ teaspoon black pepper
8 ounces pasta (vermicelli is best)
1½ pounds medium fresh shrimp, peeled and cleaned
½ cup fresh parsley, chopped
1 2½-ounce can ripe olives, sliced
¼ cup Parmesan cheese

In skillet, sauté onions and garlic in olive oil. Add tomatoes, salt, and pepper to sautéed onions and garlic; bring to boil. Lower heat, cover, and simmer for 20 minutes. Prepare pasta as directed on package and at the same time add shrimp to tomato mixture. Drain pasta and put in bowl. Fold in tomato sauce along with parsley and olives. Serve topped with Parmesan cheese. Excellent served the next day. Serves 4.

Nutritional analysis per serving: 659 cal, 4 g fiber, 25 g fat, 337 mg chol, 1497 mg sodium

Shrimp Pilau ★

4 slices bacon
½ cup chopped celery
2 tablespoons chopped green pepper
1 tablespoon all-purpose flour
1 teaspoon salt
¼ teaspoon black pepper
1 pound medium-size shrimp, cooked, peeled, and deveined
4 tablespoons Worcestershire sauce
1 tablespoon butter or margarine
1 cup rice
1 5-ounce can water chestnuts, drained
2⅔ cups water

Fry bacon until crisp. Remove bacon from skillet and reserve two tablespoons of bacon fat in pan. Sauté celery and green pepper in drippings until tender. In small bowl, combine flour, salt, and pepper. Dredge shrimp in flour mixture. Add shrimp to skillet. Stir in Worcestershire sauce. Cover and cook over low heat for 30 minutes, stirring occasionally. Melt butter in medium-size saucepan. Add rice to butter and cook over low heat until golden brown, stirring constantly. Add water chestnuts and water. Bring to full boil. Cover and reduce heat to low. Simmer for 20 minutes, or until rice is tender. Stir rice into shrimp mixture and remove from heat. Crumble the bacon and sprinkle it over the shrimp pilau. Serves 4.

Nutritional analysis per serving: 412.4 cal, 0.2 g fiber, 14 g fat, 235 mg chol, 2203 mg sodium

Shrimp Stir-Fry ★

3 slices bacon
1 cup diced celery
1 cup snow peas
¼ cup sliced red bell pepper
¼ cup sliced green bell pepper
¼ cup sliced yellow bell pepper
1 pound shrimp, peeled and deveined
1 tablespoon soy sauce
2 cups cooked rice
salt and pepper, to taste

Fry bacon until crisp, then remove from skillet. Add celery, snow peas, and peppers to bacon drippings. Cook, stirring constantly for one minute. Add shrimp and soy sauce. Cook for two minutes, or until shrimp turn pink. Add rice. Season to taste with salt and pepper. Stir to mix. Serve hot. Garnish with bacon crumbles, if desired. Serves 4.

Nutritional analysis per serving: 310.3 cal, 1.7 g fiber, 7.9 g fat, 231 mg chol, 700 mg sodium

Simple Tuna Casserole

1 6.2-ounce can white tuna packed in water, drained
1 10.75-ounce can condensed cream of mushroom soup
1 small bag of potato chips, crushed

Mix tuna with soup. Add half of crushed potato chips. Mix well. Transfer mixture to lightly greased 1-quart casserole dish. Sprinkle remaining chips on top of tuna mixture. Bake at 350°F for 20 to 30 minutes, or until mixture is bubbling and lightly browned. Serves 4.

Nutritional analysis per serving: 189 cal, 0 g fiber 10 g fat, 19.3 mg chol, 695.3 mg sodium

Southern Salmon Bake √

2 tablespoons butter
¼ cup flour
1½ cups milk
salt and pepper, to taste
½ cup grated onion

1 tablespoon chopped parsley
2 beef bouillon cubes
2 cans salmon
½ cup olives, sliced
½ cup dry bread crumbs
½ cup grated cheese

Melt butter in pan and blend in flour. Add milk, salt, pepper, onion, parsley, and bouillon cubes. Cook and stir until thickened. Place layer of salmon (drained and flaked) in bottom of greased 1½-quart casserole dish. Sprinkle olives, bread crumbs, and cheese over top, pour layer of milk mixture, then repeat layers of olives, bread crumbs, and cheese until all is used, ending with milk mixture and topping with small amount of bread crumbs and cheese. Bake at 350°F in preheated oven for 30 minutes. Serves 8.

Nutritional analysis per serving: 243 cal, 1 g fiber, 13 g fat, 40 mg chol, 979 mg sodium

Stuffed Flounder √

½ cup chopped celery
½ cup chopped onion
1 clove garlic, minced
¼ cup butter
1½ cups bread crumbs
1 cup boiled shrimp
1 cup crab meat
3 tablespoons chopped parsley
1 egg, beaten
4 flounders
salt and pepper, to taste
juice of 1 lemon

Over low heat, sauté celery, onion, and garlic in melted butter. Add bread crumbs, shrimp, crab meat, parsley, and egg, mix well. Season generously with spices. Split thick side of flounder, lengthwise and crosswise, and loosen meat from bone to form pocket for stuffing. Brush fish well with melted butter, salt, and pepper. Stuff pocket with shrimp mixture. Place fish, skin side down, on greased broiler grill. Broil 3 inches from heat until fish flakes easily with fork (about 15 minutes). Baste occasionally with lemon. Serves 4.

Nutritional analysis per serving: 397 cal, 1 g fiber, 17 g fat, 251 mg chol, 595 mg sodium

Tasty Tuna Bake

1 cup dry macaroni
1 6-ounce can tuna, drained
1 8-ounce can cream soup (mushroom or celery)
¼ cup chopped onions
1 cup milk
1 cup (4 ounces) grated Cheddar cheese
½ teaspoon crushed red pepper
salt and pepper, to taste
¼ cup toasted bread crumbs
paprika, garnish

Cook macaroni according to package directions. Drain macaroni and return to pot. Add tuna, soup, onions, milk, cheese, red pepper, and other seasonings. Mix thoroughly. Transfer to lightly greased 2-quart baking dish. Sprinkle with bread crumbs and paprika. Dot with butter. Bake at 350°F for 45 to 60 minutes, or until bubbling and lightly browned. Serves 4.

Nutritional analysis per serving: 744 cal, 0.1 g fiber, 30.7 g fat, 82.8 mg chol, 1919.5 mg sodium

Tuna-Noodle Casserole

1 can cream of celery soup
½ cup small early peas
½ cup chopped pimento
½ cup milk
1 6½-ounce can water-pack flaked tuna, drained
1 cup egg noodles, cooked
salt and pepper, to taste
1 cup grated sharp Cheddar

Heat celery soup, peas, pimento, and milk together. Remove from heat and add tuna, cooked noodles, salt, and pepper. Pour into greased 2-quart casserole. Bake in preheated 350°F oven for 25 minutes. Remove and sprinkle grated cheese over top. Continue cooking ten minutes or until brown. Serves 4.

Nutritional analysis per serving: 277 cal, 2 g fiber, 12 g fat, 56 mg chol, 638 mg sodium

Unfried Catfish √ ★

¼ cup cornmeal
1 teaspoon thyme
1 teaspoon basil
½ teaspoon lemon pepper
1½ teaspoon garlic powder
4 teaspoons creole seasoning
½ teaspoon paprika
4 4-ounce catfish fillets

Preheat oven to 400°F. Spray vegetable oil on baking sheet. Mix cornmeal, thyme, and basil. Sprinkle remaining seasonings lightly over catfish fillets. Roll fillets in cornmeal mixture. Place fillets on baking sheet and spray lightly with vegetable oil. Bake for 20 minutes at 400°F. Reduce heat to 350°F and bake about 5 minutes or until crust is golden brown. Serves 4.

Nutritional analysis per serving: 155 cal, 0 g fiber, 4 g fat, 105 mg chol, 38 mg sodium

DESSERTS

CAKES

Amalgamation Cake

4 cups sugar, divided
3 sticks (1½ cup) butter, at room
   temperature, divided
1 teaspoon vanilla extract
3¼ cups all-purpose flour,
   divided
½ teaspoon baking soda
1 cup milk
6 eggs, separated
½ teaspoon cream of tartar
1 cup chopped nuts
1 cup raisins

Preheat oven to 350°F. To make cake: Grease and lightly flour three 9-inch round cake pans. Cream 2 cups sugar and 1 stick butter. Beat in vanilla extract. Sift together 3 cups flour and baking soda. Alternately add flour and milk to creamed mixture while beating. Beat egg whites with cream of tartar until stiff peaks form. Fold egg whites into batter. Divide batter evenly among prepared pans and bake for 25 to 30 minutes, or until a toothpick inserted in the center comes out clean. Cool cake in pan for 15 minutes, then carefully turn onto wire rack to cool. Cool completely before filling. To make filling: Cream 2 sticks of butter and 2 cups of sugar together until fluffy. Add the flour to the creamed mixture while beating. Beat the egg yolks until light. Transfer creamed mixture and egg yolks to top of double boiler. Cook,

stirring constantly, until filling thickens. Cool. Stir in nuts and raisins. To complete cake: Put one layer on cake plate. Spread with a fifth of the filling. Continue with other layers. Frost with remaining filling. Serves 20.

Nutritional analysis per serving: 478 cal, 0 g fiber, 23.4 g fat, 83.4 mg chol, 191 mg sodium

Ann's Peter Paul Mound Cake

1 box devil's food cake mix, baked in
   a 9 × 13-inch pan according to
   package directions, warm
24 large marshmallows
1½ cups milk, divided
2½ cups sugar, divided
1 14-ounce package coconut
1 stick butter
1 12-ounce package of semisweet
   chocolate chips

To make coconut filling: In saucepan over medium heat, melt together marshmallows, 1 cup milk, 1 cup sugar, and coconut, stirring constantly. Keep warm. To make chocolate topping: In saucepan over medium-high heat, combine 1½ cups sugar, ½ cup milk, and butter. Boil for 1 minute. Remove from heat and add chocolate chips, stirring until melted. Spread coconut filling on warm cake. Spread chocolate topping on coconut filling. Allow cake to cool; refrigerate. Serves 12.

Nutritional analysis per serving: 675.3 cal, 0 g fiber, 36 g fat, 44 mg chol, 203.3 mg sodium

Apple Dapple Cake

3 eggs
1½ cups vegetable oil
2 cups sugar
2 teaspoons vanilla extract
3 cups all-purpose flour
1 teaspoon salt
1 teaspoon baking soda
1 teaspoon ground cinnamon
3 cups peeled, chopped apples
1 cup chopped pecans
1 cup brown sugar
¼ cup orange juice
1 stick (½ cup) margarine

Preheat oven to 350°F. Grease and lightly flour 10-inch tube cake pan. Combine eggs, oil, sugar, and vanilla extract. Beat until smooth. In separate bowl, sift together flour, salt, baking soda, and cinnamon. Add sifted mixture to egg mixture. Mix well. Stir in chopped apples and pecans. Pour batter evenly into prepared pan. Bake for 1 hour. Five minutes before cake is done prepare topping. Combine brown sugar, orange juice, and margarine in saucepan. Cook for 2½ minutes over low to medium heat, stirring constantly. Pour hot topping over hot cake. Remove cake from pan after it has completely cooled. Serves 12.

Nutritional analysis per serving: 789 cal, 0.62 g fiber, 49 g fat, 68.5 mg chol, 292.4 mg sodium

Apple Spice Cake

1 2-layer box spice cake mix
2 eggs
2 cups tart apples, peeled and chopped
1 14-ounce can condensed milk
½ cup sour cream
1 tablespoon lemon juice

Preheat oven to 350°F. Grease and lightly flour 9 × 13-inch baking pan. Mix cake according to directions on box. Fold apples into batter. Pour batter into prepared pan and bake for 30 minutes. While cake is baking, combine condensed milk, sour cream, and lemon juice, mixing well. Remove cake from oven. Poke small holes into cake with toothpick. Pour liquid mixture evenly over top of cake. Return cake to oven and bake for additional 10 minutes. Cool in pan. Serves 12.

Nutritional analysis per serving: 315.6 cal, 0.43 g fiber, 9.5 g fat, 20.9 mg chol, 210.2 mg sodium

Banana Pound Cake

1 box yellow cake mix
2 sticks (1 cup) margarine
½ cup sugar
5 large eggs
½ cup self-rising flour
1½ cups pecans, chopped
4 large bananas, well ripened

Preheat oven to 325°F. Grease and lightly flour 10-inch tube cake pan. In large mixing bowl, combine cake mix, margarine, sugar, and eggs. Mix well. Combine flour and pecans. Add to cake mixture. Add bananas. Beat until well blended. Pour batter into the prepared pan. Bake for 45 minutes, or until golden brown. Serves 12.

Nutritional analysis per serving: 647.6 cal, 0.53 g fiber, 43.4 g fat, 144.8 mg chol, 410.7 mg sodium

Basic Layer Cake

2 sticks (1 cup) margarine
2 cups sugar
5 large eggs
1 teaspoon vanilla extract
3 cups all-purpose flour
2 teaspoons baking powder
½ teaspoon salt
1 cup milk

Preheat oven to 350°F. Grease and lightly flour three 9-inch round layer cake pans. In mixing bowl, cream together margarine and sugar until light and fluffy. Add eggs 1 at a time, beating well after each addition. Add vanilla flavoring. Mix well. In a separate bowl, sift flour, baking powder, and salt. Add flour mixture alternating with milk to creamed mixture. Pour batter into prepared pans. Bake for

30 minutes or until done. Layers can be put together with chocolate or coconut frosting. Serves 12.

Nutritional analysis per serving: 424 cal, 0 g fiber, 18.5 g fat, 117 mg chol, 365 mg sodium

Blackberry Jam Cake √

Cake:
¾ cup butter
1 cup sugar
3 eggs, well beaten
1 cup blackberry jam
1 teaspoon baking soda
3 tablespoons buttermilk
1 teaspoon vanilla
1 teaspoon cinnamon
1 teaspoon allspice
3 cups flour
White boiled icing:
2 cups sugar
1⅓ cups water
2 egg whites
¼ teaspoon cream of tartar
1 teaspoon vanilla

For cake: Cream butter and sugar. Add eggs and jam. Stir soda into milk and add to other ingredients, along with vanilla. Add other seasonings sifted with flour. Bake in greased and floured layer pans at 350°F for about 20 minutes or until toothpick in center comes out clean. Use white boiled icing between layers and on top. For icing: Cook sugar and water until it spins threads when poured from the spoon. Beat egg whites until stiff, adding cream of tartar. Pour sugar-water syrup slowly over egg whites, beating constantly until thick. Add vanilla. (One cup coconut, finely grated, may be added if desired.) Serves 16.

Nutritional analysis per serving: 284 cal, 1 g fiber, 10 g fat, 51 mg chol, 148 mg sodium

Caramel Pound Cake

Cake:
2 sticks (1 cup) margarine, at room temperature
½ cup shortening

1 16-ounce (1 pound) box light brown sugar
1 cup granulated sugar
1½ teaspoons vanilla extract
5 eggs
3 cups all-purpose flour, sifted
1 teaspoon baking powder
1 cup milk
1 cup chopped pecans
Icing:
1 16-ounce (1 pound) box light brown sugar
2 tablespoons evaporated milk
1½ sticks (¾ cup) butter
¾ teaspoon baking powder

Preheat oven to 325°F. For cake: Grease and lightly flour 10-inch tube pan. Cream margarine, shortening, sugars, and vanilla extract in large mixing bowl until light and fluffy. Add eggs, 1 at a time, beating after each addition. In separate bowl, sift flour and baking powder together. Alternately add flour and milk, mixing after each addition. Stir in pecans. Pour batter into prepared pan. Bake at 325°F for 90 minutes. Allow cake to cool in pan for 15 minutes. Remove cake from pan and cool completely before icing. For icing: Combine sugar, milk, and butter in medium-sized saucepan. Bring to boil over medium heat. Boil mixture for 3 minutes. Remove from heat and add baking powder. If icing is too thick, add more milk. Serves 16.

Nutritional analysis per serving: 709.6 cal, 0 g fiber, 38 g fat, 112 mg chol, 271 mg sodium

Carolina Banana Nut Cake

1 cup shortening
3 cups sugar
5 eggs
2 teaspoons vanilla extract
3 cups self-rising flour
1 tablespoon cornstarch
¼ cup buttermilk
4 large bananas, mashed
1½ cups chopped nuts

Preheat oven to 300°F. Grease and lightly flour 10-inch tube pan. Cream shortening and sugar until light and fluffy. Add eggs, 1 at a time, beating after each addition. Beat in vanilla extract. Mix together flour and cornstarch. Alternately stir in flour and buttermilk. Mix in bananas and nuts. Spoon batter into prepared pan and bake 75 minutes, or until toothpick inserted in middle of cake comes out clean. Cool cake in pan for 10 minutes, then carefully turn onto wire rack right-side-up to cool completely. Serves 20.

Nutritional analysis per serving: 422.5 cal, 0.3 g fiber, 23 g fat, 68.6 mg chol, 340 mg sodium

Carrot Fig Cake

Puree:
2 cups dried figs
¾ cup water
2 teaspoons vanilla
Cake:
2 eggs
2 egg whites
2 cups flour
2 cups sugar
2 teaspoons baking powder
1½ teaspoons baking soda
1 teaspoon salt
1 teaspoon ground cinnamon
2 cups peeled and grated carrots
1 8-ounce can crushed pineapple, drained, with juice reserved
1 cup seedless raisins
1 cup powdered sugar, optional for glaze

For puree: Combine figs, water, and vanilla in blender or food processor and process until smooth; makes about 1½ cups (replaces 1½ cups oil). For cake: Lightly beat together eggs and egg whites in bowl. Sift together flour, sugar, baking powder, baking soda, salt, and cinnamon into mixing bowl. Stir to blend. Add pureed figs, beaten eggs, carrots, pineapple, and raisins. Stir until blended. Turn into 9 × 13-inch baking pan sprayed with nonstick vegetable cooking spray. Bake at 350°F 35 to 40 minutes or until cake tests done in center.

For optional glaze: blend together powdered sugar and 2 tablespoons reserved pineapple juice until smooth and of spreading consistency. Drizzle over cooled cake. Makes 24 servings.

Nutritional analysis per serving: 183 cal, 0.98 g fiber, 1 g fat, 18 mg chol, 150 mg sodium

Cheese Cake +

6¾ cups graham cracker crumbs
¾ cup sugar
1½ cups softened butter or margarine
3 pounds cream cheese
2½ quarts chilled milk
3 tablespoons lemon rind, grated
2 pounds instant vanilla pudding
4 tablespoons plain gelatin
½ cup cold water

Combine crumbs, sugar, and butter and mix well. Set aside ½ cup to sprinkle on top of cake. Press remainder into bottoms of four ½-inch springform cake pans or bottoms and sides of six 9-inch pie pans. Bake in moderate oven about 5 minutes. Cool. Soften cream cheese in mixer, using paddle, and blend in small amount of chilled milk. Scrape bowl; add rest of milk gradually, blending thoroughly. Add lemon rind. Insert whip. Add pie filling powder and whip at low speed until powder is dampened (about 15 seconds). Whip at medium speed until smooth (1 to 2 minutes). Soften plain gelatin in cold water. Dissolve in pan of hot water. Add to mixture. Pour at once into crumb-lined pans. Sprinkle with reserved crumbs. Chill until firm. Serves 50.

Nutritional analysis per serving: 268 cal, 0 g fiber, 18 g fat, 31 mg chol, 313 mg sodium

Cherry Pie Filling Cake

Cake:
1 cup margarine
1¾ cups sugar
3 large eggs
1 teaspoon vanilla extract
3 cups all-purpose flour
1½ teaspoons baking powder

1 15-ounce can cherry pie filling
Icing:
1 teaspoon margarine
2 cups confectioners sugar
½ teaspoon vanilla extract
2 tablespoons milk

Preheat oven to 350°F. For cake: Grease and lightly flour 9 × 13-inch pan. In large mixing bowl, combine margarine, sugar, eggs, vanilla, flour, and baking powder. Beat until well combined. Spoon ⅔ of batter into pan. Spread pie filling over batter. Dot with remaining batter. Bake for 25 to 30 minutes. Allow cake to cool before removing from pan. Drizzle icing over cooled cake. For icing: Cream margarine with sugar and vanilla extract. Add milk. Beat until icing is smooth and thin enough to drizzle. Add more milk, if needed. Serves 12.

Nutritional analysis per serving: 505.4 cal, 0 g fiber, 17.9 g fat, 91.6 mg chol, 252.3 mg sodium

Chocolate Chip Cake

½ cup margarine or butter, at room
    temperature
1 cup sugar
1 teaspoon vanilla extract
2 eggs
1 cup sour cream
2 cups all-purpose flour
¼ teaspoon salt
1 teaspoon baking powder
1 teaspoon baking soda
1 6-ounce package (1 cup) semisweet
    chocolate chips
½ cup chopped nuts

Preheat oven to 350°F. Grease and lightly flour 10-inch tube cake pan. Cream margarine and sugar until light and fluffy. Beat in vanilla extract, eggs, and sour cream. Sift together flour, salt, baking powder, and baking soda. Mix into creamed mixture. Stir in ¾ cup chocolate chips and nuts. Spoon batter into prepared cake pan. Sprinkle remaining chips over top. Bake for 45 minutes, or until toothpick

inserted into center comes out clean. Cool cake in pan for 10 minutes, then carefully turn onto wire rack right-side-up to cool completely. Serves 10.

Nutritional analysis per serving: 560 cal, 34.7 g fat, 65 mg chol, 223 mg sodium

Chocolate Layer Cake

Cake:
1⅔ cups self-rising flour
1 cup all-purpose flour
2 sticks (1 cup) margarine
1¾ cups sugar
4 large eggs
2¾ teaspoons vanilla extract
1 cup milk
Frosting:
1 stick (½ cup) plus 1 tablespoon
    margarine
2 tablespoons white corn syrup
¼ teaspoon salt
¾ teaspoon vanilla extract
½ cup plus 1 tablespoon cocoa
1 pound box plus ¾ cup sifted
    confectioners' sugar
½ cup evaporated milk

Preheat oven to 350°F. Grease and lightly flour five 9-inch round cake pans. Directions for cake: In mixing bowl, combine sifted flours. In separate bowl, cream margarine and sugar. Add eggs, 1 at a time, to creamed mixture. Beat well after each addition. Add vanilla and continue beating. Add flour, alternately with milk. Beat until ingredients are well mixed. Pour cake evenly into five prepared cake pans. Bake for 20 minutes or until top springs back when touched lightly. Cool cakes completely before frosting. Directions for frosting: In mixing bowl, cream margarine, corn syrup, salt, vanilla extract, and cocoa, using electric mixer on low speed. Gradually add sugar and milk to creamed mixture. Beat until mixture is smooth and creamy after each addition. Add enough milk to make consistency spreadable. Spread frosting between each layer, on top, and on sides of the five layers. Serves 12.

Nutritional analysis per serving: 664 cal, 0 g fiber, 28.3 g fat, 98.2 mg chol, 650 mg sodium

Chocolate Pound Cake

2 sticks (1 cup) butter or margarine, at room temperature
½ cup shortening
1 teaspoon vanilla extract
3 cups sugar
5 eggs
3 cups sifted cake flour
½ teaspoon baking powder
½ teaspoon salt
4 tablespoons cocoa
1 tablespoon instant coffee
1 cup milk

Preheat oven to 325°F. Grease and lightly flour 10-inch tube cake pan. Cream butter, shortening, and vanilla extract. Gradually beat in sugar. Add eggs, 1 at a time, beating after each addition. Sift dry ingredients together. Dissolve instant coffee in milk. Alternately add dry ingredients with milk to creamed mixture. Pour batter in prepared cake pan. Bake for 60 to 90 minutes, or until golden brown. Allow cake to cool before removing it from pan. Serves 12.

Nutritional analysis per serving: 572 cal, 0 g fiber, 27.3 g fat, 117.3 mg chol, 369.3 mg sodium

Chocolate Sheet Cake +

Cake:
2 cups sugar
2 sticks butter or margarine
1 cup water
1 teaspoon vanilla extract
1 teaspoon baking soda
2 cups cake flour
½ cup vegetable shortening
4 tablespoons cocoa
3 large eggs
½ cup buttermilk
Icing:
2–3 tablespoons cocoa
1 pound box confectioners' sugar

1 cup chopped nuts
1 stick (½ cup) butter, melted
1 teaspoon vanilla extract
milk, 1 tablespoon at a time

Preheat oven to 350°F. For cake: Grease jelly roll pan. In large mixing bowl, sift together sugar and flour. In saucepan, combine butter, shortening, water, and cocoa. Bring to rapid boil. Add boiled mixture to sifted ingredients. Beat eggs. Add vanilla to eggs. In small bowl, combine baking soda and buttermilk. Set aside for few minutes. Add buttermilk mixture to flour mixture. Add beaten eggs. Mix ingredients until well blended. Pour batter into prepared jelly roll pan. Bake for 35 to 40 minutes. Allow cake to cool in pan before removing. For icing: Combine ingredients for icing. Beat until thick and spreadable. Spread evenly over cake. Serves 48.

Nutritional analysis per serving: 171.6 cal, 0 g fiber, 9.6 g fat, 17.6 mg chol, 73.3 mg sodium

Cocoa Sponge Roll +

2¾ cups cake flour, sifted
1⅓ cups cocoa
1 cup sugar
1 tablespoon baking powder
1 teaspoon salt
20 eggs
3½ cups sugar
2 tablespoons vanilla
confectioners' sugar as necessary

Generously grease and flour 3 15 × 10-inch jelly roll pans. Line with wax paper, allowing paper to extend about 2 inches at each end; grease paper. Sift flour with cocoa, sugar, baking powder, and salt. Whip eggs at high speed until thick and light in color. Gradually add sugar, beating thoroughly after each addition. At low speed, gradually fold in flour mixture; blend in vanilla. Pour into pans, allowing about 1¼ pounds per pan. Bake at 350°F for 20 to 25 minutes or until cakes spring back when lightly pressed. Cool in pans 3 to 5 minutes; turn onto cloths which have been sprinkled lightly with confectioners' sugar. Quickly remove paper and trim crisp edges from cake. Roll up cakes in cloth. Cool on racks. Serves 24.

Nutritional analysis per serving: 263 cal, 1 g fiber, 5 g fat, 178 mg chol, 181 mg sodium

Cup Cakes

2 cups all-purpose flour
3 teaspoons baking powder
1 teaspoon salt
1¼ cups sugar
½ cup margarine
2 eggs
¾ cup milk
1 teaspoon vanilla extract

Preheat oven to 350°F. In large mixing bowl, combine sifted flour, baking powder, and salt. Stir in sugar. Blend in margarine. Mix well. Add eggs, milk, and vanilla. Beat for 2 minutes. Spoon batter into lined cup cake pan. Bake for 10 minutes, or until golden brown. Serves 24.

Nutritional analysis per serving: 127.3 cal, 0 g fiber, 5.1 g fat, 24 mg chol, 142 mg sodium

Dark Fruit Cake

1 pound (2 cups) butter, at room temperature
1 pound (2 cups) sugar
10 eggs
1¾ pounds (about 7 cups) sifted all-purpose flour
¾ pound citron, finely chopped
2 tablespoons grated orange peel
2 teaspoons cinnamon
1 teaspoon allspice
2 teaspoons baking powder
1 cup chopped pecans or almonds
3 pounds raisins
½ cup of wine combined with a pinch of baking soda

Generously grease large tube pan. In very large mixing bowl, cream butter and sugar. Add eggs, 1 at a time, beating after each addition. In separate bowl, combine flour, citron,

orange peel, cinnamon, allspice, and baking powder. Mix nuts and raisins in 1 cup of flour mixture. Add wine to raisin-nut mixture. Beat flour mixture into creamed mixture. Stir raisin-nut mixture into batter. Pour batter into prepared pan. Bake at 275°F for 3 to 3½ hours. Serves 20.

Nutritional analysis per serving: 612.5 cal, 0 g fiber, 27.4 g fat, 136.9 mg chol, 339.8 mg sodium

Fran's Applesauce Cake

1½ cups applesauce
2 teaspoons baking soda
1½ sticks (¾ cup) margarine, at room temperature, divided
1¾ cups sugar
2 eggs, beaten
2 cups all-purpose flour
1 cup chopped pecans
1 cup raisins
1 teaspoon cinnamon
1 teaspoon allspice
½ teaspoon salt
1 box (2 cups) confectioners' sugar
1 5.5-ounce can crushed pineapple, drained, with juice reserved

Preheat oven to 350°F. Grease and lightly flour three 8-inch round cake pans. In large saucepan, combine applesauce, baking soda, 1 stick margarine, sugar, eggs, flour, pecans, raisins, spices, and salt. Stir constantly to mix over low heat. Batter will be soft; do not add extra flour. Divide batter evenly among prepared pans. Bake for 25 to 30 minutes, or until toothpick inserted in center comes out clean. Cool layers in pans for 10 minutes, then turn onto wire racks to cool completely. After cake layers have cooled completely, make icing. Cream together remaining ½ stick margarine, confectioners' sugar, and crushed pineapple. Add juice to thin, if necessary. Spread icing evenly between layers and on top of cake. Do not ice sides. Serves 12.

Nutritional analysis per serving: 503 cal, 0.34 g fiber, 17.6 g fat, 45.6 mg chol, 152 mg sodium

Fresh Apple Cake

Cake:

2 cups sugar
1 cup vegetable oil
3 eggs
1 teaspoon vanilla extract
3 cups all-purpose flour
½ teaspoon baking powder
1 teaspoon baking soda
1 teaspoon salt
2 teaspoons cinnamon
3 cups peeled and chopped apples
1 cup chopped pecans
Frosting:
11 ounces cream cheese
¼ cup margarine
1 tablespoon vanilla extract
1½ boxes (1½ pounds) confectioners'
   sugar
1 cup chopped pecans

Preheat oven to 325°F. For cake: Grease and lightly flour four 9-inch round cake pans. In large mixing bowl, beat sugar, oil, eggs, and vanilla extract. In separate bowl, sift flour, baking powder, baking soda, salt, and cinnamon. Add flour mixture to creamed mixture. Beat until well mixed. Stir in chopped apples and pecans. Pour cake batter evenly among the four pans. Bake for 20 to 25 minutes, or until golden brown. For frosting: In mixing bowl, combine cream cheese and margarine. Mix until smooth. Add vanilla. Mix well. Gradually add sugar. Beat until frosting is smooth and spreadable. Frost cake between each layer, on top, and on sides. Sprinkle with chopped pecans. Serves 12.

Nutritional analysis per serving: 918.7 cal, 0.62 g fiber, 57.2 g fat, 96.6 mg chol, 331.6 mg sodium

Fresh Apple Cake

Cake:

2 cups all-purpose flour
1 teaspoon baking soda
¼ teaspoon cinnamon
2 cups sugar

2 cups apples, peeled and sliced thin
1 cup chopped pecans
1 tablespoon baking powder
¼ teaspoon salt
¾ cup margarine
2 large eggs
1 cup raisins or dates
Topping:
1 stick (½ cup) margarine, melted
2 egg yolks
milk
1 cup light brown sugar
1 cup nuts, chopped

Preheat oven to 350°F. For cake: Grease and lightly flour 9 × 13-inch baking pan. Combine flour, baking powder, baking soda, salt, and cinnamon. Mix well and set aside. In large mixing bowl, cream margarine and sugar. Add eggs, 1 at a time, to creamed mixture. Beat after each addition. Gradually add flour mixture. Mix until well blended. Stir in apples, raisins, and nuts. Batter will be thick. Pour batter evenly into prepared pan. Bake for 35 minutes. Remove cake from oven. For topping: In saucepan, combine ingredients for topping. Cook over low heat, stirring constantly, for 2 minutes. Add milk as needed to thin for a spreadable consistency. Spread hot topping on hot cake. Bake additional 10 minutes. Cool cake completely in pan. Serves 12.

Nutritional analysis per serving: 763. cal, 0.42 g fiber, 45.7 g fat, 91 mg chol, 394.8 mg sodium

Fruit Cake +

1 pound candied cherries, halved
1 pound candied pineapple, chopped
¼ pound candied citron, finely chopped
2 pounds white raisins
¼ pound lemon peel, finely chopped
¼ pound orange peel, finely chopped
8 cups chopped pecans
5 cups all-purpose flour
2 teaspoons baking powder
¾ pound butter, at room temperature
2 cups sugar
10 eggs

Grease and flour two 10-inch tube cake pans. Mix fruit and nuts in 1 cup of flour. In mixing bowl, sift together 4 remaining cups of flour and baking powder. In large mixing bowl, cream together butter and sugar. Add eggs, 1 at a time, to creamed mixture, beating well after each addition. Gradually add flour mixture to egg mixture. Stir fruits and nuts into batter. Divide batter evenly between the two pans and bake at 200°F for 90 minutes, or until golden brown. Cool cake in pan for fifteen minutes, then carefully turn onto wire rack right-side-up to cool completely. Serves 40.

Nutritional analysis per serving: 347 cal, 0 g fiber, 23.3 g fat, 87 mg chol, 117 mg sodium

Icebox Fruit Cake

1 pound marshmallows
1 pound graham crackers, crushed
4 cups pecans, chopped
2 cups black walnuts, chopped
1½ jars of cherries, chopped
1 10.5-ounce can evaporated milk

Melt marshmallows in double boiler over hot water. Add graham crackers, pecans, walnuts, cherries, and evaporated milk. Mix well. Pour mixture into lined tube cake pan. Allow cake to sit in refrigerator for 12 to 24 hours. Serves 10.

Nutritional analysis per serving: 860 cal, 0.06 g fiber, 74.5 g fat, 0.4 mg chol, 120.5 mg sodium

Ice Cream Cake

30 cookies, crushed (your choice)
½ cup margarine, melted
½ gallon ice cream (your choice)
1 12-ounce container nondairy whipped topping
½ cup shredded coconut, fresh or frozen
½ cup pecans, chopped
12 or more cherries

Combine cookies and margarine. Press mixture into bottom of 9 × 13-inch pan. Spread ice cream evenly on crumb mixture.

Top ice cream with nondairy whipped topping. Sprinkle coconut and pecans on whipped topping. Garnish with cherries. Place cake into freezer until ready to serve. Serves 16.

Nutritional analysis per serving: 338.5 cal, 0.02 g fiber, 25 g fat, 32.7 mg chol, 158.6 mg sodium

Jessie Irwin's Buttermilk Cake

2 sticks (1 cup) margarine, at room temperature
2 cups sugar
1 cup buttermilk
3 cups self-rising flour
3 eggs
1 teaspoon vanilla extract
1 teaspoon lemon extract
1 teaspoon almond extract

Preheat oven to 325°F. Grease and lightly flour 10-inch tube cake pan. In large mixing bowl, cream margarine and sugar until light and fluffy. Alternately add buttermilk and flour, beating well after each addition. Add eggs, 1 at a time, beating after each addition. Beat in extracts. Pour batter into prepared pan and bake for 60 to 75 minutes, or until toothpick inserted in center comes out clean. Cool cake in pan for 10 minutes, then carefully turn onto wire rack right-side-up to cool completely. Serves 12.

Nutritional analysis per serving: 393.3 cal, 0 g fiber, 17.1 g fat, 69.2 mg chol, 527.6 mg sodium

Lemon Buttermilk Pound Cake

Cake:
3 sticks of margarine
2 cups sugar
1 teaspoon lemon extract
4 large eggs
3½ cups all-purpose flour
½ teaspoon baking soda
½ teaspoon salt
1 cup buttermilk
Glaze:
1 tablespoon butter
2 tablespoons milk

½ confectioners' sugar
lemon juice

Preheat oven to 325°F. For cake: Grease and lightly flour 9-inch tube cake pan. Cream together margarine and sugar. Add lemon extract. Add eggs, 1 at a time, beating after each addition. In separate bowl, combine flour, baking soda, and salt. Add dry ingredients alternately with buttermilk to first mixture. Mix until well combined. Pour batter into prepared pan. Bake for 60 to 70 minutes, or until cake is golden brown. For glaze: In small bowl, combine butter, milk, and sugar. Blend until mixture is spreadable consistency. Flavor with lemon juice to your taste. Serves 12.

Nutritional analysis per serving: 549 cal, 0 g fiber, 26.3 g fat, 92.3 mg chol, 414.3 mg sodium

Lemon Pound Cake

1 cup shortening
1½ cups sugar
grated rind and juice of 1 lemon
6 eggs
1 teaspoon lemon extract
2 cups sifted cake flour

Preheat oven to 325°F. Grease and lightly flour 9-inch tube cake pan. Cream shortening, sugar, and lemon rind. Beat in lemon juice, 1 egg, and lemon extract. Beat in remaining eggs, 1 at a time, beating well after each addition. Gradually mix in flour. Pour batter into prepared pan. Bake for 75 minutes, or until golden brown. Cool for 10 to 15 minutes in pan, then turn onto wire rack to cool completely. Serves 12.

Nutritional analysis per serving: 346.3 cal, 0 g fiber, 20 g fat, 136.9 mg chol, 35.3 mg sodium

Low-Fat Lemon Poppy Seed Cake

Cake:
1 18.5-ounce package 97%-fat-free yellow cake mix
½ cup sugar
⅓ cup vegetable oil

¼ cup water
1 cup egg substitute
1 cup plain nonfat yogurt
3 tablespoons lemon juice
2 tablespoons poppy seeds
vegetable cooking spray
Lemon Glaze:
½ cup sifted powdered sugar
2 tablespoons lemon juice

For cake: Combine cake mix and sugar in large mixing bowl; add vegetable oil and next four ingredients. Beat for 6 minutes at medium speed with electric mixer. Stir in poppy seeds. Pour batter into 10-cup Bundt pan coated with cooking spray. Bake at 350°F for 40 minutes or until a wooden pick inserted in center of cake comes out clean. Cool in pan on a wire rack 10 minutes. Remove from pan; drizzle with lemon glaze. For glaze: Combine ingredients, stirring until smooth. Yield: ¼ cup. Cool glazed cake completely on wire rack. Serves 24.

Nutritional analysis per serving: 216 cal, 0.1 g fiber, 4.7 g fat, 0.2 mg chol, 168 mg sodium

Mama's Applesauce Cake

1 cup butter or margarine, at room temperature
2 cups brown sugar
4 cups all-purpose flour
4 teaspoons baking powder
1 teaspoon cloves
1 teaspoon cinnamon
1 teaspoon salt
1 cup milk
2 cups applesauce or apple butter
2 cups raisins

Preheat oven to 325°F. Grease and lightly flour 10-inch tube cake pan. In large mixing bowl, cream butter and sugar until light and fluffy. In separate bowl, combine flour, baking powder, cloves, cinnamon, and salt. Alternately add flour and milk to creamed mixture, beating well after each addition. Stir in applesauce and raisins until well blended. Bake for 75 minutes or until toothpick inserted in center comes out clean. Cool in pan for 10 minutes, then turn right-side-up onto wire rack to cool completely. Serves 12.

Nutritional analysis per serving: 529 cal, 0.32 g fiber, 16.5 g fat, 2.8 mg chol, 498.2 mg sodium

Miliette's Favorite Christmas Cake

½ pound (2 sticks) butter
1 stick (½ cup) margarine
2 cups sugar
6 eggs
4 cups cake flour
1 teaspoon baking powder
¼ teaspoon salt
½ pound candied cherries
½ pound candied pineapple
1 quart pecans, chopped
2 teaspoons vanilla extract
1 cup grape juice

Preheat oven to 250°F. Grease 10-inch tube cake pan with margarine and line with heavy brown paper. In large mixing bowl, cream butter, margarine, and sugar until light and fluffy. Add eggs, 1 at a time, beating after each addition. Sift together 3 cups flour, baking powder, and salt. Add flour mixture to creamed mixture. Mix well. Mix remaining flour with cherries, pineapple, nuts, and vanilla extract. Stir mixture into batter. Spoon batter onto paper. Bake at 250°F for 3 hours. Allow cake to cool in pan. Turn cake out from pan when slightly warm. When cake is cold, pour 1 cup of grape juice onto it. Serves 20.

Nutritional analysis per serving: 65 cal, 0 g fiber, 4.5 g fat, 10.7 mg chol, 21.5 mg sodium

1-2-3-4 Cake

3 cups all-purpose flour
1 tablespoon baking powder
¼ teaspoon salt
1 cup shortening or margarine, at room temperature
2 cups sugar
4 eggs, separated

1 teaspoon vanilla extract
1 cup milk

Preheat oven to 350°F. Grease and lightly flour three 9-inch round cake pans. In small mixing bowl, sift together flour, baking powder, and salt. Set aside. In large bowl, cream together shortening and sugar. Beat in egg yolks, 1 at a time, beating well after each addition. Beat in vanilla extract. Alternately add flour and milk while mixing. In separate bowl, beat egg whites until stiff but not dry. Fold egg whites into batter. Divide batter evenly among prepared pans and bake for 30 minutes or until toothpick inserted in center comes out clean. Cool cake layers in pan for 10 minutes, then carefully turn onto wire rack to cool completely. Assemble layers with favorite frosting. Serves 12.

Nutritional analysis per serving: 417.3 cal, 0 g fiber, 18.1 g fat, 94 mg chol, 344 mg sodium

Orange Juice Pound Cake

1 cup shortening
1¾ cups sugar
5 eggs
2 cups all-purpose flour
¼ teaspoon salt
¼ teaspoon baking powder
5 tablespoons orange juice

Preheat oven to 325°F. Grease and lightly flour 10-inch tube cake pan. Cream shortening and sugar until fluffy. Add eggs 1 at a time, beating well after each addition. Sift together flour, salt, and baking powder. Alternately add flour and orange juice to creamed mixture. Pour batter into prepared pan. Bake for 60 minutes, or until golden brown. Allow cake to cool completely in cake pan. Serves 12.

Nutritional analysis per serving: 377 cal, 0 g fiber, 19.6 g fat, 114 mg chol, 83 mg sodium

Pineapple Cake

2 cups all-purpose flour
2 teaspoons baking soda
2¼ cups sugar

2 eggs, beaten
1 15.5-ounce can crushed pineapple
½ cup chopped pecans
½ cup brown sugar
1 5-ounce can (⅔ cup) evaporated milk

Preheat oven to 350°F. Grease and lightly flour 9 × 13-inch baking pan. Sift together flour and baking soda. Add 1½ cups sugar. Mix well. Add eggs and pineapple to flour mixture. Mix until well combined. Pour batter into prepared pan. Sprinkle pecans and brown sugar over top of cake. Bake for 30 to 35 minutes, or until lightly browned. In saucepan, combine remaining ¾ cup sugar and evaporated milk. Bring to boil. Poke holes in warm cake with toothpick or fork and pour hot milk and sugar mixture over cake. Cool completely in pan before cutting into squares. Store in refrigerator. Serves 12.

Nutritional analysis per serving: 367 cal, 0.3 g fiber, 8.9 g fat, 51.8 mg chol, 37.8 mg sodium

Pineapple Layer Cake √ ★

Cake:
1 cup shortening
2 cups sugar
4 eggs
3 cups all-purpose flour
2 teaspoons baking powder
1 teaspoon salt
1 cup milk
1 teaspoon vanilla
½ teaspoon almond extract
1 teaspoon lemon juice
Pineapple Filling:
4 tablespoons flour
1 cup sugar
dash salt
2 cups crushed pineapple
White Icing:
1 box confectioners' sugar
1 teaspoon vanilla
1 stick margarine, softened
2 tablespoons milk

For cake: Cream shortening; gradually add sugar, creaming until light. One at a time, add beaten eggs and beat well. Measure 3 cups of sifted flour and sift again with baking powder and salt. Add flour alternately with milk. Stir in flavorings. Pour into three greased and floured layer pans and bake at 375°F for 20–25 minutes. For filling: Mix flour, sugar, and salt in a saucepan. Stir in pineapple. Bring to a boil and let boil until thick. Let cool. For icing: Beat sugar, vanilla, and margarine together, adding milk until of spreading consistency. To assemble cake, spread filling over first layer, add second layer, filling, and top with third layer. Spread white icing over top and sides of cake. Better if made day ahead and flavors are allowed to develop. Serves 16.

Nutritional analysis per serving: 522 cal, 1 g fiber, 20 g fat, 54 mg chol, 259 mg sodium

Pineapple Pound Cake

1 cup butter or margarine
½ cup vegetable shortening
2¾ cups sugar
6 large eggs
3 cups all-purpose flour
1 teaspoon baking powder
¼ cup milk
¾ cup crushed pineapple and juice
1 tablespoon pineapple extract
1 teaspoon vanilla extract

Grease and lightly flour 10-inch tube cake pan. In large mixing bowl, cream butter, shortening, and sugar until light and fluffy. Add eggs, 1 at a time. Mix well after each addition. In separate small bowl, sift together flour and baking powder. Add flour to creamed mixture alternately with milk. Add crushed pineapple and extracts. Pour batter into prepared pan. Place cake into cold oven. Bake at 325°F for 1 hour and 10 minutes, or until cake tests done when toothpick inserted into center of cake comes out clean. Allow cake to completely cool on wire rack. Serves 12.

Nutritional analysis per serving: 554 cal, 0.12 g fiber, 27 g fat, 137.6 mg chol, 245.7 mg sodium

Pineapple Upside Down Cake

10 tablespoons butter or margarine, at
    room temperature, divided
1 cup sugar
2 large eggs, separated
1 teaspoon vanilla extract
2 cups all-purpose flour
2 teaspoons baking powder
¼ teaspoon salt
½ cup milk
1 20-ounce can sliced pineapple
1 16-ounce bottle maraschino cherries
1 cup light brown sugar

In mixing bowl, cream together ½ cup (8 tablespoons) of butter, sugar, egg yolks, and vanilla extract. Sift together flour, baking powder, and salt. Alternately add flour mixture and milk to creamed mixture. Beat egg whites until stiff. Fold into creamed mixture. Melt 2 tablespoons of butter or margarine in 10-inch oven-proof skillet. Once butter has melted, spread it evenly in pan. Cover skillet bottom with one layer of pineapple rings. Place cherry in center of each pineapple ring. Sprinkle evenly with brown sugar. Pour cake batter over pineapple slices. Bake at 375°F for 25 minutes, or until golden brown. Cool in pan for about 10 minutes. Then turn out onto serving plate fruit-side up. Serves 12.

Nutritional analysis per serving: 340 cal, 0.5 fiber, 11 g fat, 47 mg chol, 236.3 mg sodium

Pound Cake

2 cups sugar
1 cup butter, at room temperature
5 eggs
½ teaspoon vanilla extract
½ teaspoon lemon extract
2 cups sifted cake flour

Preheat oven to 300°F. Grease 10-inch tube cake pan and line with waxed paper. In large mixing bowl, cream sugar and butter until light and fluffy (consistency of whipped cream). Add eggs, 1 at a time, beating 2 minutes after each addition. Add vanilla and

lemon extracts. Mix well. Gradually add flour while beating. Pour batter into prepared pan. Bake for 80 minutes, or until toothpick inserted in center comes out clean. Cool cake in pan for 10 minutes, then carefully turn onto wire rack right-side-up to cool completely. Serves 12.

Nutritional analysis per serving: 442 cal, 0 g fiber, 21.4 g fat, 186.6 mg chol, 223 mg sodium

Pound Cake Squares

3 sticks (1½ cups) butter, at room
    temperature
¾ cup shortening
4½ cups sugar
8 eggs
1½ teaspoons lemon or vanilla extract
5½ cups sifted cake flour
1½ teaspoons baking powder
¾ teaspoon salt
1½ cups milk

Preheat oven to 325°F. Lightly grease one 12 × 18 × 2-inch or two 9 × 13 × 2-inch baking pans with shortening or nonstick cooking spray. In large mixing bowl, cream butter, shortening, and sugar until fluffy. Add eggs, 1 at a time, beating well after each addition. Beat in desired extract. In separate bowl, sift together dry ingredients. Alternately add dry ingredients and milk to creamed mixture. Pour batter into pan(s) and bake for 50–60 minutes, or until toothpick inserted in center comes out clean. Cool completely in pan before cutting into squares. Serves 36.

Nutritional analysis per serving: 291 cal, 0 g fiber, 14 g fat, 83 mg chol, 156.5 g sodium

Pumpkin Cake with Cream Cheese Frosting

2 cups sugar
1¼ cups cooking oil
2 cups pumpkin, cooked or canned
4 eggs
2 cups all-purpose flour
1 teaspoon salt

2 teaspoons baking powder
2 teaspoons baking soda
2 teaspoons cinnamon
1 cup chopped pecans, divided
1 cup shredded coconut, divided
1 stick margarine, room temperature
8 ounces cream cheese, room
    temperature
½ teaspoon vanilla extract
1 pound (3½ cups) confectioners' sugar

Preheat oven to 350°F. Grease and lightly flour 9 × 13-inch pan. In large mixing bowl, combine sugar, oil, pumpkin, and eggs. Beat well. In separate bowl, sift together remaining dry ingredients. Add dry ingredients to pumpkin mixture. Stir in half of nuts and coconut. Pour batter into prepared pan and bake for 35 minutes or until toothpick inserted in center of cake comes out clean. Cool cake in pan. When cake is completely cool, beat margarine, cream cheese, and vanilla extract together. Gradually beat in confectioners' sugar. Stir in remaining nuts and coconut. Spread icing evenly on cake. Serves 12.

Nutritional analysis per serving: 853 cal, 0 g fiber, 54 g fat, 112 mg chol, 518.3 mg sodium

Russian Cake

2 cups sugar
2 eggs
2 cups all-purpose flour
2 teaspoons baking soda
1 20-ounce can crushed pineapple and
    juice
2 teaspoons vanilla extract, divided
½ cup chopped nuts
1 stick (½ cup) butter, at room
    temperature
8 ounces cream cheese, at room
    temperature
1 cup confectioners' sugar

Preheat oven to 350°F. Grease and lightly flour 9 × 13-inch pan. In large mixing bowl, combine sugar, eggs, flour, baking soda, pineapple with juice, and 1 teaspoon vanilla ex-

tract. Mix thoroughly. Stir in nuts. Spoon batter into prepared pan. Bake for 35 to 45 minutes, or until toothpick inserted in center comes out clean. Allow cake to cool in pan before removing. When cake is cool, cream together butter and cream cheese. Add 1 teaspoon vanilla extract. Gradually beat in confectioners' sugar. Beat until frosting peaks. Spread frosting evenly on cooled cake. Serves 12.

Nutritional analysis per serving: 482.5 cal, 0.4 g fiber, 21.4 g fat, 66 mg chol, 157.3 mg sodium

Sour Cream Cake

2 sticks (1 cup) butter, at room
    temperature
2¾ cups sugar
6 eggs
8 ounces sour cream
1 teaspoon vanilla extract
2 teaspoon lemon extract
3 cups all-purpose flour
½ teaspoon salt
¼ teaspoon baking powder

Preheat oven to 350°F. Grease and flour 10-inch tube cake pan. In large mixing bowl, cream butter and sugar until light and fluffy (consistency of whipped cream). Add eggs, 1 at a time, beating 2 minutes after each addition. Add sour cream and vanilla and lemon extracts. Mix well. Sift flour, salt, and baking powder together. Gradually add flour while beating. Pour batter into prepared pan. Bake for 75 to 80 minutes, or until toothpick inserted in center comes out clean. Cool cake in pan for 10 minutes, then carefully turn onto wire rack right-side-up to cool completely. Serves 10.

Nutritional analysis per serving: 687.2 cal, 0 g fiber, 36 g fat, 174.5 mg chol, 578 mg sodium

Spiced Apple Pound Cake

Cake:
2¼ cups all-purpose flour
½ teaspoon salt
1 teaspoon vanilla extract

3 large eggs
2 cups sugar
½ teaspoon baking soda
1 cup butter or margarine, softened
1 8-ounce container spiced apple yogurt
Glaze:
1 cup confectioners' sugar
2 tablespoons milk
1 teaspoon cinnamon
1 cup pecans, chopped

Preheat oven to 325°F. Grease and lightly flour 10-inch Bundt pan. For cake: In large mixing bowl, combine all ingredients for cake. Mix on low speed. Beat at medium speed for 3 minutes, scraping bowl occasionally. Pour batter into prepared pan. Bake for 60 to 65 minutes or until cake tests done when toothpick is inserted in center and comes out clean. Allow cake to cool for 15 minutes before removing from pan. For glaze: In small mixing bowl, combine sugar, milk, and cinnamon. Beat until smooth. Drizzle glaze over cooled cake. Sprinkle with pecans. Serves 12.

Nutritional analysis per serving: 554 cal, 0 g fiber, 29.4 g fat, 69.6 mg chol, 298 mg sodium

Strawberry Cake

1 4-serving package strawberry gelatin
4 eggs
¾ cup water
1 2-layer package yellow cake mix
¾ cup cooking oil
1 teaspoon vanilla extract
2 tablespoons butter or margarine, at room temperature
1 10-ounce box frozen strawberries, thawed
2 cups confectioners' sugar

Preheat oven to 350°F. Grease and lightly flour 10-inch tube cake pan. Combine gelatin, eggs, water, yellow cake mix, cooking oil, and vanilla extract. Beat for 2 minutes. Spoon batter into prepared pan. Bake for 1 hour. Allow cake to cool in pan 10 to 15 minutes before removing it. After removing cake from oven, combine butter, strawberries, and confectioners' sugar. Mix well. Pour over warm cake as frosting. Serves 10.

Nutritional analysis per serving: 574.4 cal, 0 g fiber, 29.5 g fat, 146.4 mg chol, 257.9 mg sodium

Whipped Cream Pound Cake

1 cup vegetable shortening
3 cups sugar
6 eggs
1 tablespoon lemon juice, fresh or bottled
3 cups all-purpose flour
½ pint whipping cream
1 tablespoon butternut flavoring

Preheat oven to 300°F. Grease and lightly flour 10-inch tube pan. In mixing bowl, cream vegetable shortening and sugar. Add eggs, 1 at a time, beating well after each addition. Add lemon juice and 1 cup of the flour. Continue to beat until well mixed. Add whipping cream, remaining flour, and butternut flavoring. Beat until well mixed. Pour batter into prepared pan. Bake at 300°F for 1 to 1½ hours. Serves 10.

Nutritional analysis per serving: 669.6 cal, 0 g fiber, 31.6 g fat, 202.3 mg chol, 51.4 mg sodium

Yam Coffee Cake √

Cake:
2 cups sifted flour
1½ teaspoons baking soda
¾ teaspoons salt
1 cup raisins
1 cup pecans
½ cup soft shortening
¼ teaspoon cinnamon
¼ teaspoon ground cloves
¼ teaspoon nutmeg
¼ teaspoon allspice
2 tablespoons cocoa
1½ cups sugar
2 eggs, unbeaten
1 No. 2 can yams
¼ cup orange juice

Frosting:
¾ cup sifted confectioners' sugar
1 tablespoon orange juice

Preheat oven to 350°F. Spray vegetable oil in a Bundt pan. Sift flour, soda, and salt. Toss 2 tablespoons flour mixture with raisins and pecans. In large bowl, cream shortening, cinnamon, cloves, nutmeg, allspice, and cocoa. Gradually add sugar, beating until fluffy. Add eggs, one at a time, beating well after each addition. At low speed, or blend, alternately add flour mixture, yams, and orange juice. Stir in pecan mixture. Pour into baking pan. Bake about 1 hour. Remove from oven and cool. Combine confectioners' sugar and orange juice. When cake is cool, drizzle frosting on top, letting some run down sides. Looks nice on platter with orange slices around bottom of cake. Serves 12.

Nutritional analysis per serving: 393 cal, 2 g fiber, 16 g fat, 36 mg chol, 252 mg sodium

CANDIES

Candy Pecans

    1 large egg white
    ¾ cup brown sugar
    ½ teaspoon vanilla
    2 cups pecan halves

Beat egg white until stiff. Gradually add brown sugar and vanilla. Fold in pecan halves and coat well. Separate pecan halves and place on lightly greased cookie sheet. Bake at 250°F for 20 minutes. Turn off oven and allow pecans to sit for 30 minutes. Store in airtight container. Pecans can be stored in refrigerator for long storage. Serves 60.

Nutritional analysis per serving: 57 cal, 0 g fiber, 4.9 g fat, 0 mg chol, 1.5 mg sodium

Chocolate Fudge

    3 cups sugar
    ½ cup light corn syrup
    1 cup evaporated milk
    3 1-ounce squares unsweetened
       chocolate

    4 tablespoons butter or margarine
    1 teaspoon vanilla extract
    1 cup chopped nuts

In large saucepan, combine sugar, corn syrup, milk, and chocolate. Stir constantly over low heat until sugar is dissolved. Increase heat slightly and cook, stirring frequently, until drop of candy forms soft ball in cold water or until candy thermometer reaches soft-ball stage (238–240°F). Remove from heat, add butter, and let stand until candy is warm, not hot. You should be able to rest hand comfortably on bottom of pan. Add vanilla and beat until firm and no longer glossy. Stir in nuts. Spread into buttered 5 × 9-inch pan. Cool thoroughly before cutting into squares. Serves 45.

Nutritional analysis per serving: 121.2 cal, 0 g fiber, 5.7 g fat, 1.6 mg chol, 21 mg sodium

English Toffee

    2 sticks (1 cup) butter
    1 cup brown sugar, packed
    1 box saltine crackers
    12 ounces (2 cups) semisweet chocolate
       chips
    1 cup chopped pecans

Preheat oven to 350°F. In saucepan, boil butter and brown sugar for 5 minutes, stirring constantly. Line 9 × 13-inch pan with foil. Line pan with saltine crackers, so they are close together without overlapping. Pour boiled mixture over saltines, spreading evenly with spoon. Bake for 5 to 7 minutes. When mixture begins to bubble, remove it from oven. Pour chocolate chips evenly over mixture and spread to cover surface. Sprinkle top with pecans. Put candy in refrigerator to cool. Peel off foil when candy is hard and break into chunks. Serves 48 1-inch pieces.

Nutritional analysis per serving: 142 cal, 0 g fiber, 9 g fat, 10.3 mg chol, 143.7 mg sodium

Minted Nuts

    1½ cups sugar
    ½ cup milk
    1 tablespoon white corn syrup

4 drops oil of peppermint
2½ cups pecan halves

Combine sugar, milk, and corn syrup in saucepan. Cook, stirring frequently, until mixture reaches 238°F on candy thermometer. Add oil of peppermint and pecan halves. Mix until creamy. Spread nuts on waxed paper and separate into individual halves. Store in airtight container. Serves 75.

Nutritional analysis per serving: 67 cal, 0 g fiber, 5 g fat, 0.2 mg chol, 1.1 mg sodium

Old-Fashioned Fudge

4 tablespoons cocoa
2 cups sugar
1 cup milk
1 tablespoon light corn syrup
¼ teaspoon salt
2 tablespoons butter
1 teaspoon vanilla extract
½ cup chopped nuts

In large saucepan, combine cocoa, sugar, milk, corn syrup, and salt. Stir constantly over low heat until sugar is dissolved. Increase heat slightly and cook, stirring frequently, until drop of candy forms soft ball in cold water or until candy reaches 238–240°F on candy thermometer. Remove from heat, add butter, and let stand until candy is warm, not hot. You should be able to rest hand comfortably on bottom of pan. Add vanilla and beat until firm and no longer glossy. Stir in nuts. Spread into buttered 5 × 9-inch pan. Cool thoroughly before cutting. Serves 45.

Nutritional analysis per serving: 65 cal, 0 g fiber, 2.4 g fat, 2.3 mg chol, 26.8 mg sodium

Peanut Brittle Deluxe

2 cups sugar
1 cup dark corn syrup
¼ cup water
1½ cups salted peanuts
2 tablespoons butter
1 teaspoon vanilla
2 teaspoons baking soda

In 3-quart saucepan combine sugar, corn syrup, and water. Mix well. Cook over medium heat, stirring constantly, until candy reaches 285°F (light-crack stage) on candy thermometer. Add peanuts and butter. Continue stirring until candy reaches 295°F (hard-crack stage) on thermometer. Remove candy from heat. Add vanilla and baking soda. Stir until well mixed. Pour mixture onto well-oiled cookie sheet and spread out as thin as possible. Be sure to work fast, before brittle begins to set. Loosen from side of pan, flip brittle over, and pull at it until very thin. When cold, break into pieces. Serves 32.

Nutritional analysis per serving: 124.6 cal, 0 g fiber, 4.2 g fat, 2.1 mg chol, 70.5 mg sodium

Pecan Pralines √

1 cup brown sugar
1 cup white sugar
½ cup light cream
2 tablespoons butter
1 cup pecan halves

Dissolve sugars in cream and boil to thread test (228°F), stirring occasionally. Add butter and pecans and cook until syrup reaches soft-ball test (236°F). Cool; beat until thickened, but not until it loses its gloss. Drop by tablespoonfuls onto greased marble slab or on double thicknesses of waxed paper. Candy will flatten out into large cakes. Serves 12.

Nutritional analysis per serving: 222 cal, 1 g fiber, 11 g fat, 14 mg chol, 26 mg sodium

Pulled Molasses Taffy

2 cups molasses
¼ cup butter
1 cup sugar (optional)

Cook all ingredients slowly to 265°F or until hard ball is formed. Pour onto greased platter and let cool until dent is left when pressed with finger. Gather into lump and pull with tips of fingers until very light and porous. Break into desired size pieces. Nuts, benne seeds, or any flavoring may be added while pulling. Adding a few drops of peppermint makes a pleasing flavor. Serves 48.

Nutritional analysis per serving: 60.5 cal, 0 g fiber, 0.96 mg fat, 2.59 mg chol, 11.9 mg sodium

Sewing Candy

2 cups sugar
⅔ cup light corn syrup
1 cup water
¼ teaspoon oil of cinnamon or wintergreen
red or green food coloring
1 pound confectioners' sugar

In saucepan, combine sugar, corn syrup, and water. Cook over medium heat, stirring constantly, until sugar dissolves. Cook without stirring until mixture reaches 300°F on candy thermometer (hard-ball stage). Add flavored oil and food coloring. Mix well. Prepare two cookie sheets by sprinkling even layer of confectioners' sugar on them. Draw tunnels with your finger into sugar. Pour candy into tunnels. Cut into 1-inch pieces with scissors.

Nutritional analysis per serving: 60.2 cal, 0 g fiber, 0 g fat, 0 mg chol, 4.2 mg sodium

COOKIES

Angel Kisses

1 cup granulated sugar
3 egg whites, stiffly beaten
1 teaspoon vanilla extract
1 cup pecans, finely chopped

Fold sugar gently and gradually into stiffly beaten egg whites. Fold in chopped nuts and vanilla. Drop by tablespoonsful onto baking sheet covered with aluminum foil. Bake in 350°F oven for 20 to 30 minutes. Serves 36.

Nutritional analysis per serving: 42 cal, 0 g fiber, 2.0 g fat, 0 mg chol, 4 mg sodium

Black Walnut Oatmeal Cookies

1 cup all-purpose flour
½ cup old-fashioned oatmeal
½ cup sugar

¼ cup margarine, room temperature
1 egg
⅓ cup skim milk
¼ cup chopped black walnuts
1 teaspoon black walnut extract

Preheat oven to 350°F. In large mixing bowl, combine flour, oatmeal, and sugar. Add margarine, egg, and skim milk. Stir until well combined. Add walnuts and extract. Drop by teaspoonfuls onto greased cookie sheet. Bake for 10 minutes, or until golden brown on bottom of cookie. Allow cookies to cool completely on wire rack before storing. Serves 24.

Nutritional analysis per serving: 68 cal, 0 g fiber, 3 g fat, 11.5 mg chol, 35 mg sodium

Brownies

2 1-ounce squares unsweetened chocolate
½ cup margarine
2 eggs
1 cup sugar
1 teaspoon vanilla extract
½ cup sifted all-purpose flour
⅛ teaspoon salt
¾ cup chopped nuts

Preheat oven to 350°F. Grease 8-inch square baking pan. In saucepan, melt chocolate and margarine over low heat. Cool completely. In mixing bowl, beat eggs. Gradually add sugar until fluffy and thick. Stir in chocolate and vanilla extract. Stir in flour, salt, and nuts. Bake for 30 minutes. Cool completely before cutting into squares. Serves 9.

Nutritional analysis per serving: 373 cal, 0 g fiber, 27 g fat, 61 mg chol, 164.6 mg sodium

Butter Cookies +

3 sticks butter
1 cup sugar
4 cups flour
1 egg, unbeaten
1 teaspoon vanilla

Cream butter and sugar. Add flour gradually. Add egg and vanilla. Roll into logs on waxed paper. Chill or freeze. Cut in thin slices and bake at 350°F for 10 minutes or until light brown. Serves 80.

Nutritional analysis per serving: 53 cal, 0 g fiber, 2 g fat, 9 mg chol, 24 mg sodium

Butter Fingers

1 cup butter, room temperature
5 tablespoons powdered sugar
2 cups all-purpose flour
1 teaspoon vanilla extract
1 cup chopped nuts
½ cup confectioners' sugar

Preheat oven to 350°F. In large mixing bowl, cream butter and sugar until smooth. Gradually add flour until soft dough forms. Add vanilla extract and nuts. Roll dough into shape of fingers. Place dough on ungreased cookie sheet. Bake for 15 minutes or until light brown. Cool and roll cookies in confectioners' sugar. Serves 36.

Nutritional analysis per serving: 116 cal, 0 g fiber, 9.3 g fat, 13.8 chol, 52.3 mg sodium

Butterscotch Bars +

3 pounds sifted flour
1 ounce salt
1 ounce baking powder
2 pounds shortening
3 pounds brown sugar, packed
4 teaspoons vanilla
1 quart milk
4½ quarts rolled oats
2 cups dry coconut, shredded
powdered sugar

Sift together flour, salt, and baking powder into mixer bowl. Add shortening, sugar, vanilla, and milk. Mix until smooth, about 2 minutes on low speed. Add oats and coconut; mix only until blended. Spread ½-inch thick on two greased baking sheets and bake at 350°F for 25 to 30 minutes. Cut into bars while warm; cool and remove from pan. Sprinkle with powdered sugar. Note: shortening must be at room temperature in order to blend easily with other ingredients. Serves 100.

Nutritional analysis per serving: 244 cal, 1 g fiber 10 g fat, 0 mg chol, 140 mg sodium

Chinese Chewies

1 stick (½ cup) margarine
1 16-ounce box light brown sugar
2 eggs, beaten
2 cups self-rising flour
1 teaspoon vanilla extract
1 cup chopped pecans

Preheat oven to 350°F. Lightly grease a 9 × 13-inch baking pan. In saucepan, melt margarine. Remove from heat. Add brown sugar, eggs, flour, vanilla extract, and nuts. Mix until well blended. Pour batter into prepared pan. Bake for 25 to 30 minutes. Cool before cutting into squares. Serves 24.

Nutritional analysis per serving: 167 cal, 0 g fiber, 7.4 g fat, 22.8 mg chol, 167.6 mg sodium

Chocolate Marble Cookies

½ cup oil
4 squares unsweetened chocolate, melted
1 cup sugar
2 teaspoons vanilla
4 eggs
2 cups flour
2 teaspoons baking powder
¼ teaspoon salt
powdered sugar

Combine oil, chocolate squares, sugar, and vanilla. Beat in eggs, 1 at a time. Add flour, baking powder, and salt. Chill well, form balls, and roll in sifted powdered sugar to cover well. Place on ungreased cookie sheet and bake 12 to 15 minutes in 350°F oven. Serves 36.

Nutritional analysis per serving: 97 cal, 0 g fiber, 5 g fat, 24 mg chol, 22 mg sodium

Cloud Cookies

1½ cups margarine, at room temperature
1 cup brown sugar
1 cup sugar

2 eggs
2 teaspoons vanilla extract
3 cups all-purpose flour
2 teaspoons cream of tartar
2 teaspoons baking soda

Preheat oven to 350°F. Combine all ingredients in large bowl, mixing well. Drop by teaspoonfuls onto ungreased baking sheet. Bake for 8 to 10 minutes. Serves 84.

Nutritional analysis per serving: 66.2 cal, 0 g fiber, 3.5 g fat, 6.5 mg chol, 45.6 mg sodium

Coconut-Nut Bars

⅓ cup margarine, room temperature
2 tablespoons confectioners' sugar
1 cup plus 2 tablespoons all-purpose flour
2 eggs, beaten
1¼ cups light brown sugar
1 teaspoon vanilla extract
½ teaspoon salt
¼ teaspoon baking powder
½ cup shredded coconut
1 cup chopped nuts

Preheat oven to 350°F. Grease and lightly flour 8-inch square pan. Cream margarine. Add confectioners' sugar and 1 cup of flour, mixing until smooth. Pat mixture evenly into pan and bake for 15 minutes. Beat eggs with sugar and vanilla extract. Mix together remaining 2 tablespoons of flour, salt, and baking powder. Gradually add flour mixture to egg mixture, mixing well. Stir in coconut and nuts. Spread batter evenly over pastry-lined pan. Bake for 25 minutes. Cool in pan. Cut into 1-inch by 4-inch bars. Serves 12.

Nutritional analysis per serving: 221 cal, 0 g fiber, 13.2 g fat, 45.6 mg chol, 175 mg sodium

Forgotten Kisses

4 egg whites
1½ cups sugar
1 12-ounce package chocolate chips, or 1 6-ounce package for milder flavor

Heat oven to 350°F. Beat egg whites until stiff. Add sugar gradually, beating until they hold peaks. Add chocolate chips to egg whites and mix in well. Drop by teaspoonsful onto wax paper–lined cookie sheet. Place in oven. Turn off oven. When oven is cool, cookies are done. Serves 60.

Nutritional analysis per serving: 45 cal, 0 g fiber, 1.6 g fat, 0 mg chol, 3.8 mg sodium

Fruit Balls ★

½ cup dates, pitted
½ cup apricots, dried
½ cup raisins
½ cup walnuts
½ teaspoon lemon rind, grated
½ teaspoon orange rind, grated
confectioners' sugar, optional

Put dates, apricots, raisins, and walnuts through food chopper, using medium-coarse cutter. Add lemon and orange rinds and blend thoroughly. Shape into small balls; coat with confectioners' sugar if desired. Serves 24.

Nutritional analysis per serving: 41 cal, 0 g fiber, 1.5 g fat, 0 mg chol, 1.0 mg sodium

Ginger Snaps

¾ cup margarine
1 cup sugar
1 egg, slightly whipped
¼ cup molasses
2½ cups flour
2 teaspoons baking soda
1 teaspoon cinnamon
1 teaspoon ginger

Preheat oven to 350°F. Cream margarine and sugar. Beat in egg and molasses. Sift flour with soda and spices and mix with wet ingredients. Chill dough. Roll dough to ⅛-inch thickness on lightly floured board. Cut out with seasonal cookie cutters. Bake 8 to 10 minutes at 350°F. Decorate, if desired. Makes 3 to 4 dozen cookies depending on size of cookie cutter. Dough may be rolled into walnut-size balls, dipped into sugar, and baked for an old-fashioned ginger snap. Serves 36.

Nutritional analysis per serving: 93.9 cal, 0.27 g fiber, 4.0 g fat, 5.9 mg chol, 98.7 mg sodium

Graham Cracker Delights

Cookies:
2 sticks margarine
1 cup sugar
1 egg, beaten
½ cup milk
1 cup graham cracker crumbs, crushed
1 cup shredded coconut
1 cup chopped nuts
1 box graham crackers
Icing:
2 cups 4X confectioners' sugar
6 tablespoons margarine
milk, as needed

In saucepan, bring 2 sticks margarine, sugar, egg, and milk to boil. Remove from heat. Stir in crushed graham crackers, coconut, and nuts. Place layer of whole graham crackers on cookie sheet. Spread filling on crackers. Place another layer of crackers over top of filling. Icing: In small saucepan, combine 4X sugar and 6 tablespoons margarine. Cook over low heat, stirring until margarine melts. Add only enough milk to make consistency smooth and spreadable. Smooth icing over top of crackers. Place cookie sheet in refrigerator to cool before cutting. Serves 72.

Nutritional analysis per serving: 118.4 cal, 0 g fiber, 6.7 g fat, 4 mg chol, 91 mg sodium

Hello Dollies

1 cup butter or margarine
1 cup graham cracker crumbs
1 cup shredded coconut
1 cup chopped walnuts or pecans
1 cup (6 ounces) chocolate chips
1 cup sweetened condensed milk

Preheat oven to 350°F. Melt butter and pour it into 9 × 13 × 2-inch baking pan. Sprinkle graham cracker crumbs, coconut, nuts, and chocolate chips evenly over butter

(in order given). Pour condensed milk over top. Bake for 25 minutes, or until light brown. Cool completely before cutting into squares. Serves 60.

Nutritional analysis per serving: 82 cal, 0 g fiber, 6.3 g fat, 2 mg chol, 55 mg sodium

Hungarian Filled Pastries

½ cup raisins
1 cup ground nuts
½ cup sugar
1 teaspoon cinnamon
1 pound cream cheese, room temperature
6 cups flour
½ pound butter, room temperature
½ pound margarine, room temperature
2 cups confectioners' sugar

To prepare filling: Soften raisins in hot water for 15 minutes. Drain. Mix raisins with nuts, sugar, and cinnamon. To make pastries: In large mixing bowl, mix cream cheese, flour, butter, and margarine. Chill dough in refrigerator for 12 to 24 hours. Roll out pastry as you would for pie crust, except use confectioners' sugar to keep from sticking to board and rolling pin. Cut into 3½-inch squares. Place teaspoon of filling on each square and roll up. Bake at 350°F for 15 to 20 minutes, or until they are light brown on bottom. Serves 50.

Nutritional analysis per serving: 195.4 cal, 0 g fiber, 13.6 g fat, 19.8 mg chol, 107.3 mg sodium

Micky's Oatmeal Cookies

1¾ cups sugar
2 tablespoons cocoa
6 tablespoons milk
1 stick (½ cup) margarine
¾ cup peanut butter, creamy or crunchy, room temperature
1 teaspoon vanilla extract
3 cups quick-cooking oatmeal, uncooked

In large saucepan, combine sugar, cocoa, and milk. Add margarine and bring mixture to boil. Remove from heat and add peanut butter, vanilla extract, and oatmeal. Stir well. Drop by teaspoonfuls onto waxed paper. Allow cookies to cool and harden before serving. Serves 48.

Nutritional analysis per serving: 98.2 cal, 0.12 g fiber, 4.5 g fat, 0.3 mg chol, 117 mg sodium

Mother's Oatmeal Cookies

1½ cups raisins
2 cups all-purpose flour
2 cups quick-cooking oats, uncooked
1½ teaspoons baking powder
2 teaspoons cinnamon
½ teaspoon salt
½ teaspoon baking soda
1½ cups sugar
¾ cup shortening
2 eggs, beaten
1½ cups chopped nuts

Preheat oven to 350°F. Place raisins in boiling water and allow to sit. In mixing bowl, combine flour, oats, baking powder, cinnamon, salt, and baking soda. In large mixing bowl, beat sugar, shortening, and eggs. Gradually add dry ingredients to sugar mixture. Squeeze raisins out and add with nuts to batter. Batter will be stiff. Drop by teaspoonfuls onto ungreased cookie sheet. Bake for about 12 minutes. Allow cookies to cool before removing from pan. Serves 36.

Nutritional analysis per serving: 204 cal, 0 g fiber, 11.2 g fat, 15.2 mg chol, 112.4 mg sodium

No Bake Cookies

1½ cups sugar
1 cup milk
4 teaspoons cocoa
1 teaspoon vanilla
3 cups graham cracker crumbs
½ cup butter
1 12-ounce jar marshmallow creme

In large, heavy pot, mix sugar, milk, and cocoa. Bring to boil and cook to soft-ball stage. Remove from heat. Add vanilla, butter,

marshmallow creme, and graham cracker crumbs. Mix well. Pour onto cookie sheet that has been greased with butter. When almost cool, cut like fudge. Serves 24.

Nutritional analysis per serving: 198 cal, 0 g fiber, 6 g fat, 11 mg chol, 131 mg sodium

Oatmeal Crispies

1 cup margarine, at room temperature
1 cup light brown sugar
1 cup sugar
2 eggs, beaten
1 teaspoon vanilla extract
1½ cups all-purpose flour
1 teaspoon salt
1 teaspoon baking soda
3 cups quick-cooking oats, uncooked
½ cup chopped walnuts

In large mixing bowl, combine all ingredients in order listed. Form dough into two 6-inch-long rolls. Chill dough at least 12 hours. Slice rolls into ¼-inch thick rounds and place cookies 2 inches apart on ungreased cookie sheet. Bake for 10 minutes at 350°F, or until cookie bottoms are golden brown. Serves 48.

Nutritional analysis per serving: 119 cal, 0 g fiber, 5.3 g fat, 11.4 mg chol, 164.7 mg sodium

Peanut Butter Cookies

1 cup sugar
1 cup white corn syrup
1 cup peanut butter, smooth or crunchy
6½ cups crisped rice cereal
1 cup halved roasted peanuts

In saucepan, combine sugar and syrup. Cook over medium heat, stirring constantly, until mixture begins to boil. Remove from heat. Immediately add peanut butter to hot syrup. Stir until peanut butter has melted. Add cereal and peanuts. Mix until well coated. Drop by teaspoonfuls onto waxed paper. Allow balls to harden before removing them. Serves 48.

Nutritional analysis per serving: 33.4 cal, 0.02 g fiber, 1.4 g fat, 0 mg chol, 19.5 mg sodium

Peanut Butter Cookies

1 cup peanut butter
1 egg
1 cup sugar, brown or white

Preheat oven to 350°F. In mixing bowl, combine peanut butter, egg, and sugar. Mix until consistency of stiff dough. Drop dough by teaspoonfuls onto ungreased cookie sheet. Bake for 10 minutes. Cool on wire rack before storing. Serves 24.

Nutritional analysis per serving: 100.7 cal, 0 g fiber, 5.6 g fat, 11.4 mg chol, 57 mg sodium

Pecan Confections

1 egg white
1 cup light brown sugar
1 tablespoon all-purpose flour
⅛ teaspoon salt
1 cup nuts, chopped

Preheat oven to 250°F. In mixing bowl, beat egg white until frothy. In separate bowl, combine sugar, flour, and salt. Gradually add sugar mixture to egg, beating constantly. Stir in chopped nuts. Drop by teaspoonful on greased wax paper. Place wax paper on baking sheet. Bake for 20 minutes. Remove from paper when cookies cool. Serves 24.

Nutritional analysis per serving: 98.4 cal, 0 g fiber, 6 g fat, 0 mg chol, 16 mg sodium

Pecan Tassies ★

½ cup butter or margarine, room temperature
3 ounces cream cheese, room temperature
1 cup all-purpose flour
¾ cup brown sugar, packed
1 egg
1 teaspoon vanilla extract
1 cup chopped pecans

Preheat oven to 325°F. In bowl, combine margarine, cream cheese, and flour. Mix well. Chill. Mix together brown sugar, egg, and vanilla extract. Beat until combined. Stir in pecans. Form chilled dough into 24 small balls. Press balls into small muffin tins, filling only until ¾ full. Fill with pecan mixture to top of dough. Bake for 25 to 30 minutes. Remove from oven and cool for 5 minutes before removing from tins.

Serves 24.

Nutritional analysis per serving: 155 cal, 0 g fiber, 11.4 g fat, 15.3 mg chol, 60.2 mg sodium

Snowballs

8 ounces cream cheese, room temperature
2 cups confectioners' sugar
1 cup crushed pineapple
1 box vanilla wafer cookies
1 12-ounce container nondairy whipped topping
¼ cup coconut, to garnish
16 maraschino cherries, to garnish

In mixing bowl, combine cream cheese, sugar, and pineapple. Mix until well combined. For each dessert portion, put a vanilla wafer in bottom of dessert cup. Top vanilla wafer with heaping tablespoon of pineapple mixture and then another vanilla wafer. Repeat layers once more. Cover dessert with whipped topping. Sprinkle with coconut and top with a cherry. Serves 16.

Nutritional analysis per serving: 189 cal, 0.12 g fiber, 8 g fat, 20 mg chol, 82 mg sodium

Stuffed Date Drops

Cookies:
1 pound pitted dates
1 cup pecan halves
¼ cup shortening
¾ cup light brown sugar
1 egg
½ teaspoon lemon extract
1¼ cups sifted all-purpose flour
½ teaspoon baking powder
½ teaspoon baking soda
½ teaspoon salt
½ cup sour cream

Frosting:

½ cup butter, room temperature

3 cups sifted confectioners' sugar

¾ teaspoon vanilla extract

3 tablespoons warm water

Preheat oven to 400°F. Stuff dates with pecan halves. Cream shortening and sugar until fluffy. Add egg and lemon extract. Beat until smooth. In separate bowl, sift flour, baking powder, baking soda, and salt. Alternately add flour mixture and sour cream to egg mixture. Stir in dates. Drop by teaspoonfuls onto greased cookie sheet, 1 date per cookie. Bake for 8 to 10 minutes. Transfer to wire rack to cool. To make frosting: In mixing bowl, cream butter with sugar. Add vanilla extract and water. Beat until frosting is smooth and spreadable. Frost cookies when they are completely cool. Serves 22.

Nutritional analysis per serving: 256 cal, 0 g fiber, 11.3 g fat, 26 mg chol, 108 mg sodium

Super Cookies

1 stick (½ cup) margarine, melted

¼ cup corn oil

¾ cup brown sugar

¾ cup granulated sugar

2 eggs, beaten

1 tablespoon vanilla extract

¾ cup regular oatmeal

¾ cup corn flakes, crushed

2 cups self-rising flour

1 teaspoon baking soda

½ cup chopped pecans or walnuts

½ cup shredded coconut

½ cup raisins

In large bowl, combine margarine, oil, sugar, eggs, and vanilla extract. Beat well. Add oatmeal, crushed corn flakes, flour, and baking soda. Mix well. Add nuts, coconut, and raisins. Stir until combined. Form batter into balls the size of walnuts. Press balls out 2 inches apart on ungreased cookie sheet. Bake at 325°F for 12 minutes. Serves 48.

Nutritional analysis per serving: 75 cal, 0.03 g fiber, 3.3 g fat, 8.6 mg chol, 93 mg sodium

World's Best Cookies

1 cup butter

1 cup granulated sugar

1 cup brown sugar

1 egg

1 cup oil

1 cup rolled oats

½ cup coconut

1 cup crushed corn flakes

½ cup nuts

3½ cups flour

1 teaspoon soda

1 teaspoon salt

1 teaspoon vanilla

Cream butter and sugar. Add egg and oil. Stir in rest of ingredients. Drop by teaspoonfuls onto cookie sheet. Bake at 350°F for 10 to 12 minutes or until light brown. Serves 48.

Nutritional analysis per serving: 167.4 cal, 0.51 g fiber, 10.1 g fat, 14.8 mg chol, 119.3 mg sodium

Zoo Cookies

1 cup finely crushed vanilla wafers

1 cup finely chopped toasted almonds

2 to 3 tablespoons milk

1 cup confectioners' sugar

2 tablespoons light corn syrup

In medium bowl, stir all ingredients until well combined. Roll into 1-inch balls, or form into animal shapes and decorate accordingly. Use your imagination and have fun decorating them. Suggestions for eyes, noses, ears, etc., are the following items: raisins, slivered almonds, string licorice (red or black), gumdrops, marshmallows, and cinnamon candies. Serves 24.

Nutritional analysis per serving: 82.4 cal, 1.0 g fiber, 4.0 g fat, 3.2 mg chol, 14.6 mg sodium

FROSTINGS

Easy Chocolate Frosting

3 cups sugar

¾ cup cocoa

¾ cup milk

1 stick (½ cup) margarine or butter
1 teaspoon vanilla extract

Combine sugar, cocoa, milk, and margarine in a saucepan. Bring to a boil over medium heat, stirring constantly. Allow mixture to boil for 5 minutes. Remove from heat and add vanilla extract. Beat until thick and spreadable. If frosting is too thick, add small amount of milk.

Nutritional analysis (total): 3853 cal, 0 g fiber, 104 g fat, 33.4 mg chol, 2024.3 mg sodium

Caramel Filling

1½ cups light brown sugar
1½ cups sugar
¾ cup milk
1 stick (½ cup) butter or margarine
1 teaspoon vanilla extract

Combine all ingredients except vanilla extract in saucepan. Bring mixture to boil over medium heat, stirring constantly. Boil for 3 minutes. Remove mixture from heat. Add vanilla extract. Beat until thick and spreadable. If too thick to spread, add small amount of milk. Makes enough for a 3-layer cake.

Nutritional analysis (total): 3313.3 cal, 0 g fiber, 97.4 fat, 25 mg chol, 1261.5 mg sodium

Cherry Sauce

1 16.4-ounce can sour pitted cherries
2 tablespoons cornstarch
¼ cup sugar
¼ teaspoon salt
3 drops almond extract
3 drops red food coloring

Drain syrup from cherries into measuring cup. Add enough water to syrup to make 1¼ cups liquid. Reserve cherries. Combine cornstarch, sugar, and salt in saucepan. Add liquid. Bring to boil over medium heat, stirring constantly. Boil for 3 minutes. Remove from heat. Stir in almond extract and food coloring. Serve over cheese souffle, roast duck, or dessert. Serves 8.

Nutritional analysis per serving: 78.6 cal, 0 g fiber, 0.6 g fat, 0 mg chol, 71 mg sodium

Chocolate Frosting

¼ cup cocoa
6 tablespoons hot coffee
1 stick butter or margarine, at room temperature
1 teaspoon vanilla extract
1 14-ounce box of confectioners' sugar (about 3 cups)

Beat together cocoa, coffee, butter, and vanilla in large mixing bowl. Gradually beat in confectioners' sugar. Beat until thick and spreadable. If frosting is too thick, add small amount of water.

Nutritional analysis (total): 1830 cal, 0 g fiber, 93.6 g fat, 3 mg chol, 1360 mg sodium

Fluffy Coconut Frosting

3 egg whites
¼ teaspoon cream of tartar
1 cup sugar
½ cup light corn syrup
3 tablespoons water
¼ teaspoon salt
1½ teaspoons coconut extract
1 16-ounce bag shredded coconut

Beat egg whites and cream of tartar until foamy. Combine egg whites with sugar, syrup, water, and salt in top of double boiler over simmering water. Beat ingredients with mixer until peaks form. Remove from heat. Beat in coconut extract and ½ cup coconut. Continue beating frosting until it reaches spreadable consistency. To frost cake: Spread frosting on layer and sprinkle with coconut. Repeat until all layers have been iced. Ice sides of cake and coat with coconut. Makes enough for 3-layer cake.

Nutritional analysis (total): 4293.4 cal, 0 g fiber, 293.2 g fat, 0 mg chol, 1016.6 mg sodium

Lemon Curd

4 large lemons
2 cups sugar
1 cup butter or margarine
4 eggs

Grate lemon peel and squeeze juice. Place grated peel, juice, sugar, and butter in top of double boiler over simmering water. Cook, stirring constantly, until butter melts and sugar dissolves. Remove top of double boiler from heat. In mixing bowl, beat eggs until light. Gradually add hot mixture to eggs, stirring constantly. Beat until smooth. Return mixture to top of double boiler. Return double boiler top over simmering water. Cook, stirring constantly, until mixture coats back of spoon. Remove from heat. Cover and allow to cool. Refrigerate until ready to use. To serve, spread on toast, muffins, or cake layers or use to fill small tarts. Serves 48.

Nutritional analysis per serving: 74.4 cal, 0 g fiber, 4.3 g fat, 22.8 mg chol, 50.7 mg sodium

Orange Blossom Frosting

2 oranges
2 lemons
1½ pounds (about 5 cups) 4X sugar

Finely grate rind from 1 orange and 1 lemon. Juice all fruit. Beat grated rinds, juices, and sugar together until smooth. Dip miniature cupcakes in icing while they are still warm. Drain on wire rack. Store cooled cupcakes in covered tins in refrigerator. Cakes also freeze well. Store leftover icing in freezer.

Nutritional analysis (total): 1506.6 cal, 0 g fiber, 1 g fat, 0 mg chol, 11.8 mg sodium

MISCELLANEOUS DESSERTS

Banana Pudding

2 cups milk
1 egg
¾ cup sugar
2 tablespoons all-purpose flour
pinch of salt
3 tablespoons butter or margarine
1 teaspoon vanilla extract
vanilla wafers or graham crackers
3 small bananas

Mix together milk, egg, sugar, flour, salt, and butter. Pour mixture into 2-quart microwaveable bowl. Microwave on high power for 6 minutes. Add vanilla and mix well. Place layer of vanilla wafers or graham crackers on bottom of 2-quart casserole dish. Slice bananas onto cookies. Pour pudding mixture over bananas. Serve warm or cold. Serves 4.

Nutritional analysis per serving: 410 cal, 1.2 g fiber, 11 g fat, 91 mg chol, 148 mg sodium

Banana Split Dessert

1 stick (½ cup) margarine, melted
2 cups graham cracker crumbs
2 large eggs
2 cups confectioners' sugar
1 stick (½ cup) margarine
5 bananas
1 20-ounce can crushed pineapple, drained
1 large container nondairy whipped topping
pecans or maraschino cherries (optional)

Combine melted margarine and graham cracker crumbs. Mix until moistened. Place crumb mixture into 14 × 10-inch pan. In saucepan, over low heat, combine eggs, sugar, and margarine. Stir constantly until thickened. Pour this mixture over cracker crumbs. Slice bananas lengthwise and place them over custard. Add pineapple on top of custard mixture. Top custard evenly with whipped topping. Sprinkle top with pecans and cherries. Allow dessert to set 12 to 24 hours in refrigerator before slicing to serve. Serves 12.

Nutritional analysis per serving: 470 cal, 1 g fiber, 21.4 g fat, 10.3 mg chol, 344 mg sodium

Blueberry Pudding

2 cups blueberries
juice of ½ lemon (1 tablespoon)
½ cup sugar
3 tablespoons butter or margarine, softened
½ cup milk
1 cup flour
1 teaspoon baking powder

¼ teaspoon salt
½ to ¾ cup sugar (according to your
    taste and sweetness of fruit)
1 tablespoon cornstarch
dash of salt
¾ cup boiling water

Line well-greased 8 × 8 × 2-inch pan with blueberries; sprinkle lemon juice over. Cream ½ cup sugar with butter; add milk. In small bowl, stir together flour, baking powder, and salt. Add to creamed mixture. Spread batter over blueberries. Mix together ½ cup sugar with cornstarch and salt. Sprinkle over batter; pour boiling water over top; do not stir. Bake at 375°F for 1 hour. Serves 6.

Nutritional analysis per serving: 288 cal, 2 g fiber, 6 g fat, 16 mg chol, 206 mg sodium

Brandied Fruit

    1 16-ounce can sliced peaches
    1 16-ounce can pear halves
    1 15.5-ounce can pineapple chunks
    1 16-ounce can apricot halves
    1 16-ounce can pitted dark sweet
        cherries
    approximately ½ cup sugar
    ½ cup peach brandy

Drain fruits, reserving syrup from all except cherries. Mix fruit together in 9 × 13-inch dish. Strain and measure juices. Add water to yield 3 cups liquid. For each cup of water used, add ½ cup sugar. Bring liquid to boil. Remove from heat and add brandy. Cool liquid completely. Pour liquid over fruit and refrigerate 12 to 24 hours before serving. Serve cold or warm. Fruit may be warmed on medium-high for 2 minutes in microwave oven. Serves 10.

Nutritional analysis per serving: 268.6 cal, 0.9 g fiber, 0.12 g fat, 0 mg chol, 8.4 mg sodium

Bread Pudding

    2 cups stale bread, diced
    3 cups milk, scalded
    2 eggs, beaten

1 cup sugar
¼ teaspoon salt
½ teaspoon cinnamon
½ teaspoon vanilla
½ cup raisins
½ cup chopped apples
½ cup crushed pineapple, drained

Soak bread in milk in greased 2-quart baking dish. Mix eggs, sugar, salt, vanilla, and cinnamon and stir into bread mixture. Add raisins, apples, and pineapple and mix well. Set dish in pan of hot water and bake in preheated 350°F oven about 40 to 45 minutes (until knife inserted in center comes out clean). Serves 8.

Nutritional analysis per serving: 205 cal, 1 g fiber, 2 g fat, 54 mg chol, 173 mg sodium

Cheese Custard Tarts +

    2 pounds cream cheese, softened
    3 quarts milk
    ½ cup sugar
    1 18-ounce package custard mix
    1 tablespoon lemon rind, grated
    48 3-inch tart shells
    canned pie filling, blueberry, peach, or
        cherry as preferred

Blend cream cheese with small amount of milk in saucepan until smooth. Blend in remaining milk and sugar and heat. Add custard mix to hot milk mixture. Stir well with wire whip until well blended. Add lemon rind and pour at once into tart shells, allowing ⅓ cup for each. Let cool 15 minutes. Chill until set—about 4 hours. Top with pie filling. Serves 48.

Nutritional analysis per serving: 278 cal, 1 g fiber, 11 g fat, 97 mg chol, 207 mg sodium

Cherry Delite

    1 box yellow cake mix, divided in half
    1 21-ounce can cherry pie filling
    1 cup sugar
    1½ sticks butter
    1 20-ounce can crushed pineapple
    1 cup milk

Preheat oven to 350°F. Place pie filling in bottom of 9-inch square baking dish. Add half of cake mix to pie filling. Add ½ cup sugar and ½ stick of butter and distribute evenly. Add pineapple and remaining ½ cup sugar, then top with remaining cake mix. Spread all ingredients evenly. Dot top with remaining butter. Pour milk over top. Bake for 1 hour, or until brown. Serves 8.

Nutritional analysis per serving: 690 cal, 0.6 g fiber, 29.3 g fat, 97 mg chol, 414 mg sodium

Cherry Tarts +

2¼ cups sugar
1 48-ounce package cream cheese
6 eggs
3 teaspoons vanilla
3 teaspoons lemon extract
vanilla wafers
3 cans cherry pie filling

Cream sugar into cream cheese. Add eggs, vanilla, and lemon extract. Place a vanilla wafer in bottom of paper baking cup in muffin tin. Pour mixture into baking cups, filling them ½ to ⅔ full. Bake at 375°F for 25 minutes or until starting to brown. (They will be muffin-shaped when taken from the oven but will sink to tart shell shape as they cool.) Remove paper baking cups when cool. Top with cherry pie filling. Use about 3 cherries on each tart. Refrigerate. Serves 60.

Nutritional analysis per serving: 152 cal, 0 g fiber, 10 g fat, 46 mg chol, 91 mg sodium

Chocolate Souffle

2 tablespoons butter
1 tablespoon all-purpose flour
1 cup milk
1 ounce unsweetened baking chocolate
⅓ cup sugar
3 eggs, separated
1 teaspoon vanilla extract

Preheat oven to 350°F. Melt butter in saucepan. Add flour and stir until blended. Add milk, chocolate, and sugar, stirring con-stantly. Heat until hot, but not boiling. In mixing bowl, beat egg yolks until light. Add half of sauce to egg yolks, stirring constantly. Then add egg mixture to remaining sauce, stirring constantly. Cook over low heat, stirring constantly, until thick. Remove from heat and allow to cool. Stir in vanilla. Whip egg whites until stiff, but not dry. Fold egg whites into chocolate mixture. Pour batter into 9-inch souffle dish. Set dish in pan of hot water. Bake for 20 minutes or until firm. Serves 4.

Nutritional analysis per serving: 254 cal, 0 g fiber, 15.7 g fat, 229.2 mg chol, 141 mg sodium

Coconut Cream Dessert

3 cups Ritz crackers, crushed
1 stick (½ cup) margarine or butter, melted
3 tablespoons sugar
1 3-ounce package instant coconut pudding
1½ cups cold milk
1½ quarts vanilla ice cream, softened
1 small container nondairy whipped topping

Combine crackers, margarine, and sugar. Mix until moistened. Reserve ¾ cup of mixture. Press remaining crumb mix in bottom of 9 × 13-inch pan. In mixing bowl, beat pudding and milk. Add ice cream and continue beating until thick. Pour mixture over crumbs and spread evenly. Cover top with whipped topping. Sprinkle reserved crumbs over topping. Place in freezer until ready to serve. Serves 15.

Nutritional analysis per serving: 483 cal, 0 g fiber, 23 g fat, 33.4 mg chol, 695 mg sodium

Congealed Lemon Bisque

1 4-serving box lemon-flavored gelatin
¼ cup boiling water
½ cup sugar
¼ cup freshly squeezed lemon juice
2 tablespoons freshly grated lemon rind

1 cup evaporated milk, frozen until
 slushy
2¼ cups graham cracker crumbs

Dissolve lemon gelatin in hot water. Add
sugar, lemon juice, and lemon rind. Chill until
partially set. Whip evaporated milk until stiff.
Fold gelatin mixture into whipped milk.
Grease bottom of 8-inch square glass dish.
Sprinkle 2 cups of graham cracker crumbs
evenly on bottom of dish. Pour gelatin mixture over crumbs. Garnish top with remaining
crumbs. Chill for 12 to 24 hours. Serve cold.
Serves 8.

Nutritional analysis per serving: 224 cal,
0 g fiber, 4.6 g fat, 9.3 mg chol, 227.6 mg
sodium

Cream Puffs

1 4-serving package vanilla pudding mix
2 cups milk
1 cup water
1 stick (½ cup) margarine
¼ teaspoon salt
1 cup all-purpose flour
4 large eggs
1 container chocolate frosting

Prepare pudding with milk according to
package instructions and refrigerate. Preheat
oven to 400°F. Combine water and margarine
in saucepan and bring to boil. Lower heat and
stir in salt and flour. Stir constantly for 1 minute or until mixture forms ball. Remove from
heat and put into mixing bowl. Add eggs, 1 at
a time, beating until mixture is smooth and
glossy. Drop by teaspoonfuls onto ungreased
baking sheet. Bake for 25 minutes, or until
brown and dry. Remove puffs from oven and
prick tops with toothpick to allow steam to
escape. Allow to cool. Cut off tops. Fill puffs
with vanilla pudding. Return tops; ice with
chocolate frosting. Refrigerate. Puffs may be
filled with other puddings or with chicken
salad. Serves 24.

Nutritional analysis per serving: 142 cal,
0 g fiber, 7.2 g fat, 50 mg chol, 89 mg sodium

Dirt

1 16-ounce package Oreo cookies
2 cups cold milk
1 4-serving size package Jello instant
 pudding and pie filling
1 8-ounce tub Cool Whip, thawed

Crush cookies in food processor or in zip-
per-style plastic bag with rolling pin. Pour
milk into large bowl. Add pudding mix. Beat
with wire whisk 1 to 2 minutes. Let stand for
5 minutes. Stir in whipped topping and half of
crushed cookies. Reserve remaining cookies
for top. Place in refrigerator for 1 hour or
until ready to serve. Serves 12.

Nutritional analysis per serving: 294.2
cal, 0.57 mg fiber, 13.95 fat, 3 mg chol, 401.8
mg sodium

English Trifle for Americans

1 3-ounce package vanilla pudding mix
2 cups milk
1 angel or sponge cake
1 cup sherry wine
1 large container nondairy whipped
 topping
½ cup nuts, chopped

Prepare pudding according to directions
on package. Place approximately one-third of
cake into bottom of large, round, deep trifle
bowl. Dribble half of sherry wine over top of
cake. Next, pour layer of pudding, reserving
half. Place even layer of whipped topping over
custard. Repeat layers, starting with cake and
finishing with whipped topping. Sprinkle nuts
on top of cake for garnish. Serves 10.

Nutritional analysis per serving: 288 cal,
0 g fiber, 10 g fat, 136.5 mg chol, 134.3 mg
sodium

Fresh Peach Shake √ ★

½ cup sugar
½ cup water
4 soft, ripe peaches
1 pint frozen vanilla yogurt
2 cups milk, cold
½ teaspoon almond extract

Place sugar and water in saucepan and bring to boil. Remove from heat. Add peaches and pour mixture into blender. Cover and puree. Add frozen yogurt and blend on high speed for 30 seconds. Add milk and blend on high speed until foamy. Stir in almond extract. Serve in chilled glasses. Serves 6.

Nutritional analysis per serving: 190 cal, 1 g fiber, 3 g fat, 3 mg chol, 85 mg sodium

Fruit Dessert

½ stick (¼ cup) margarine or butter
1 cup sugar
1 cup self-rising flour
1 cup milk
3 cups of berries or other fruit

Preheat oven to 350°F. Melt margarine in 2-quart casserole dish. Combine sugar, flour, and milk in mixing bowl. Mix well. Pour batter over melting margarine and spread evenly. Pour fruit over batter. Bake for 30 to 45 minutes, or until lightly browned. Serves 8.

Nutritional analysis per serving: 278 cal, 0.4 g fiber, 12.7 g fat, 4.2 mg chol, 318 mg sodium

Fruit Marinade

1½ cups water
½ cup sugar
2 tablespoons cornstarch
4 tablespoons lemonade concentrate
4 tablespoons orange concentrate
pineapple, kiwi, cantaloupe, bananas, apples, grapes, etc.

Bring water, sugar, and cornstarch to boil. Boil until liquid becomes clear, stirring constantly. Add lemonade and orange concentrate and mix. Pour liquid over prepared fruit and refrigerate. Serves 8.

Nutritional analysis per serving: 95 cal, 0 g fiber, 0 g fat, 0 mg chol, 4 mg sodium

Hot Fruit Casserole

1 stick (½ cup) margarine
1 cup sugar
2 tablespoons flour or cornstarch
1 cup sherry or cooking wine
1 20-ounce can pineapple, drained
1 16-ounce can peach halves, drained
1 16-ounce can pear halves, drained
1 jar apple rings, drained
1 jar maraschino cherries, drained

Combine margarine, sugar, flour, and sherry. Bring to boil over medium heat, stirring constantly. Arrange fruit in 9 × 13-inch baking dish. Pour sauce evenly over fruit. Bake at 325°F for 15–20 minutes, or until sauce bubbles. Serves 6.

Nutritional analysis per serving: 267.4 cal, 1.4 g fiber, 7.8 g fat, 0 mg chol, 91 mg sodium

Ice Cream Custard

8 large eggs, separated
2 cups sugar
4 quarts milk
1 teaspoon vanilla extract

Separate eggs. Beat egg yolks and sugar until light. In separate bowl, beat egg whites until stiff. Fold egg whites into yolk and sugar mixture. In saucepan, heat milk until hot. Slowly add egg mixture to milk and bring to boil. Remove from heat immediately. Allow to cool before freezing. Add vanilla or extract of choice and/or any fruit just before placing custard into freezer. Serves 30.

Nutritional analysis per serving: 152.4 cal, 0 g fiber, 6 g fat, 91 mg chol, 82.3 mg sodium

Ice Cream Delight +

1 cup saltine cracker crumbs
1 cup graham cracker crumbs
½ cup melted butter or margarine
1 quart butter-pecan ice cream, softened
2 3¾-ounce packages instant vanilla pudding and pie filling mix
2 cups milk
1 12-ounce carton frozen whipped topping, thawed
3 1¼-ounce chocolate-covered toffee bars, chopped

Combine cracker crumbs and butter, stirring well; press into 9 × 13 × 2-inch baking pan. Bake at 350°F for 5 to 8 minutes. Allow to cool. Combine ice cream, pudding mix, and milk; beat at low speed of electric mixer 2 minutes. Pour ice cream mixture over crust and chill until set. Spread whipped topping over ice cream, and sprinkle with candy. Serves 15.

Nutritional analysis per serving: 359 cal, 0 g fiber, 22 g fat, 29 mg chol, 310 mg sodium

No-Bake Orange Rolls +

2 4-pound boxes vanilla wafers, crushed
12 cups grated coconut
12 cups confectioners' sugar (4 pounds)
8 cups frozen orange juice concentrate

Mix wafers, coconut, and sugar. Add thawed orange juice. Form into 1-inch balls. Roll balls in additional confectioners' sugar. Serves 230.

Nutritional analysis per serving: 128 cal, 0 g fiber, 4 g fat, 10 mg chol, 52 mg sodium

Old South Bread Pudding √

⅓ loaf stale French bread (cut into small cubes)
¼ cup raisins
2 tablespoons butter
2 eggs, separated
6 tablespoons sugar
1¼ cups milk
1 teaspoon vanilla
¼ teaspoon cream of tartar
¼ cup sugar
1 small package vanilla pudding mix
1 teaspoon grated nutmeg
2⅔ cups milk
1 jigger whiskey

Moisten bread cubes with water and squeeze dry. Mix with raisins and butter in a 1-quart baking dish. Beat egg yolks with 6 tablespoons sugar. Stir in milk until smooth. Add vanilla. Pour mixture over bread. Bake at 350°F for 45 minutes. For meringue: Beat egg whites until foamy, add cream of tartar, and gradually add ¼ cup sugar. Beat until stiff but not dry. Spoon on top of pudding and brown in 350°F oven for 12 to 15 minutes. The authentic southern bread pudding was served with whiskey sauce. You may substitute lemon sauce if you prefer. For whiskey sauce: Put pudding mix in saucepan and add nutmeg. Add 2⅔ cups milk slowly and stir. Cook over moderate heat about 15 minutes. Remove from heat and add whiskey. Serves 4.

Nutritional analysis per serving: 494 cal, 1 g fiber, 10 g fat, 118 mg chol, 455 mg sodium

Old South Peach Ice Cream √

6 eggs
juice of 1 lemon
1 can sweetened condensed milk
1 cup sugar
½ pint whipping cream
6 soft ripe peaches, mashed
1 quart milk

Separate eggs. Beat egg whites until stiff. Set mixture aside. Beat egg yolks in large bowl and add lemon juice. Add sweetened condensed milk and sugar to yolk mixture and beat. Add cream and beat 5 minutes (until thick). Fold in egg whites, add mashed peaches, and pour into 1-gallon freezer container of ice cream maker. Add milk to fill freezer to line. Freeze as directions indicate for your ice cream maker. Serves 8.

Nutritional analysis per serving: 428 cal, 1 g fiber, 17 g fat, 209 mg chol, 166 mg sodium

Peach Crepes √ ★

Crepes:
½ cup all-purpose flour
1 large egg
2 tablespoons nondairy creamer, Amaretto flavor
½ cup skim milk
⅛ teaspoon nutmeg
1 teaspoon vanilla extract

Filling:

2 cups fresh orange juice

2 tablespoons orange liqueur

8 peaches, peeled and sliced

1 teaspoon honey

1 teaspoon cinnamon

1 teaspoon orange zest

Place flour in mixing bowl. Add egg. While stirring, pour in nondairy creamer and skim milk. Stir until batter is free of lumps. Add nutmeg and vanilla. Cover and set aside for 30 minutes. Preheat small, heavy frying pan over medium heat. Spray with vegetable oil. Spoon batter into pan to coat bottom evenly. Cook crepe 1 to 2 minutes until edge is firm. Flip crepe and cook about 1 minute on other side. Remove to sheet of waxed paper. Continue to cook crepes, stacking them on waxed paper until all crepes are made. Combine orange juice, liqueur, peaches, and honey in medium frying pan. Cook about 10 minutes, until liquid is thick and syrupy. Place a crepe on serving plate. Spoon ⅓ cup peaches on bottom half of crepe, then flip top half over peaches. Spoon peach syrup over each and dust with cinnamon. Sprinkle orange zest on top. Serves 8.

Nutritional analysis per serving: 128 cal, 2 g fiber, 1 g fat, 27 mg chol, 19 mg sodium

Peanut Butter Chocolate Pudding +

1 30-ounce box rice pudding mix

5 quarts milk

1½ pounds chocolate-flavored baking chips

8 ounces miniature marshmallows

2 cups creamy or chunky peanut butter

Add pudding mix to milk in saucepan. Cook, stirring often, until mixture comes to full boil. (Mixture will be thin; it thickens as it cools.) Remove from heat; stir in chips, marshmallows, and peanut butter, blending until smooth. Pour into a shallow pan. Cool 15 minutes, stirring occasionally to prevent formation of skin. Stir well; cover surface with plastic wrap. Serve warm or chilled. Garnish with pre-pared whipped topping and chocolate sprinkles or chopped peanuts. Serves 56.

Nutritional analysis per serving: 211 cal, 1 g fiber, 7 g fat, 2 mg chol, 155 mg sodium

Pineapple-Lemon Gelatin Mold

1 4-serving package lemon gelatin

1 20-ounce can crushed pineapple, drained, with juice reserved

8 ounces cream cheese, at room temperature

2 tablespoons lemon juice

2 tablespoons sugar

5 cups miniature marshmallows

1 12-ounce container nondairy whipped topping

Combine gelatin and 1 cup of hot boiling water. Stir until dissolved. Add enough cold water to pineapple juice to equal 1 cup of water, and add liquid to gelatin. In separate bowl, combine pineapple, cream cheese, lemon juice, and sugar. Mix well. Gradually add gelatin to pineapple and cream cheese mixture. Mix all ingredients with electric mixer. Add marshmallows. Pour mixture into Bundt pan and refrigerate until semigelled (about 2 hours). Stir in container of whipped topping and refrigerate again. Unmold and serve when set. Serves 12.

Nutritional analysis per serving: 230 cal, 0 g fiber, 9.6 g fat, 21 mg chol, 94 mg sodium

Pineapple Pavlova

Pavlova:

4 egg whites

2 teaspoons cornstarch

1 teaspoon vanilla extract

1 cup sugar

2 teaspoons white vinegar

Filling:

1 15-ounce can crushed pineapple, fruit and syrup

2 teaspoons vanilla extract

2 tablespoons cornstarch

sweetened whipped topping (garnish)

4 egg yolks

2 tablespoons butter

½ cup sugar
2 fresh pears, chopped fine

For pavlova: Beat egg whites until stiff, while gradually adding sugar. Beat in cornstarch, vinegar, and vanilla. Pile large circle of meringue on parchment paper–lined cookie sheet. Bake in 300°F oven for 1 hour. Meringue is done when it can be gently pushed loose. Do not force; it breaks easily and will budge only when ready to do so. For filling: Prepare filling by combining all ingredients in large saucepan. Bring to boil, stirring constantly. Cool. Pile into pavlova and garnish with sweetened whipped cream. Note: Any type custard filling may be used to fill pavlova case. Decorate case with fruit or combine whipped topping and fruit to use as filling. Serves 12.

Nutritional analysis per serving: 184 cal, 0.7 g fiber, 4 g fat, 96 mg chol, 40 mg sodium

Rainbow Pies +

Crust:
10 cups graham crackers
1 pound margarine, melted
1½ cups sugar
Filling:
½ package lime gelatin
½ package strawberry gelatin
8 cups hot pineapple juice
1½ pounds lemon gelatin
14 ounces sugar
3 quarts whipped topping

Combine crust ingredients, press into pans, and bake in 400°F oven for 12 to 15 minutes or until done. Make lime and strawberry gelatins in separate pans the day ahead. Cut into small cubes. Mix hot pineapple juice, lemon gelatin, and sugar and let set until like egg whites. Fold in 3 quarts whipped topping and gelatine cubes. Pour into crusts and top with crumbs. Chill. Serve with whipped topping. Serves 60.

Nutritional analysis per serving: 237 cal, 0 g fiber, 10 g fat, 0 mg chol, 201 mg sodium

Scalloped Pineapple

5 slices white bread, cubed
¼ cup margarine
2 eggs
1 20-ounce can crushed pineapple
½ cup sugar
3 tablespoons all-purpose flour

In skillet, brown bread cubes in margarine. Put half of cubes into 9 × 13-inch casserole dish. In large mixing bowl, beat eggs. Add pineapple, sugar, and flour. Mix until just combined. Pour mixture over layer of bread cubes. Top with remaining cubes. Bake at 350°F for 35 minutes. Serves 6.

Nutritional analysis per serving: 355 cal, 0.8 g fiber, 17.8 g fat, 92 mg chol, 308.2 mg sodium

Vanilla Delight

1 cup all-purpose flour
½ cup margarine or butter, at room temperature
1 cup chopped pecans
1 12-ounce container nondairy whipped topping
8 ounces cream cheese, at room temperature
1 cup confectioners' sugar
2 3-ounce packages instant vanilla pudding mix
3 cups cold milk

In small bowl, combine flour, margarine, and chopped pecans. Mix well. Spread this mixture evenly on bottom of 9 × 13-inch baking pan. Bake crust at 375°F oven for 15 minutes. Remove from oven and allow to cool. In large mixing bowl, combine 1 cup whipped topping, cream cheese, and confectioners' sugar. Beat until light and creamy. Spread mixture on cooled crust. Combine pudding mix and milk. Beat with electric mixer until thick. Pour pudding mix over second layer. Spread remaining whipped topping over top. Garnish with additional nuts, chocolate curls, cherries, or coconut, if desired. Refrigerate for at least 4 hours before serving. Serves 12.

Nutritional analysis per serving: 356 cal, 0 g fiber, 25.3 g fat, 30.6 g chol, 203 mg sodium

Watermelon-Strawberry Ice ★

2 cups watermelon
½ cup sugar
2 cups strawberries, hulled and halved
2 tablespoons lemon juice

Measure all ingredients into blender; blend on low speed (puree). Pour into ice tray and freeze. Let stand for 15 minutes at room temperature before serving. Garnish with mint. Serves 4.

Nutritional analysis per serving: 140 cal, 2 g fiber, 1 g fat, 0 mg chol, 3 g sodium

PIES

Apple Pie

3 large cooking apples, peeled and sliced
1 cup sugar
1½ teaspoons apple pie spice
2 unbaked 9-inch pie shells
3 tablespoons margarine

Preheat oven to 375°F. In small bowl, combine apples, sugar, and spice. Toss until well mixed. Pour apples into pastry-lined pie plate. Dot pie with margarine. Cover with second pie shell and crimp edges together. Pierce pie with fork to allow steam to escape. Bake for 40 minutes, or until the crust is golden brown. Cool before slicing. Serves 8.

Nutritional analysis per serving: 382.4 cal, 1 g fiber, 19 g fat, 0 mg chol, 319.5 mg sodium

Blender Lemon Pie

4 eggs
½ stick (¼ cup) margarine, room
  temperature
1 lemon
2 cups sugar
1 9-inch unbaked pie shell

Preheat oven to 350°F. Combine eggs and margarine in blender. Blend until well com-

bined. Cut lemon into 8 pieces, removing seeds. Put 1 piece of lemon at a time into blender, blending well after each piece. Add sugar, 1 cup at a time, blending well after each addition. Pour mixture into pie shell. Bake for 35 to 40 minutes, or until filling is firm. Cool before slicing. Serves 8.

Nutritional analysis per serving: 449 cal, 0 g fiber, 21.8 g fat, 137 mg chol, 306.7 mg sodium

Buttermilk Pie

1⅓ cups sugar
3 tablespoons all-purpose flour
2 eggs, beaten
½ cup margarine, melted
1 cup buttermilk
2 teaspoons vanilla extract
1 teaspoon lemon extract
1 unbaked pie shell

Preheat oven to 400°F. Combine sugar and flour. Add eggs, margarine, and buttermilk. Mix well. Stir in extracts. Pour mixture into unbaked pie shell. Bake for 10 minutes. Reduce oven temperature to 325°F and bake for additional 30 to 35 minutes. Cool completely before slicing. Serves 8.

Nutritional analysis per serving: 389 cal, 0 g fiber, 20.6 g fat, 69.5 mg chol, 321 mg sodium

Calypso Pie

20 chocolate sandwich cookies, crushed
1 quart vanilla ice cream, softened
¼ cup margarine, room temperature
1½ ounces unsweetened chocolate
⅔ cup sugar
⅔ cup evaporated milk
1 teaspoon vanilla extract
⅛ teaspoon salt
1 12-ounce container nondairy whipped
  topping
chopped nuts or shaved chocolate
  (garnish)

Press crushed cookies into pie plate to form crust. Spread ice cream over cookies.

Freeze mixture. In medium saucepan, combine margarine, chocolate, sugar, milk, vanilla extract, and salt. Cook over medium heat for 5 minutes, stirring constantly until mixture thickens. Remove from heat and cool completely. Pour sauce over frozen ice cream. Refreeze. Top pie with whipped topping and garnish before serving. Serves 8.

Nutritional analysis per serving: 460 cal, 0 g fiber, 25.2 g fat, 46 mg chol, 320 mg sodium

Cheesecake Pie

  8 ounces cream cheese, room
    temperature
  ½ cup plus 2 tablespoons sugar, divided
  1 tablespoon lemon juice
  1 teaspoon vanilla extract, divided
  ⅛ teaspoon salt
  2 eggs
  1 9-inch graham cracker crust
  1 cup sour cream

Preheat oven to 350°F. Beat cream cheese until fluffy. Add ½ cup sugar, lemon juice, ½ teaspoon vanilla extract, and salt. Add eggs 1 at a time, beating after each addition. Pour batter into graham cracker crust. Bake for 30 minutes or until set. Remove from the oven and allow pie to sit undisturbed for 10 minutes. In small mixing bowl, combine 1 cup sour cream, 2 tablespoons sugar, and ½ teaspoon vanilla extract. Spoon topping over pie. Bake an additional 10 minutes. Cool completely before slicing. Store in refrigerator. Serves 8.

Nutritional analysis per serving: 176 cal, 0 g fiber, 11.4 g fat, 99 mg chol, 184.6 mg sodium

Egg Custard Pie

  1½ cups sugar
  3 tablespoons cornstarch
  5 eggs, separated
  1 teaspoon vanilla or lemon extract
  1 14.5-ounce can evaporated milk
  1 14.5-ounce can whole milk
  2 unbaked 9-inch pie crust shells

Preheat oven to 375°F. Combine sugar and cornstarch. Beat egg yolks and extract with sugar mixture until thick. Add evaporated milk and whole milk. Beat egg whites. Fold egg whites into mixture. Pour mixture evenly into the unbaked pie crust shells. Bake for 35 to 40 minutes, or until knife comes out clean when inserted into center of pie. Serves 16.

Nutritional analysis per serving: 382 cal, 0 g fiber, 20 g fat, 97.6 mg chol, 340 mg sodium

Fresh Blueberry Pie

  1 baked 9-inch pie shell
  4 cups fresh blueberries, divided
  ¼ cup water
  1 cup sugar
  3 tablespoons cornstarch
  ¼ teaspoon salt
  1 teaspoon butter

Line pie shell with 2 cups of blueberries. Over medium heat, cook remaining blueberries, water, sugar, cornstarch, and salt in saucepan, stirring constantly, until thick. Remove from heat. Add butter. Allow mixture to cool. Pour over blueberries in pie shell. Serves 8.

Nutritional analysis per serving: 265 cal, 0 g fiber, 8.3 g fat, 1.4 mg chol, 214 mg sodium

Fruit Pie

  2 pounds crushed pineapple with juice
  ½ cup sugar
  4 tablespoons flour
  2 baked 9-inch pie shells
  2 bananas, sliced
  ½ cup chopped pecans
  whipped cream to garnish

In medium saucepan over low heat, cook pineapple, sugar, and flour until thick. Remove from heat and allow to cool. Line both pie shells with sliced bananas. Sprinkle pecans evenly over bananas. Pour cooled pineapple mixture over bananas. Chill. Garnish with whipped cream to serve. Serves 16.

Grandma's Strawberry Pie

¾ cup water
1½ tablespoons cornstarch
½ cup sugar
1 tablespoon strawberry gelatin
2 cups strawberries, sliced thin
1 9-inch baked pie shell
whipped topping

Combine water, cornstarch, and sugar; cook over medium heat until thick. Remove from heat, add jello; mix well. Stir in strawberries. Pour into baked pie shell. Chill for several hours before serving. Top with whipped topping. Serves 8.

Nutritional analysis per serving: 185 cal, 1 g fiber, 9 g fat, 0 mg chol, 150 mg sodium

Lemon Pie

2 cups sugar
2 tablespoons butter
4 large eggs
rind from 1 lemon, grated
2 unbaked pastry pie shells

Preheat oven to 350°F. In mixing bowl, cream sugar and butter. Add beaten eggs and lemon rind. Stir mixture until well blended. Pour mixture into two pie shells. Bake for 50 minutes, or until filling is firm. Serves 16.

Nutritional analysis per serving: 242.4 cal, 0 g fiber, 10.4 g fat, 72.3 mg chol, 170 mg sodium

Mom's Green Tomato Pie

4 green tomatoes, peeled and sliced
1 cup sugar
2½ tablespoons flour
pinch of salt
1 teaspoon cinnamon
1 teaspoon nutmeg
⅓ cup water

1 teaspoon lemon juice
pastry for 2-crust pie
margarine

Place tomato slices in mixing bowl. Combine sugar, flour, salt, cinnamon, and nutmeg. Sprinkle over tomatoes. Add water and lemon juice. Gently mix together. Pour into pie crust. Dot with margarine. Cover pie with top crust, seal edges, and prick top. Bake at 450°F for 15 minutes. Reduce heat to 350°F and bake for 30 minutes. Serves 8.

Nutritional analysis per serving: 380 cal, 1 g fiber, 18 g fat, 0 g chol, 330 mg sodium

Never Fail Pie Crust

One Crust:
1 cup plus 2 tablespoons flour
½ teaspoon salt
⅓ cup cooking oil
2 tablespoons cold water
Two Crust Pie:
1¾ cups flour
1 teaspoon salt
½ cup cooking oil
3 tablespoons cold water

Mix flour and salt; blend in oil, then cold water. Roll out between 2 pieces of waxed paper. For unfilled pie crust, bake at 450°F for 12 to 15 minutes. Or fill and bake according to pie recipe.

Nutritional analysis per serving: 191 cal, 1 g fiber, 12 g fat, 0 g chol, 178 mg sodium

Old-Fashioned Egg Custard Pie

1 cup plus 2 tablespoons sugar, divided
2½ tablespoons all-purpose flour
⅛ teaspoon nutmeg
4 eggs, separated and divided
1 cup milk
2 tablespoons butter, melted and slightly cooled
1 unbaked pie shell

Preheat oven to 400°F. In large mixing bowl, combine 1 cup of sugar with flour and nutmeg. In separate small bowl, beat together 4 egg yolks and 2 egg whites. Add eggs to dry ingredients and beat well. Add milk and melted butter, mixing thoroughly. Pour custard into unbaked pie crust. Bake at 400°F for 10 minutes. Reduce heat to 325°F and bake for 20 minutes longer, or until knife inserted in center of custard comes out clean. Gently remove pie from oven. To make meringue: Beat egg whites until foamy. Sprinkle with 2 tablespoons sugar and continue beating until fluffy and stiff. Gently spread over top of pie. Return pie to oven and bake for 10 minutes, or until meringue is golden brown. Allow to cool at room temperature. Store in refrigerator. Serves 8.

Nutritional analysis per serving: 305 cal, 0 g fiber, 14.4 g fat, 149 mg chol, 216 mg sodium

Peach Cobbler

1 cup all-purpose flour
2 cups sugar, divided
½ teaspoon baking powder
½ teaspoon salt
½ cup milk
½ stick (¼ cup) margarine, melted
4 cups peaches, fresh or frozen
1 cup water
1 4-serving package peach gelatin

Preheat oven to 350°F. Lightly grease 8 × 12-inch oven-proof glass dish. In mixing bowl, sift flour, 1 cup of sugar, baking powder, and salt. Mix in milk and melted margarine. Spread evenly on bottom of baking dish. In saucepan, bring peaches, water, 1 cup of sugar, and gelatin to boil. Spoon peach mixture into baking dish. Bake for 45 minutes, or until golden brown. Serves 8.

Nutritional analysis per serving: 404 cal, 0.6 g fiber, 6.4 g fat, 2.1 mg chol, 248 mg sodium

Peach Cobbler

1 quart peaches, sliced
1 cup sugar
2 4-serving boxes peach gelatin
1 2-layer box yellow cake mix
1 stick (½ cup) butter or margarine
1½ cups water

Preheat oven to 400°F. Place peaches into 9 × 13-inch baking dish and spread evenly. Sprinkle sugar, then the gelatin, then dry cake mix evenly over peaches. Slice butter evenly over cake mix. Pour water evenly over cake mix to moisten. Bake for 40 minutes, or until golden brown. Serve warm or cold. Serves 8.

Nutritional analysis per serving: 687 cal, 0.6 g fiber, 21.6 g fat, 99.2 mg chol, 507.5 mg sodium

Peach Cobbler

1 stick butter or margarine
1 cup self-rising flour
1 cup sugar
½ cup milk
2 cups sliced peaches

Melt butter in casserole dish in preheated oven. Combine flour, sugar, and milk. Pour into casserole. Add peaches and bake at 350°F for 45 minutes. Top should be brown and cobbler should be set when gently shaken. Serves 6.

Nutritional analysis per serving: 368 cal, 4 g fiber, 16 g fat, 42 mg chol, 432 mg sodium

Peach Cobbler √

3 cups fresh peaches, cup up and cooked
    until soft
1 cup sugar
1 stick margarine, melted
1 cup self-rising flour
½ teaspoon nutmeg
1 cup milk
1 teaspoon baking powder
1 teaspoon vanilla
½ teaspoon cinnamon

Cook peaches and sugar until peaches are soft. In baking dish, pour warm peaches over melted margarine. Mix other ingredients and pour over peaches. Cook at 350°F for 30 minutes or until brown. Put cookie sheet in oven under cobbler dish to catch juice if it runs over. Serves 8.

Nutritional analysis per serving: 297 cal, 1 g fiber, 12 g fat, 32 mg chol, 364 mg sodium

Pecan Pie

4 eggs, beaten
1 16-ounce box light brown sugar
1 stick (½ cup) margarine, melted
1 tablespoon vanilla extract
½ teaspoon salt
2 tablespoons cornmeal
2 tablespoons water
2 cups chopped pecans
2 9-inch unbaked pie shells

Preheat oven to 300°F. In large mixing bowl, combine eggs, brown sugar, margarine, vanilla extract, salt, cornmeal, water, and pecans. Divide mixture evenly between pie shells. Bake for 35 to 45 minutes, or until firm. Cool before slicing. Serves 16.

Nutritional analysis per serving: 379.4 cal, 0 g fiber, 23.8 g fat, 68.5 mg chol, 296.7 mg sodium

Piña Colada Pie

1 10¾-ounce pound cake
3 tablespoons dark rum
1 20-ounce can crushed pineapple
 (drain and reserve juice)
3 envelopes unflavored gelatin
1½ cups plain yogurt
½ cup confectioners' sugar
1 teaspoon coconut extract
1 5.5-ounce can pineapple slices,
 drained and halved
mint leaves (garnish)

Cut cake into 12 slices. Line bottom and sides of ungreased 9-inch pie plate with cake slices, cutting to fit. Cut leftover cake into small cubes and set aside. Sprinkle cake in pie plate with rum. Place reserved pineapple juice from crushed pineapple into saucepan. Sprinkle with gelatin and let stand 5 minutes before heating. Over low heat, stir until gelatin is completely dissolved. Transfer to large bowl and add yogurt, confectioners' sugar, coconut extract, and crushed pineapple. Stir until gelatin mixture is very thick. Beat with electric mixer at high speed until smooth. Chill until almost set and then beat again until smooth.

Fold in reserved cake cubes. Spoon mixture into cake-lined pie plate. Top with pineapple slices and chill until firm, approximately 2 to 3 hours. Garnish with mint leaves. Serves 8.

Nutritional analysis per serving: 477 cal, 0.6 g fiber, 20 g fat, 89.3 mg chol, 130.4 mg sodium

Quick and Easy Watermelon Pie

1 can sweetened condensed milk
1 4-ounce container nondairy whipped
 topping, thawed
¼ cup lime juice
2 cups watermelon balls
1 9-inch graham cracker crust

Fold together milk and topping. Add lime juice. Fold in watermelon balls, reserving about 5 balls for garnish. Pour into graham cracker crust. Place remaining watermelon balls on pie to garnish. Chill for 2 or more hours before serving. Serves 8.

Nutritional analysis per serving: 251 cal, 1 g fiber, 11 g fat, 10 mg chol, 171 mg sodium

Ritz Cracker Pie

25 Ritz crackers, crushed
1¼ cups chopped pecans
¾ teaspoon vanilla extract
1 cup sugar, divided
3 egg whites
1 8-ounce container nondairy whipped
 topping

Preheat oven to 325°F. Lightly grease 11-inch pie plate. Combine crackers, nuts, vanilla, and ½ cup sugar. Mix well. In separate bowl, beat egg whites until stiff, beating in remaining sugar as soft peaks begin to form. Fold 2 mixtures together. Pour batter into prepared pie plate and bake for 30 minutes. After pie cools completely, spread nondairy whipped on top. Serves 8.

Nutritional analysis per serving: 394 cal, 0 g fiber, 25.5 g fat, 0 mg chol, 138 mg sodium

Southern Pecan Pie √

1 cup dark corn syrup
½ cup sugar
⅓ cup butter or margarine
1 teaspoon vanilla extract
3 eggs, beaten
1½ cups chopped pecans
1 9-inch unbaked pie shell

Preheat oven to 350°F. Mix corn syrup and sugar over high heat, stirring constantly. Remove from heat. Add butter and stir until melted. Set mixture aside until just warm. Pour syrup over beaten eggs, stirring constantly. Slowly add vanilla extract and nuts. Pour into pie shell. Bake for about 50 minutes, or until filling is firm. Serves 8.

Nutritional analysis per serving: 639 cal, 1 g fiber, 39 g fat, 105 mg chol, 331 mg sodium

Strawberry Cream Cheese Pie

8 ounces light cream cheese
1 cup sour cream
½ pint whipping cream
1 teaspoon vanilla extract
1 baked 9-inch pie shell
½ pint (1 cup) fresh strawberries, halved

Beat cream cheese until smooth. Add sour cream and continue to beat. Whip whipping cream until thick. Add to cheese mixture. Stir in vanilla. Mix until well combined. Pour batter into pie crust. Chill. Add strawberries to top of pie. Serves 8.

Nutritional analysis per serving: 321 cal, 0.4 g fiber, 28 g fat, 60 mg chol, 241 mg sodium

Sweet Potato Pie

3 large sweet potatoes, cooked, peeled, and mashed
½ cup margarine
2 eggs
1 14-ounce can sweetened condensed milk
1 cup sugar
1 teaspoon vanilla extract
2 9-inch partially baked pie shells

Preheat oven to 425°F. In mixing bowl, combine sweet potatoes with margarine, eggs, condensed milk, sugar, and vanilla extract. Beat with electric mixer until well blended. Pour mixture into partially baked pie shells. Bake for 10 minutes, reduce heat to 300°F, and bake for about 50 minutes more, or until filling is firm. Cool before slicing. Serves 16.

Nutritional analysis per serving: 335 cal, 0 g fiber, 16.2 g fat, 42.8 mg chol, 249.3 mg sodium

Sweet Potato Pie

2¼ cups mashed sweet potatoes
½ cup butter or margarine
1¼ cups sugar
1 tablespoon flour
½ teaspoon salt
½ teaspoon ground nutmeg
½ teaspoon ground ginger
½ teaspoon ground cinnamon
⅛ teaspoon ground cloves
2 eggs, beaten
2 5-ounce cans (1⅓ cups) evaporated milk
⅔ cup milk
2 9-inch unbaked pie shells

Preheat oven to 425°F. In large mixing bowl, combine sweet potatoes and butter. Mix until blended. Add sugar, flour, salt, and spices to batter. Beat until well blended. Add eggs and milks. Beat until mixture is smooth. Divide mixture evenly between pie shells. Bake for 10 minutes. Reduce heat to 300°F and bake for about 50 minutes more, or until filling is firm. Cool before slicing. Serves 16.

Nutritional analysis per serving: 308.2 cal, 0 g fiber, 14.5 g fat, 36.4 mg chol, 315 mg sodium

Sweet Potato Pie √

Crust:
2 cups graham cracker crumbs
1 large egg white
2 teaspoon cinnamon
Filling:
4 baked sweet potatoes

¼ teaspoon nutmeg
¼ teaspoon allspice
2 tablespoons vanilla extract
1 tablespoon honey
¼ cup fresh orange juice
6 large egg whites
¼ teaspoon cloves
¼ teaspoon ginger
5 tablespoons maple syrup
6 ounces light cream cheese

Preheat oven to 350°F. Spray pie pan with vegetable oil. Mix crust ingredients in food processor. Transfer to pie pan and press in firmly to cover pan evenly. Peel and mash sweet potatoes. Transfer to blender and add remaining filling ingredients. Blend until mixture is smooth and blended well. Pour filling into crust. Bake about 45 minutes, until center of pie is firm and not sticky to touch. Cool 30 minutes, then refrigerate at least 1 hour. Serve with spoonful of light whipped cream sprinkled with cinnamon. Serves 12.

Nutritional analysis per serving: 202 cal, 1 g fiber, 5 g fat, 5 mg chol, 222 mg sodium

Tasty Pear Pie

4 large, ripe pears, peeled and thinly
  sliced
1 unbaked pie shell (deep-dish)
1 cup sugar
½ cup flour
¾ teaspoon cinnamon
¼ teaspoon salt
1 stick (½ cup) margarine, melted

2 eggs, slightly beaten
1 teaspoon vanilla extract

Preheat oven to 325°F. Evenly distribute pears over bottom of pie shell. Mix sugar, flour, cinnamon, and salt together. Add margarine, eggs, and vanilla extract. Mix until smooth. Pour batter over pears. Put pie on cookie sheet to reduce spillover into oven. Bake for 55 minutes, or until edges of pie crust are golden brown. Serves 8.

Nutritional analysis per serving: 408.5 cal, 2 g fiber, 21 g fat, 68.5 mg chol, 355.6 mg sodium

Two-Tone Lemon Pie

1 4-serving box of lemon pie filling
  (not instant)
½ cup sugar
2¼ cups water
1 egg
1 baked 9-inch pie shell
1 8-ounce container of nondairy
  whipped topping

In saucepan, combine pie filling mix, sugar, water, and egg. Cook over medium heat, stirring constantly until pudding begins to boil. Pour 1 cup of pudding into baked pie shell and chill. Chill remaining pudding. When chilled, mix together remaining pudding with 1 cup of whipped topping. Spread mixture on pie. Top pie with remaining whipped topping. Serves 8.

Nutritional analysis per serving: 205 cal, 0 g fiber, 9.7 g fat, 34.2 mg chol, 159 mg sodium

RECIPE CONTRIBUTORS

Allen, Dorothy
Allen, Tina
Anderson, Carolina
Anderson, Pauline
Anthony, Mavis
Appel, Ruth
Averill, Mildred

Baker, Betty
Barber, Robert
Beasley, Linda
Beckman, Mary
Bell, Ida
Berkaw, Mary
Berley, Peggy
Bixby, Shirley
Black, Mertie H.
Bledsoe, Gladys
Boatwright, Nell
Boling, Misty
Boyer, Patricia
Bozard, Becca
Branham, Margie
Branham, Paula
Brannon, Marcia
Broome, Isabelle
Brown, Emma
Brown, Rebecca
Bruce, Doris
Buff, Betty
Burnett, Juliette
Burton, LaGarr
Busch, Nell

Cain, Jeannie
Cantey, Lucille
Carrington, Eddie M.
Carroll, June
Carter, Dorothy
Casey, Pam

Catoe, Mamie
Cauthern, Rosemary
Chamberlain, Elizabeth
Chaney, Rachel
Chapman, Caroline
Cheatham, Simmie
Clark, Elizabeth
Clowny, Annette
Crawford, Elizabeth
Crumpton, Edie
Curry, Doris

Davis, Danielle
Davis, Dot
Day, Mary Sue
DeLo, Lou
Dicks, Sallie D.
Dixon, Carol
Dodson, Alma
Domonick, Ophelia
Drew, Carol

Earle, Bobbie
Easter, Marilyn
Ellis, Lizzelle
Ellison, Angela
Evans, Carolyn
Evans, Eather
Evans, Gladys

Fagan, Tina
Fairey, Mary Nell
Faulkner, Sara
Finley, Ora
FitzSimons, Carmen
Floria, Donna
Floyd, Mamie
Folsom, Annie
Foster, Sara
Frick, Pattie

Fuller, Lib
Furse, Sara

Gaddy, Nancy
Gaines, Gladys
Gambrell, Cleo
Garrett, Grace
Glass, Theresa
Glenn, Susan W.
Goodwin, Mattie
Gustafson, Mildred

Hall, April
Hall, Louise
Hallman, Jessie R.
Hamm, Gene
Hampton, Magdalene
Hanckel, Sally
Hannah, Annie
Harned, Christy
Harris, Blondy
Hawkins, Connie
Hendricks, Mark
Hendricks, Sylvia
Henley, Jennifer
Hollings, Mrs. Fritz
Howe, Cindy
Howell, Nelda
Huddleston, Maribeth
Huffman, Eva Mae
Hyde, Charlotte

Irwin, Betty

Jackson, Alma
Jefferies, Mrs. G. P.
Johnson, Hazel
Joe, Mary
Jones, Addie Mae
Jones, Grace
Jones, Martha S.

176

Kaufman, Katherinea
Kelly, Margie
Kennedy, Miley
Kneece, Josie

Lacy, Ellen
Langford, Romona
Ledford, Muriel
Leitner, Lotie
Linda, Ann
Linder, Lila
Lintner, Gretta
Lowery, Eleanor

Mabry, Joye
Mason, Evelyn
McCants, Luvenia
McCarthy, Cheryl
McDowell, Betty
McDowell, Marcella
McGhee, Doris
McGregor, Betty
McInvaille, Betty
McLaurin, Eulalie
McRee, Janice
Melton, Ruby
Metcalfe, Ruth
Montgomery, Carol
Moore, Betty
Morrison, Margaret
Mosely, Elizabeth
Moss, Mavis
Mounter, Judi
Murray, Robin G.

Nabors, Irene
Napper, Stephanie
Nations, Margaret
Newsom, Annie
Nichols, T. C.
Nichols, Trudie
Norsworthy, Yvonne

Nuernberg, Gladys
Nunnery, Annie

Ogburn, Clarine
Osgood, Betty
Owens, Vivian

Pardue, Juanita
Perry, Jackie
Phillips, Floride
Phillips, Ouida
Preacher, Lyda

Rama, John
Ramsey, Lorraine
Ready, Carol
Renwick, Virginia
Ricard, JoAnn
Rich, Martha
Richardson, Fanny
Rinehart, Mary J.
Risinger, Maude
Roberts, Alice
Robinson, Genevieve
Rollins, Helen
Roof, Lois
Rose, Mary N.
Ross, Betty K.
Ruff, Ada
Rushing, Jean

Sanders, Letitia
Sanders, Ruth
Sandifer, Carol
Sanford, Mary Ee.
Schall, Mary
Seegars, Lucille
Senn, Jane
Shadel, Letha
Shealy, Willene
Shramek, Cordelia
Shuler, Candice

Simons, Allison
Simpson, Dorothy
Simpson, Ella
Smith, Frances
Smith, Lois
Smoak, Josefa M.
Snelgrove, Miliette
Snyder, Brenda
South Carolina Department
of Agriculture
Sowell, Vivian
Stephens, Betsy
Stewart, Nell
Stoudemire, Martha
Stump, Mary
Sturkie, Lorene

Thompson, Geraldine
Thurmond, Strom
Till, Vira
Tripp, Evelyn
Tumbleson, Mrs. Ray

Vansant, Beth
Vansant, Martha

Wall, Betty
Wallace, Grace
Walpoole, Mrs. John
Walters, Frankie
Watson, Jean
Webb, B. K.
Weed, Nellie
Weir, Mary L.
Werts, Elizabeth
Wiedeman, Barbara
Williams, Audrey
Wilson, Marty C.
Wingo, Edith
Wright, Hazel

Yelton, Ann
York, Sherlyn

INDEX

(+ Cooking for a Crowd, √ Palmetto Favorites, ★ Lower in Fat)